Reality Check

Reality Check

Lessons from 25 Policies Advancing a Low-Carbon Future

WORLD BANK GROUP

ISBN (paper): 978-1-4648-1996-4
ISBN (electronic): 978-1-4648-1997-1
DOI: 10.1596/978-1-4648-1996-4

Cover design: Bill Pragluski, Critical Stages, LLC.

Library of Congress Control Number: 2023910918

Climate Change and Development

The Climate Change and Development Series was created in 2015 to showcase economic and scientific research that explores the interactions between climate change, climate policies, and development. The series aims to promote debate and broaden understanding of current and emerging questions about the climate-development nexus through evidence-based analysis.

The series is sponsored by the Sustainable Development Vice Presidency of the World Bank, and its publications represent the highest quality of research and output in the institution on these issues. The group is committed to sharing relevant and rigorously peer-reviewed insights on the opportunities and challenges present in the climate-development nexus with policy makers, the academic community, and a wider global audience.

Contents

Box

Figures

Map

Tables

Foreword

In the past year, records for extreme weather events continued to be broken, as our changing climate swept in a new round of storms, heat waves, flooding, and drought, bringing life-changing devastation to millions of people. Although climate change affects every corner of the world, poor people and developing countries are more severely affected by its negative effects. In the summer of 2022, flash flooding in Pakistan triggered by glacial melt and monsoon rains submerged vast swaths of the country, providing a devastating example of the magnitude of climate-induced destruction. As of October 2022, around 33 million people—that is, one in seven of Pakistan's population—had been affected. For countries like Pakistan, climate change is a serious risk multiplier that hinders sustainable and inclusive development and will do so more in the future.

Eight years after the historic signing of the Paris Agreement, governments across the globe face two mutually dependent challenges: investing in resilience to ensure a disaster-resistant future and accelerating the decarbonization of energy and land-use systems. Without decarbonization, global emissions will continue to march upward, exacerbating climate risk for all countries.

The good news is that the number of countries announcing pledges to achieve net zero emissions continues to grow. Looking back over the past three decades, countries have already made significant efforts to decarbonize. Since the Intergovernmental Panel on Climate Change published its first assessment report in 1990, individual policies and regulations around the world have sparked myriad decarbonization initiatives.

Now, as we forge a pathway to reduce the addition of greenhouse gases to net zero, we need to identify the policies that have provided the most effective solutions. This World Bank report, *Reality Check: Lessons from 25 Policies Advancing a Low-Carbon Future*, fills a critical gap in the research to date, documenting policy trends for decarbonization, with a series of case studies across sectors and geographies. The 25 case studies presented here provide country context and policy or project details, examine results and impacts, and outline key takeaways and lessons learned for enabling further reductions around the world.

The case studies outlined in this report give us reason to hope. The rapid expansion of solar power in India, a growing market for climate-smart agriculture in China, greener financial systems in Colombia, and the removal of fossil fuel subsidies in the Arab Republic of Egypt are the result of well-designed policies and successful implementation and provide evidence that, with the right mix of political support and policy design, we can decarbonize development. These policies are not necessarily the first-best policies advocated by analysts and economists, and some may not be best practice. But they are real policies that have been implemented in countries with very different income levels and political contexts, and they provide many insights on how countries can design and implement climate policies—and on the compromises that doing so can require.

The World Bank is sharing these case studies to inform current and future climate actions, but our work does not stop here. These case studies offer a useful snapshot of the current policy landscape, but they will be updated over time as policies evolve and improve and, hopefully, become more ambitious and more efficient. The case studies presented here also highlight a big gap in knowledge: most of them do not have a rigorous ex post assessment of their outcomes and performance, which would help countries improve design and learn from each other. More work is definitely needed to make sure we learn from the early movers, and this will be a key priority for the World Bank moving forward.

Dr. Juergen Voegele
Vice President for Sustainable Development
World Bank

Acknowledgments

The report was prepared under the guidance of Juergen Voegele, vice president for sustainable development, by a team led by Stephane Hallegatte and Thomas Kerr, composed of Catrina Godinho, David Groves, Jia Li, Penelope Mealy, Katie Polkinghorne, and Khyati Rathore.

The policy case studies and key contributions have been prepared by Zubin Bamji, Sandra Baquié, Eliza Barnea, Diji Behr, Edward Beukes, Cecilia Briceno-Garmendia, Alexandru Cosmin Buteică, Georges Darido, Felipe DeLeon, Mariza de Oca Leon, Corinne Figueredo, Gershwin Fortune, Vivien Foster, Harikumar Gadde, Defne Gencer, David Groves, Dirk Heine, Grace Henry, Ruth Hill, Mehul Jain, Silpa Kaza, Min Lee, Bethany Linton, Alexander Lotsch, Cecilia Lozada Andrade, Tom Moerenhout, Mumba Ngulube, Emeka Nwangele, Samuel Okullo, Gerald Ollivier, Nicolas Peltier, Adam Pollard, Joseph Pryor, Wenxin Qiao, Martijn Regelink, Sarah Santucci, Bandita Sijapati, Jas Singh, Fiona Stewart, William Sutton, and Felipe Targa.

We gratefully acknowledge the invaluable comments and advice provided by our internal and external peer reviewers Diego Arias, Benoit Bosquet, Barbara Buchner (Climate Policy Initiative), Sudharshan Canagarajah, Louise Cord, Richard Damania, Christophe de Gouvello, Etienne Espagne, Marianne Fay, Anup Jagwani, Marc Sadler, Seynabou Sakho, and Martien Van Nieuwkoop.

Support with communications was provided by Ferzina Banaji, Donna Barne, and the World Bank communications team. We are also grateful to Lucy Southwood for her skillful edit of the manuscript. Bill Pragluski, Critical Stages, was the designer. Mary Fisk managed the book production process.

Finally, the team acknowledges the generous support of the Climate Support Facility and the guidance from Jennifer Sara, director of the Climate Change Group, and Renaud Seligmann, director for strategy and operations of the Sustainable Development Practice Group.

Abbreviations

°C	degrees Celsius
AMAN	The National People's Organization, Aliansi Masyarakat Adat Nusantara (Indonesia)
ASC	Adaptation Sub-Committee
BAU	business-as-usual
BBVA	Banco Bilbao Vizcaya Argentaria
BC	British Columbia
BCA	Border Carbon Adjustment
BRGM	Peat and Mangrove Restoration Agency, Badan Restorasi Gambut dan Mangrove (Indonesia)
BRT	bus rapid transit
CAGR	compound annual growth rate
CAMACOL	Colombian Chamber of Commerce
CAR	Rural Environmental Registry (Brazil)
CBAM	Carbon Border Adjustment Mechanism
CCC	Climate Change Committee
CCDR	Country Climate and Development Report
CCRA	climate change risk assessment
CDM	Clean Development Mechanism
CERs	certified emissions reductions
CESL	Convergence Energy Services Limited
CNG	compressed natural gas
CO_2	carbon dioxide
CO_2e	carbon dioxide equivalent
COP	UNFCCC climate change conference (Conference of the Parties)
COP26	26th United Nations Climate Change Conference of the Parties
COVID-19	coronavirus
CPI	Climate Policy Initiative
CTF	Clean Technology Fund
DCC	Costa Rica Climate Change Directorate, Dirección de Cambio Climático de Costa Rica
DETER	Deforestation Detection in Real Time
DPF	Development Policy Financing
EE	energy efficiency

ERC	Energy Regulatory Commission
ESCO	energy service company
ESG	environmental, social, and governance
ETS	Emissions Trading System
EU	European Union
EV	electric vehicle
FAME	Faster Adoption and Manufacturing of Electric (and Hybrid) Vehicles in India
FAME-II	second phase
FCPF	Forest Carbon Partnership Facility
FiT	feed-in tariff
FOLU	forestry and land use
FY	fiscal year
G20	Group of Twenty
GDP	gross domestic product
GEF	Global Environment Facility
GHG	greenhouse gas
Gt	metric gigatons (billion tons)
$GtCO_2e$	metric gigatons of CO_2 equivalent
GW	gigawatt
GWh	gigawatt hours
HICs	high-income countries
IBRD	International Bank for Reconstruction and Development (of the World Bank)
ICR	Implementation Completion and Results (World Bank)
IDB	Inter-American Development Bank
IEA	International Energy Agency
IFC	International Finance Corporation
IMF	International Monetary Fund
INEI	National Institute of Statistics and Informatics (Peru)
IPCC	Intergovernmental Panel on Climate Change
IPPs	independent power producers
IPTN	Integrated Public Transport Network
IRP	Integrated Resource Plan
JET	Just Energy Transition
JETF	Just Energy Transition Framework
JET IP	Just Energy Transition Investment Plan
$ktCO_2e$	metric kilotons of CO_2 equivalent (thousand tons)
kWh	kilowatt hour
LAP	Latin America Cycles, Latinoamérica Pedalea
LFG	landfill gas

LFR	legal forest reserve
LICs	low-income countries
LMICs	lower-middle-income countries
LPG	liquefied petroleum gas
LTS	long-term strategy
MDB	multilateral development bank
MEE	Ministry of Ecology and Environment
MICs	middle-income countries
MME	Ministry of Mines and Energy
MoEF	Ministry of Environment and Forestry
MoF	Ministry of Finance
$MtCO_2e$	metric megatons of CO_2 equivalent (million tons)
MW	megawatt
MWh	megawatt hour
NDC	nationally determined contribution
NDP	National Decarbonization Plan
NSM	National Solar Mission
NZEB	near-zero energy building
PCC	Presidential Climate Commission
PLI	Production-Linked Incentive
PM	particulate matter
PM2.5/10	concentrations of particulate matter less than 2.5 or 10 micrometers, respectively, in diameter
PPA	permanent preservation area
PPCDAm	Plan for the Prevention and Control of Deforestation in the Legal Amazon
PPP	public-private partnership
PRODES	Project to Calculate Deforestation in the Amazon
PV	photovoltaic
RE	renewable energy
REDD+	Reducing Emissions from Deforestation and forest Degradation, conservation of forest carbon stocks, sustainable forest management, and enhancement of forest carbon stocks in developing countries
REDZ	Renewable Energy Development Zone
RfP	request for proposal
SFC	Financial Superintendence of Colombia, Superintendencia Financiera de Colombia
STP	Servicio de Transporte de Personas
tCO_2e	metric tons of CO_2 equivalent
TWh	terawatt hour
UK	United Kingdom
UMICs	upper-middle-income countries

UNFCCC	United Nations Framework Convention on Climate Change
US	United States
ZRF	Zero Routine Flaring

A Note on Currencies

$	All dollar amounts are US dollars unless otherwise indicated
Can$	Canadian dollars
Col$	Colombian pesos
EGP	Egyptian pounds
Rs	Indian rupees
S/	Peruvian soles
¥	Chinese yuan

1. Introduction and Overview

Addressing climate change is no longer about high-level commitments: it is about transformative policies and action. While countries' pledges and targets are increasingly consistent with global objectives, the world is still on track for unprecedented climate change. The 2018–22 global mean temperature average is now estimated to be 1.17 ± 0.13 degrees Celsius (°C) above the 1850–1900 average, rapidly approaching the 1.5°C target of the Paris Agreement (United Nations 2022).

Greenhouse gas (GHG) emissions continue to rise. Although global energy-related carbon dioxide (CO_2) emissions dipped slightly in 2020 due to the COVID-19 (coronavirus) pandemic, they rebounded in 2021, reaching the highest-ever annual level of 36.3 gigatons (Gt) (figure 1.1). Models estimate that current policies are insufficient and would likely lead to a temperature increase of 2.6–2.9°C.

To meet their commitments and achieve the Paris Agreement's objective, countries will need ambitious packages of new policies that catalyze and coordinate the full decarbonization of their economies. They will need to invest in decarbonizing the electricity supply; electrifying, substituting fuel, and taking efficiency measures in transport, buildings, and industry; adopting low-carbon agriculture practices; and protecting and expanding forests and other natural carbon sinks (Kuramochi et al. 2018). Implementing such policies will require changes in infrastructure, lifestyle, and behavior and will include actions such as switching cars for public and active transport modes, designing low-carbon livable cities, adopting plant-based and healthier diets, improving material use and recycling, implementing circular economy principles, and preparing current and future workers for the green economy.

The economic benefits of following such a low-carbon development pathway are increasingly evident, but the transition requires policy reforms that face hard institutional and political economy barriers. The World Bank's new Country Climate and Development Reports (CCDRs) show that, while following a low-carbon development pathway requires an additional annual investment of 1 to 10 percent of gross domestic product (GDP) for a select set of countries, the net economic benefits of the transformation over the next several decades would be positive (World Bank 2023). Investing in decarbonization could add more than 60 million net new jobs globally (ILO 2012). However, the transition toward low-carbon pathways faces important barriers, including the need for large upfront investments, the lack of institutional capacity, significant distributional impacts (especially in coal regions), and challenging political economy issues.

FIGURE 1.1   Total Annual Global CO$_2$ Emissions from Energy Combustion and Industrial Processes and Their Annual Change, 1900–2021

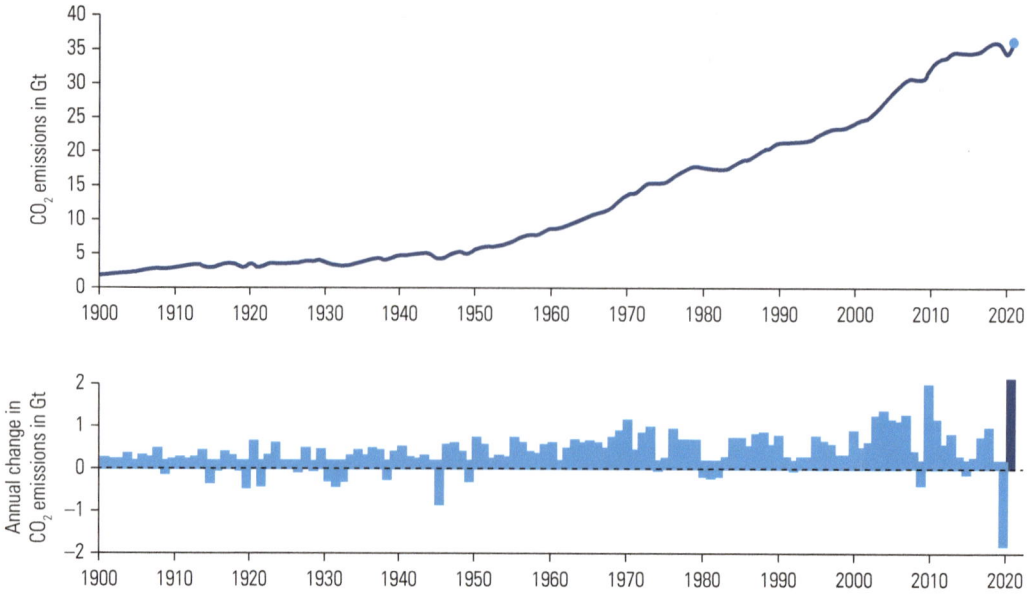

Source: IEA 2022.

Note: CO$_2$ = carbon dioxide; Gt = gigatons.

The scale of the climate challenge often appears daunting, but the rich history of climate policy implementation experiences across countries provides important lessons and pointers for how to advance policies in different contexts. Over the past three decades, countries around the world have introduced a variety of different climate policy responses. While high-income countries (HICs) pioneered the implementation of many climate policies in earlier periods, middle-income countries (MICs) and low-income countries (LICs) are increasingly active. We now have many examples of climate policies being implemented in a variety of different economic, cultural, and political contexts.

Aiming to leverage learnings from the past to inform future policy design, this report provides an overview of past climate change mitigation policy trends and discusses insights from case studies across the world. It builds on two sources. The first is the New Climate Institute's Climate Policy Database (New Climate Institute 2022), which allows for an exploration of global trends in climate change mitigation policies across time, countries with different income levels and contexts, and different sectors. The second is a set of 25 decarbonization policy case studies collected for this report that covers countries at all income levels. This report focuses on climate change mitigation or decarbonization policies, leaving policies to advance adaptation and resilience for a future analysis.

According to the Climate Policy Database, countries have introduced more than 4,500 climate policies over the past three decades (figure 1.2). Two United Nations Framework Convention on Climate Change (UNFCCC) COP events—Copenhagen in 2009 and Paris in 2015—were major catalysts for the announcement of climate policies, even though the number of policies announced has fallen over the years. In line with their emissions contributions, higher institutional capacity, and large financial resources, HICs have tended to move sooner on climate policy, but other countries are increasingly coming to the table, especially big emitters like China, India, and Indonesia. In terms of sectors, climate policies relating to electricity and heat tend to account for the largest share of country climate policies, but agriculture and forestry-related climate policies are often prevalent in LICs. Although the announcement of sector-specific climate policies has slowed down, economy-wide policy announcements remain high.

The objective of this report is not to draw conclusions around which policies are most effective or efficient in reducing emissions; rather, it aims to provide examples of real-world implementation of climate policies in multiple sectors, mobilizing various instruments. They are not necessarily first-best policies or even best practices: to make them feasible, governments often had to compromise with institutional capacity constraints or other policy objectives. Some are just a first step, and governments expect to adjust their design as they draw lessons from them.

To organize the analysis and the case studies, this report relies on a simple typology for decarbonization policies. This is derived from the 2015 World Bank report

FIGURE 1.2 **Climate Policy Announcements, by Country Income Group and by Sector**

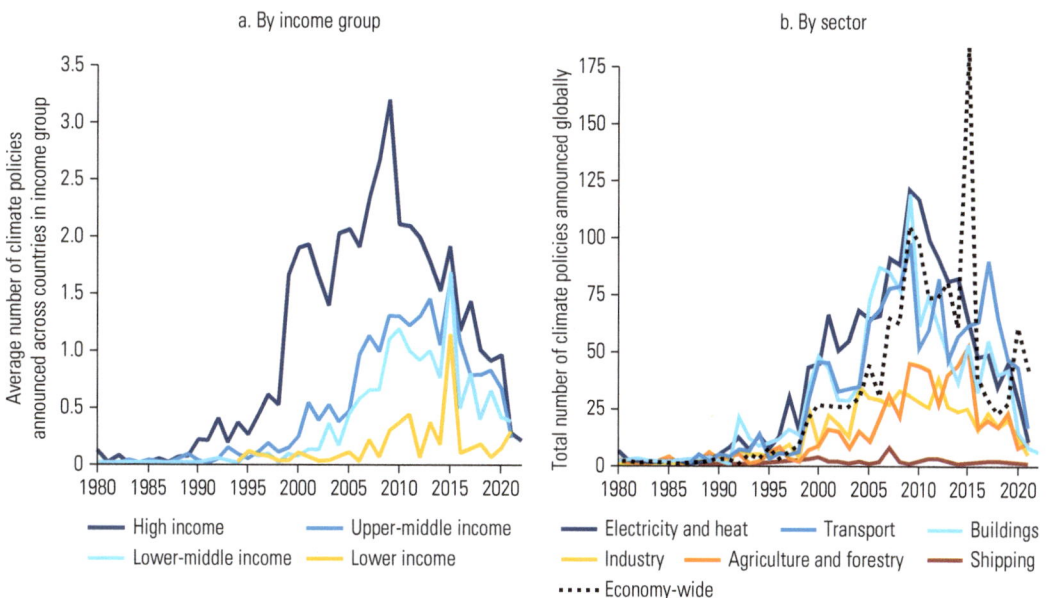

a. By income group

b. By sector

Source: World Bank calculations based on data from the Climate Policy Database 2022.

Decarbonizing Development: Three Steps to a Zero-Carbon Future (Faye et al. 2015), which highlighted the need for (1) a strategic approach that considers the end goal of full decarbonization of the economy to define short-term priorities; (2) packages of policies that can target the many market and government failures that impair decarbonization, including—but going beyond—carbon externality; and (3) a strong focus on the distributional impacts and political economy barriers. Building from this approach, we classify policies into five categories:

- **Planning for a future with zero net emissions.** The first step is to set up long-term objectives—for instance, to 2050—that are consistent with the end goal of full decarbonization. From there, countries can design sector-specific, shorter-term targets—to 2025 or 2030—and establish a way to track progress over time. Monitoring, auditing, reporting, verifying, information sharing, and training are all crucial for the success of climate policies. Building in such learning and feedback channels allows countries to identify and respond to emerging issues.

- **Getting the prices right.** Countries will need to implement policy reforms, including on pricing and taxes, to develop economic incentives that encourage efforts toward decarbonization. Encouragingly, the world is making progress on market-based mechanisms such as carbon pricing schemes and emissions trading systems, and despite being politically unpopular, some countries are also managing to reform fossil fuel subsidies. However, with less than 4 percent of global GHG emissions priced at or above the range required to meet climate stabilization goals outlined in the Paris Agreement, there is still much work to be done.

- **Facilitating, enabling, and triggering sectoral transitions.** A climate policy package will often incorporate various policies and actions—ranging from labels and regulations to subsidies and direct investments—to trigger transitions in key systems, such as the energy or food systems. They do so by providing support to certain technologies and practices (often referred to as "*supply-push*") or by creating a demand for them and facilitating their diffusion (often referred to as "*demand-pull*"). Supply-push policies reduce the cost of technology development through funding for research, development, and demonstration activities, while demand-pull policies stimulate demand for innovative solutions through financial incentives for adopters or by developing codes and standards, among other approaches.

- **Getting the finance flowing.** To support decarbonization efforts around the world, climate finance needs to quadruple by 2030. Policies to both grow and green the financial pie will be crucial to scaling up necessary resources. Policies to incentivize and attract financing and involvement from the private sector will be particularly important as sources of public finance are highly constrained. In addition, policies to encourage green investment and manage climate-related risks (such as climate stress tests and improved governance and disclosure) will be key.

- **Ensuring a just transition.** Where climate policies create winners and losers, governments need to ensure that the most vulnerable populations are protected.

Effective civic engagement, communication, and active management of distributional impacts can help build support for unpopular policies.

Table 1.1 summarizes the case studies explored in this report and classifies them within these five policy categories. It highlights the diversity of policies implemented in various countries across income levels and with diverse sectoral focus, including economy-wide policies. It further highlights the corresponding policy instruments used for the case studies, primary policy objectives, cobenefits incurred through policy implementation, and their political economy considerations.

With a few exceptions, the case studies discussed in this report do not offer an ex post assessment of their results and impact. This is due to either a lack of data or methodological challenges in causally linking policy interventions to observed emissions changes. It is also because emission reductions are not always the best result indicator. For instance, some policies are critical enablers for further climate action without necessarily reducing emissions directly. Climate change framework laws, power sector reforms, green skill development programs, and land tenure regularizations do not immediately reduce emissions. Nevertheless, these actions play a critical role in coordinating action across ministries, enabling private investment, facilitating the transition of affected workers, and enforcing policies to stop deforestation. Multiple indicators are needed to track the results and performance of climate policies beyond their direct effects on GHG emissions.

Every country has unique policy requirements based on its industrial structure, economic priorities, political system, and national circumstances. As a result, determining the appropriate national policy package involves understanding its specific needs and contexts and how best to implement policies to achieve the desired outcome. There is no unique best practice or policy recommendation that can be derived from these examples.

Even without an ex post impact assessment, every case study in this report offers valuable learnings and insights about the process through which countries have implemented policies or instruments. Each case study (1) examines the country context, including the rationale behind the policy and how it has been presented and communicated; (2) describes the policy and its design; and (3) discusses identified results and impacts, including necessary compromises in policy design. The case studies conclude with a set of key takeaways, focusing on how to navigate design and implementation challenges.

There are three main takeaways from the analysis. First, countries have introduced a vast number of climate policies over the past few decades across most sectors and geographies. Sector-specific policies are often the first to be implemented, but they are gradually being supplemented with economy-wide approaches. Key policies—such as removing fossil fuel subsidies and carbon pricing—are progressing, but there is some distance to go before they make a significant contribution to decarbonization.

TABLE 1.1 Policies and Approaches Examined in This Report

Case study	Policy instrument/program details	Primary objectives and cobenefits	Political economy considerations
Planning for a future with zero net emissions			
1. Costa Rica *Economy-wide*	Long-Term Strategy and National Decarbonization Plan	**Primary objectives:** Decarbonize all sectors; governance **Cobenefits:** Macroeconomic benefits: employment; poverty reduction	Policy development process strongly engaged technical and nontechnical stakeholders, including for climate justice and just transition considerations
2. Indonesia *Agriculture*	Moratorium on New Forest Concessions (2011) and Forest and Peatland Restoration Program (2016) as part of REDD+ strategy	**Primary objective:** Reduce deforestation **Cobenefits:** Biodiversity conservation; climate change mitigation; water conservation	Includes a feedback and grievance redress mechanism
3. United Kingdom *Economy-wide*	UK Climate Change Act (2008)	**Primary objectives:** Decarbonize all sectors; economy-wide resilience and adaptation; governance **Cobenefits:** Collaboration and knowledge-sharing	Act adopted through political consensus and strong civil society engagement; continued public engagement to ensure accountability from the government
Getting the prices right: economy-wide policies to promote structural change			
4. Canada *Economy-wide*	British Columbia carbon tax	**Primary objectives:** Climate fiscal policies; decarbonize all sectors **Cobenefits:** Economic growth; reduced income inequality; positive impact on aggregate employment	Shifted tax burden away from labor and households; included revenue recycling to address distributional impacts; conducted regular public outreach
5. China *Economy-wide$*	National emissions trading system (2021)	**Primary objectives:** Decarbonize all sectors; governance; energy efficiency **Cobenefits:** Reduced air pollution	Included stakeholder engagement and capacity building
6. Egypt, Arab Rep. *Energy$*	Energy subsidy reform with support from WB and Energy Sector Management Assistance Program (2014–16)	**Primary objectives:** Improve macroeconomic and enabling environment **Cobenefits:** Reduced GHG emissions; growth of solar and wind power generation; creating fiscal space for social spending; reduced air pollution	Included a public outreach campaign; strengthened social protection mechanisms; used targeted mechanisms with cash transfers; used fiscal savings to increase health and education spending

(Continued)

Note: **$** = Case studies with a strong link to private sector finance. Countries shaded green = high-income countries; orange = upper-middle-income countries; yellow = lower-middle-income countries; blue = low-income countries.

TABLE 1.1 *continued*

Case study	Policy instrument/program details	Primary objectives and cobenefits	Political economy considerations
7. European Union *Economy-wide*	EU Carbon Border Adjustment Mechanism (October 1, 2023)	**Primary objectives:** Reduce the risk of carbon leakage by ensuring that the price of imported goods reflects their carbon footprint **Cobenefits:** Promoting fair competition; encouraging global emission reductions; incentivizing companies to adopt cleaner technologies; and generating revenue for the EU's climate initiatives	Balancing different member states' and sectors' interests; addressing concerns of trade partners and WTO compliance; managing the potential impact on consumer prices; and ensuring the effectiveness of the mechanism in achieving its climate goals
Facilitating, enabling, and triggering sectoral transitions (technology support policies)			
8. Japan *Industry*	Act on the Rational Use of Energy (1979)	**Primary objective:** Decarbonize industry **Cobenefits:** Resource productivity	Japan is now less reliant on imported energy resources (and vulnerable to price fluctuations and supply disruptions), helping bolster Japan's economic competitiveness; also includes provisions for promoting the use of energy-efficient technologies and practices in industry, which can help reduce costs and enhance productivity
9. Mexico *Municipal solid waste*$	The Monterrey waste-to-energy project demonstrated an institutional and management framework for LFG capture and use at an existing facility turning waste into energy	**Primary objectives:** Waste management; reduce methane emissions **Cobenefits:** Public cost savings; generated carbon credits; avoided pollution (clean energy); community benefits from clean and cheaper electricity	The government provided financing and regulatory support to help ensure its success; the involvement of the private sector has been critical in ensuring the project's financial viability and long-term sustainability; community involvement has helped ensure that the project meets the needs of locals and addresses their concerns
10. Brazil *Agriculture*	Plan for the Prevention and Control of Deforestation in the Legal Amazon, enforcement of the Forest Code, and launch of Deforestation Detection in Real Time satellite system for the reduction in deforestation	**Primary objectives:** Reduce deforestation **Cobenefits:** Reduced GHG emissions; increased biodiversity; and ecosystem services	Multistakeholder engagement including monitoring, environmental control and accountability, land use, creation of protected areas, and promotion of sustainable production activities, particularly with farmers, who form a large special-interest group

Note: $ = Case studies with a strong link to private sector finance. Countries shaded green = high-income countries; yellow = lower-middle-income countries; orange = upper-middle-income countries; blue = low-income countries.

(Continued)

7

TABLE 1.1 *continued*

Case study	Policy instrument/program details	Primary objectives and cobenefits	Political economy considerations
11. Sahel Region *Agriculture*	Low-cost technologies and indigenous practices coupled with information and training to improve soil quality and agricultural outcomes	**Primary objectives:** Climate-smart agriculture **Cobenefits:** Carbon sequestration; socioeconomic outcomes; improved food security	Engaged local communities via information and training; included cash transfers
12. Egypt, Arab Rep. *Transport*	Egypt Vehicle Scrapping and Recycling Program (2008)	**Primary objectives:** Decarbonize transport **Cobenefits:** Reduced air pollution; improved traffic safety; economic growth; job creation	Offered financial incentives for owners to scrap their old vehicles and purchase new ones, as well as provided support for the development of local recycling facilities
13. Peru *Transport*	Several policies that promoted infrastructure development plans and investment to improve bicycle adoption including Law 29593 (2010) to improve biking conditions and promote cycling as a means of sustainable transportation; Law 30936 (2019) promotes and regulates bicycle use as a sustainable mode of transport and Lima's more recent Bicycle Infrastructure Plan	**Primary objectives:** Decarbonize transport; improve air quality; improve urban planning **Cobenefits:** Economic savings; social and health benefits	Lima government officials organized knowledge exchange programs; representatives from civil society, media outlets, and business chambers participated
14. South Africa *Transport*	Launched a Bus Rapid Transport strategy in 2007 with recent updates and the Integrated Public Transport Network Strategy in 13 cities	**Primary objectives:** Decarbonize transport; improve public transportation safety and efficiency **Cobenefits:** Reduced GHG emissions; reduced air pollution; reduced fuel consumption	Pilot supported by business and consulting services facilitated by the city
15. Türkiye *Buildings*	Launched the Turkish Energy Performance of Buildings Regulation or "Binalarda Enerji Performansı Yönetmeli" to improve energy efficiency in public building projects	**Primary objectives:** Green buildings; energy efficiency **Cobenefits:** Replicated in the private building market	Included training for energy auditors, design companies, and construction firms to learn from early experiences, share good practices, and build market capabilities; will share knowledge with market actors to facilitate replication

Note: **$** = Case studies with a strong link to private sector finance. Countries shaded green = high-income countries; orange = upper-middle-income countries; yellow = lower-middle-income countries; blue = low-income countries.

(Continued)

TABLE 1.1 *continued*

Case study	Policy instrument/program details	Primary objectives and cobenefits	Political economy considerations
Facilitating, enabling, and triggering sectoral transitions (demand support policies)			
16. India *Power*$	The National Solar Mission (2010). feed-in tariff and utility power purchase obligations, fiscal incentives including solar project subsidies and tax incentives (for example, 2019 Pradhan Mantri Kisan Urja Suraksha evam Utthan Mahabhiyan)	**Primary objectives:** Decarbonize energy **Cobenefits:** Avoided air pollutant emissions; improved electricity access; green jobs	Platform for broad communication and engagement; placed emphasis on local production of solar panels and equipment to enhance self-sufficiency and promote domestic manufacturing
17. Colombia *Gas flaring*	Ecopetrol Company's Climate Change Strategy to Reduce Gas Flaring (linked to NDC); Global Gas Flaring Reduction Partnership (2021)	**Primary objectives:** Decarbonize energy **Cobenefits:** Environmental, health, and economic benefits of reduced black carbon particulate matter; improved domestic energy supply	Colombia joined the Zero Routine Flaring by 2030 initiative to support cooperation between all relevant stakeholders to find solutions to gas flaring
18. India *Transport*$	Faster Adoption and Manufacturing of Electric (and Hybrid) Vehicles in India (FAME-II) scheme (2019–2021)	**Primary objectives:** Decarbonize transport **Cobenefits:** Improved mobility access; reduced air pollution; job creation by boosting domestic electric vehicle manufacturing	Provides incentives for domestic production of EV components to generate new employment opportunities
19. Colombia *Buildings*$	Green Building Code and appropriate tax incentives to bolster the interest of the private sector to build green	**Primary objectives:** Green buildings; climate finance **Cobenefits:** Energy efficiency; higher resale value	Worked with a local chamber of commerce to deliver trainings to developers and municipal governments
20. China *Agriculture*	Introduced the Guangdong Agricultural Pollution Control Project (2013) and developed standards and regulations for safe, green agricultural products	**Primary objectives:** Pollution reduction **Cobenefits:** Reduced GHG emissions; promoting the rural circular economy; reduced costs to farmers; increased crop yields; provincial economic savings; avoided health care costs; reduced deforestation	Training for key stakeholders including agricultural officers, farmers, cooperatives, and enterprises; secured the collaboration of farmers and the private sector by promoting cost reductions
Getting the finance flowing			
21. Chile *Transport*$	In addition to the National Electromobility Strategy, the government used public-private partnership to overcome financial, operational, and infrastructure challenges to e-bus development	**Primary objectives:** Decarbonize transport **Cobenefits:** Air pollution reduction; energy cost saving	Built a cooperative partnership between private companies (bus operators, bus manufacturers, and financiers) and the public sector to gain support

Note: $ = Case studies with a strong link to private sector finance. Countries shaded green = high-income countries; orange = upper-middle-income countries; yellow = lower-middle-income countries; blue = low-income countries.

(Continued)

TABLE 1.1 *continued*

Case study	Policy instrument/program details	Primary objectives and cobenefits	Political economy considerations
22. Colombia *Economy-wide*$	Climate risk stress test, regulatory reforms, and a green taxonomy to classify green investments	**Primary objectives:** Climate finance; risk management governance **Cobenefits:** Growth of green-labeled products	Created a green taxonomy with a large group of stakeholders, including various ministries, agencies, and international initiatives
23. Kenya *Power*$	Revising the Energy Act (2006), Kenya's Energy Regulatory Commission initiated a Least Cost Power Development Plan for the power sector; this introduced institutional and regulatory reforms to attract private investment and support privately financed independent power producers	**Primary objectives:** Improve macroeconomic and enabling environment **Cobenefits:** Energy transition to renewable sources; increased access to electricity, economic growth, jobs, productivity, incomes, health outcomes, and human capital development	Planning involved multistakeholder steering and technical committees
Ensuring a just transition			
24. South Africa *Coal*	Created a Presidential Climate Commission (2021) that has developed national, sectoral, and regional Just Energy Transition strategies to start decommissioning/retrofitting coal power stations while also increasing RE sources	**Primary objectives:** Just transition; decarbonize energy **Cobenefits:** Environmental; air pollution reduction; improved domestic energy supply; attract foreign investment; job protection	In 2012, the PCC launched the Social Partner Dialogues on Pathways for a Just Transition with government, labor workers/unions, business, and civil society to build a common vision for the Just Transition and create pathways to achieve this vision
25. United Kingdom, Germany, and the Netherlands *Coal*	UK Coal Phase-Out Policy (2015); Netherlands Coal Phase-Out Act (2019); Germany's Coal Exit Law (2020)	**Primary objectives:** Just transition; decarbonize energy **Cobenefits:** GHG emissions reduction; air pollution reduction; environmental and health benefits	Included policies such as strengthened social safety nets and alternative employment; used inclusive processes that involved local unions and public, private, and nongovernmental actors to build consensus around the need to transition

Note: **$** = Case studies with a strong link to private sector finance. Countries shaded green = high-income countries; blue = low-income countries; orange = upper-middle-income countries; yellow = lower-middle-income countries. https://datahelpdesk.worldbank.org/knowledgebase/articles/906519. EU = European Union; EV = electric vehicle; GHG = greenhouse gas; LFG = landfill gas; NDC = nationally determined contribution; PCC = Presidential Climate Commission; RE = renewable energy; REDD+ = Reducing Emissions from Deforestation and forest Degradation, conservation of forest carbon stocks, sustainable forest management, and enhancement of forest carbon stocks in developing countries; UK = United Kingdom; WTO = World Trade Organization.

Planning and coordination play a key role, including through commitments and targets, but a combination of long-term targets and short-term milestones is needed. The former will help set the trajectory and coordinate expectations; the latter will keep governments on track and send the short-term signals and incentives needed to influence investors and decision-makers.

Second, high-visibility failures, or even citizen unrest, hide a large and growing number of climate policies that are being successfully implemented. Case studies show that political and public buy-in are critical, with strong public institutions, cross-party support, and ongoing public engagement being crucial elements for effective implementation. A large group of stakeholders—including ministries, regulators, private sector actors, civil society actors, and academics—need to work together to design tools, create policies, socialize findings, drive implementation, and monitor results. In this context, capacity building is essential to ensure that officials at all levels of government and representatives in both public and private institutions are better able to design and implement climate policies. A follow-up report will provide a deeper analysis of the key determinants of a successful implementation of climate policies in spite of the political economy challenges, bearing in mind that some policy implementation successes (or failures) may be context-specific and cannot be directly applied to other jurisdictions.

Third, there is a critical gap in credible, ex post analysis of the impacts of decarbonization policy implementation to show the emissions reductions and other benefits that they have delivered and derive best practices that can be generalized to other countries. This makes it challenging to correlate the clear growth in markets for low-carbon technologies or the declines in carbon intensity or emissions with specific policies. It is important for governments not only to monitor policy implementation and outcomes on emissions but also to analyze costs and distributional impacts. This will allow them to adjust policies to address new challenges or unexpected and unwelcome developments; it will also allow other countries and jurisdictions to learn from their experience and improve their own actions.

This report is only a start. Evaluating the full impact of the case studies featured in this report will take time, as many describe recently enacted policies that will produce results over decades. The World Bank aims to continue collecting, analyzing, and sharing examples of successful (and less successful) climate policies or interventions to inform decision-making across the world.

As with all policy processes, the learning journey for climate policies is never complete; rather, it continues to evolve and adapt in light of new approaches, technologies, and climate challenges. As such, the insights, case studies, and lessons learned included in this report are not the final word. They are more of a stock-take on where the world is currently at with climate policy, what we have learned, and what we still need to figure out.

References

Fay, M., S. Hallegatte, A. Vogt-Schilb, J. Rozenberg, U. Narloch, and T. Kerr. 2015. "Decarbonizing Development: Three Steps to a Zero-Carbon Future." World Bank, Washington, DC. https://openknowledge.worldbank.org/handle/10986/21842.

IEA (International Energy Agency). 2022. *Global Energy Review: CO$_2$ Emissions in 2021*. https://www.iea.org/reports/global-energy-review-co2-emissions-in-2021-2.

ILO (International Labour Organization). 2012. *Working towards Sustainable Development: Opportunities for Decent Work and Social Inclusion in a Green Economy*. https://www.ilo.org/global/publications/ilo-bookstore/order-online/books/WCMS_181836.

Kuramochi, T., N. Höhne, M. Schaeffer, J. Cantzler, B. Hare et al. 2018. "Ten Key Short-Term Sectoral Benchmarks to Limit Warming to 1.5°C." *Climate Policy* 183: 287–305. https://doi.org/10.1080/14693062.2017.1397495.

New Climate Institute. 2022. Climate Policy Database. https://climatepolicydatabase.org/.

United Nations. 2022. "United in Science: We Are Heading in the Wrong Direction." Press release 13092022, September 13. https://unfccc.int/news/united-in-science-we-are-heading-in-the-wrong-direction.

World Bank. 2023. *Country Climate and Development Reports*. https://www.worldbank.org/en/publication/country-climate-development-reports.

2. Climate Policies: Past Trends and Insights on Implementation

Over the past three decades, climate policy announcements grew steadily, peaking at the 21st Climate Change Conference of the Parties in Paris. According to the Climate Policy Database, countries have introduced more than 4,500 climate policies in this time frame (figure 2.1). Two key United Nations Framework Convention on Climate Change (UNFCCC) COP events—in Copenhagen in 2009 and Paris in 2015—were major catalysts for the announcement of climate policies, but the number of policies announced has fallen over the years.

What ultimately matters for decarbonization is not how many climate policies are announced but how much emissions are reduced. Some policies, such as large fossil fuel subsidy reforms, will have a large impact on emissions; others target sectors with small emissions and may only have a marginal impact. Studies have shown, however, that these are significantly related; each new piece of climate legislation reduced annual carbon dioxide (CO_2) emissions per unit of gross domestic product (GDP), on average, by 0.78 percent nationally in the first three years and 1.79 percent in the long term (Eskander, Fankhauser, and Setzer 2020). In the absence of a policy-per-policy impact analysis, which would face difficult methodological and data availability challenges, we use the number of climate policies here as a crude proxy for policy action in different sectors, using various instruments.

Global Trends in Climate Policies across Time, Space, and Sectors

In line with their emissions contributions, higher institutional capacity, and large financial resources, high-income countries (HICs) have tended to move sooner on climate policy, but other countries are increasingly coming to the table (box 2.1). Since the 1990s, HICs introduced more climate policies on average (figure 2.2a), but upper-middle-income countries (UMICs) and lower-middle-income countries (LMICs) also increased the average number of policies they announced in 2005–15; some of the more populous countries—such as China, India, and Indonesia—introduced a comparably large number of climate policies (figure 2.2b). Although low-income countries (LICs) have tended to announce relatively few climate policies over the past three decades, average policy announcements increased significantly in 2015.

FIGURE 2.1   **Climate Policies Announced Globally, 1980–2020**

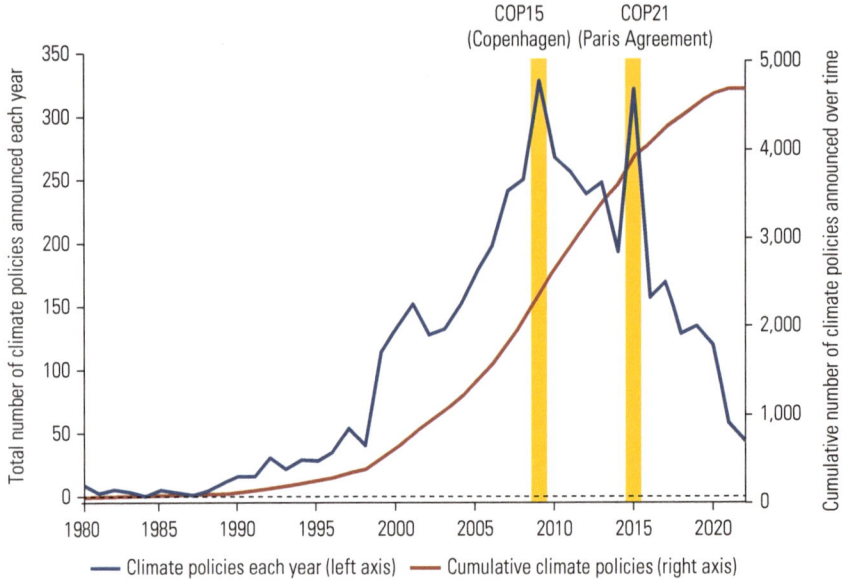

Source: World Bank calculations based on data from the Climate Policy Database 2022.
Note: COP15 = the 15th Conference of the Parties in Copenhagen; COP21 = the 21st Conference of the Parties in Paris.

FIGURE 2.2   **Climate Policy Announcements, by Country Income Group**

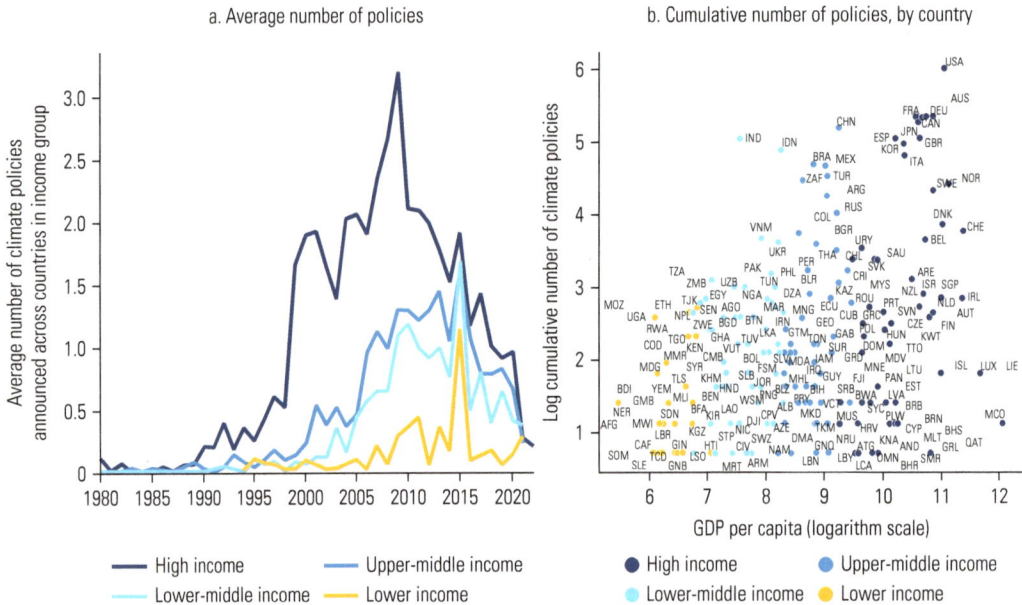

Source: World Bank calculations based on data from the Climate Policy Database 2022.
Note: GDP = gross domestic product.

Climate policies have become increasingly more widely adopted in all countries in recent decades (map 2.1). In the early 2000s, it was mostly HICs that announced climate policies, but there has since been a rapid increase in climate policy announcements by LMICs. From 2010–15, China overtook the United States in announcing more climate policies than any other country. India took over the lead from 2015–22, announcing nearly 50 climate policies—a reflection of its drive to increase the adoption of renewables, especially solar power (see Case Study 16, which details other contributory factors and shows how India has become one of the world's most attractive solar energy markets).

Compared with other regions, Sub-Saharan Africa made fewer climate policy announcements. South Africa is a notable exception, announcing more than 85 climate policies from 2000–22. More than half of all Sub-Saharan African countries have announced fewer than five climate policies, and only South Africa and Malawi have announced 2050 net zero targets. Others have set later targets or are still in discussions. Although Sub-Saharan Africa currently only contributes around 2 to 3 percent of global emissions, an excessive lock-in to fossil-fuel-based technologies could be detrimental to its long-term growth and development prospects.

The announcement of sector-specific climate policies has slowed down, but economy-wide policies are on the rise. Given their significant role in decarbonization, the electricity and heat sectors have accounted for the largest number of climate policy announcements globally. There has also been a steady increase in policy announcements relating to transport and buildings over the past two decades (figure 2.3). Growth in climate policies relating to industry, as well as agriculture and forestry, has been more muted; shipping—a notoriously hard-to-abate sector— has been the target of very few climate policies. Although policy announcements have declined across all sectors in recent years, economy-wide policies, including greenhouse gas (GHG) reduction, energy efficiency, and renewable energy (RE) targets (many of which were announced at COP21 in 2015), have been steadily increasing.

Climate policies relating to electricity and heat tend to account for the largest share of country climate policies, but agriculture- and forestry-related climate policies are often prevalent in LICs. Looking at the distribution of climate policies by sector across country income groups, HICs tend to have higher shares of climate policies relating to transport and buildings, while LICs (largely located in East Asia and Pacific and Sub-Saharan Africa) have a greater share of policies relating to agriculture and forestry (figure 2.4). This greater share largely reflects differences in economic structure across countries and the tendency for agriculture to be a dominant sector (both in terms of employment and GDP) in many low-income countries.

MAP 2.1   **Climate Policy Announcements over Time and Space**

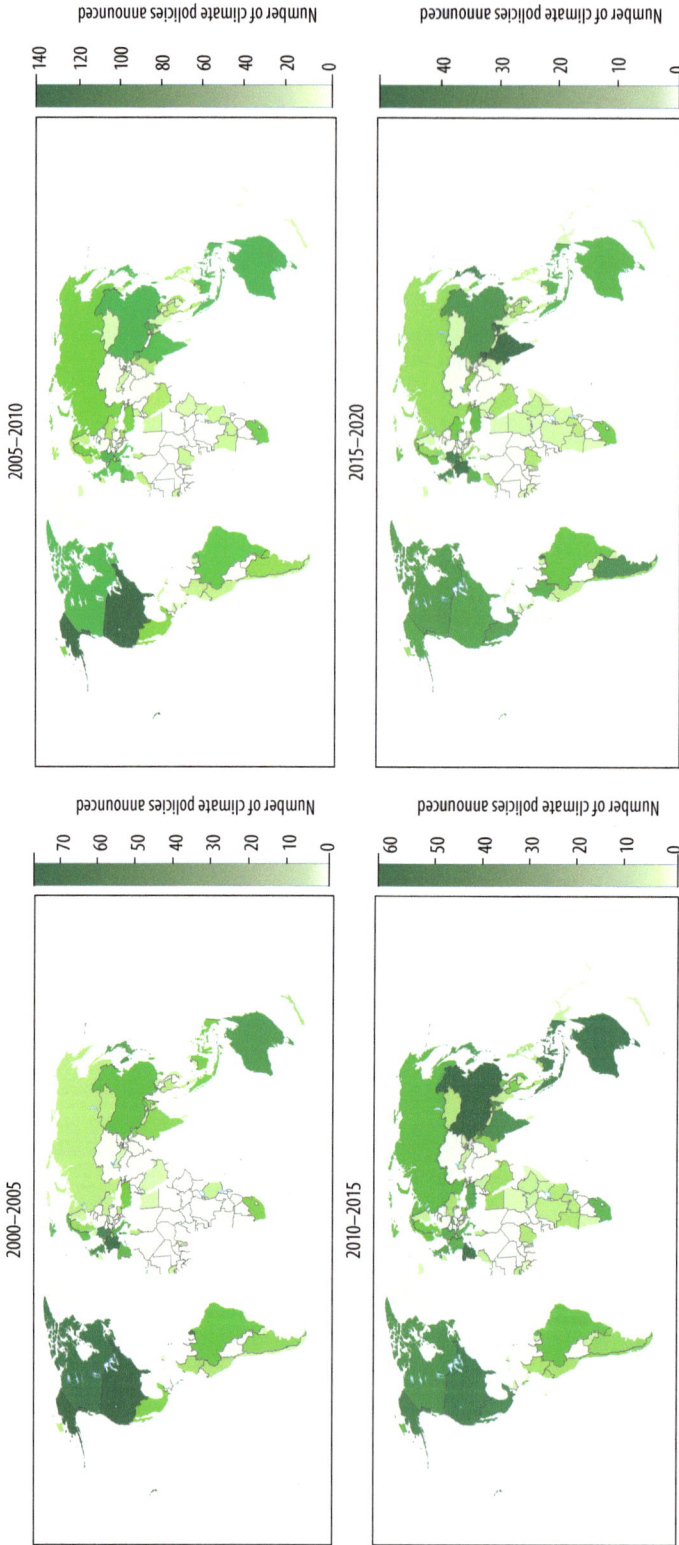

IBRD 47263 | MAY 2023

Source: World Bank calculations based on data from the Climate Policy Database 2022.

16

FIGURE 2.3   **Climate Policy Announcements Globally, by Sector**

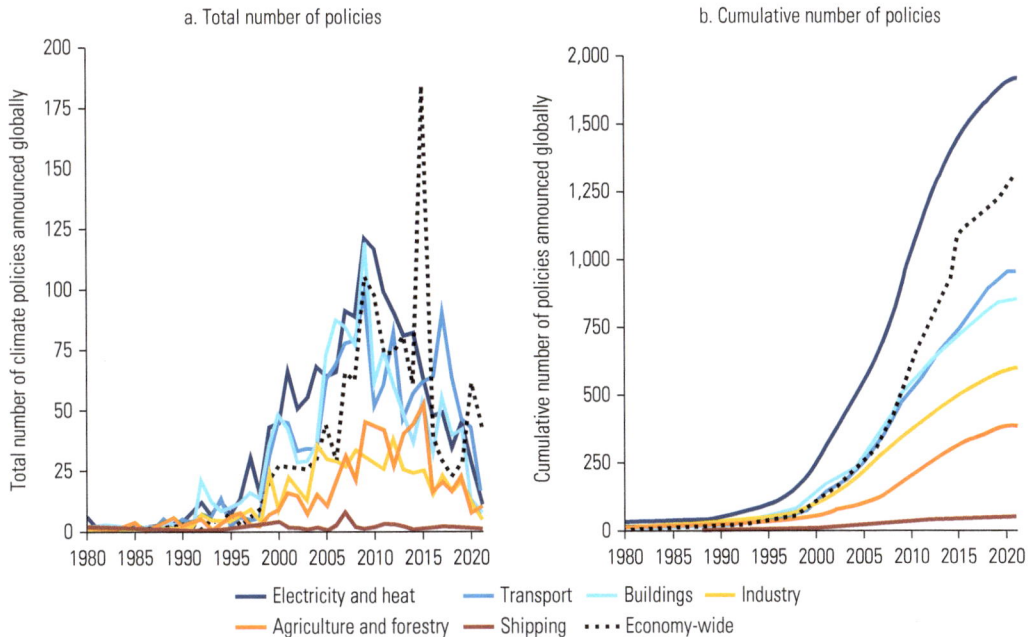

a. Total number of policies

b. Cumulative number of policies

Legend: Electricity and heat — Transport — Buildings — Industry — Agriculture and forestry — Shipping — Economy-wide

Source: World Bank calculations based on data from the Climate Policy Database 2022.
Note: Where policies relate to more than one sector, they appear more than once.

Present Insights on Climate Policy Implementation

No single policy can ensure an efficient and least-cost, low-carbon transition because there are many obstacles to overcome. To implement a least-cost transition, governments will need a set of policies to internalize the climate externality and manage other obstacles (figure 2.5). These include barriers to innovation and economies of scale, network effects, and the need for supportive infrastructure—such as electricity grids, metro systems, and electric vehicle (EV) charging stations—imperfect markets, and a lack of access to financing. To make the transition possible and cost-effective, governments can implement a package of measures and policies in parallel to manage all the other market and government failures that make the transition impossible or more expensive.

Efficiency is not the only criterion for designing climate policies: fairness, equity, and political economy constraints are also important. Policies are always driven by multiple goals and objectives, and climate policy is no exception. Policies that take into account other objectives—such as regional equity or national or energy security—will be more attractive and feasible. Particularly important for climate action is the concept of a "just transition," which aims to ensure that emissions reductions do not lead to unfair impacts on specific communities or regions, especially the poorest and

FIGURE 2.4 **Distribution of Climate Policies by Sector across Income and Regional Country Groups**

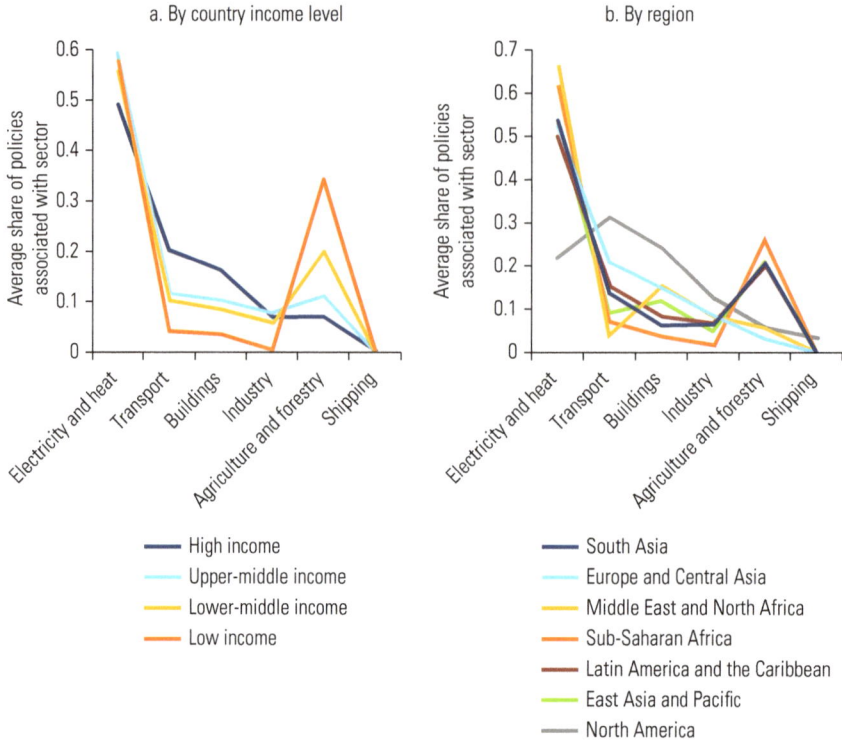

a. By country income level

b. By region

High income
Upper-middle income
Lower-middle income
Low income

South Asia
Europe and Central Asia
Middle East and North Africa
Sub-Saharan Africa
Latin America and the Caribbean
East Asia and Pacific
North America

Source: World Bank calculations based on data from the Climate Policy Database 2022.

FIGURE 2.5 **Obstacles to the Low-Carbon Transition**

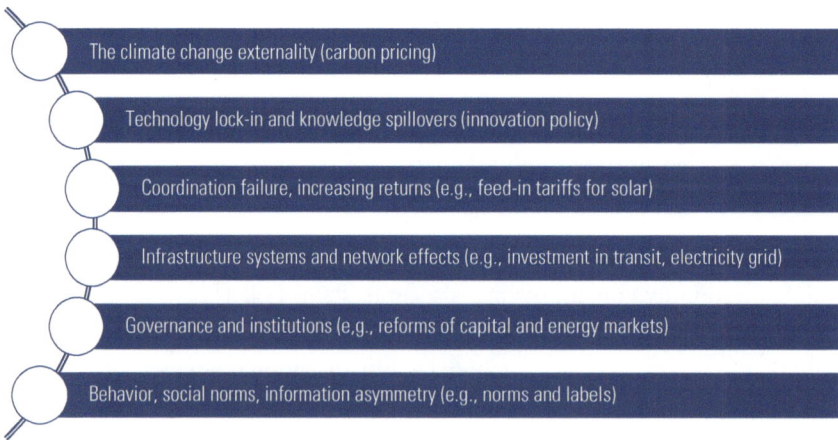

The climate change externality (carbon pricing)

Technology lock-in and knowledge spillovers (innovation policy)

Coordination failure, increasing returns (e.g., feed-in tariffs for solar)

Infrastructure systems and network effects (e.g., investment in transit, electricity grid)

Governance and institutions (e,g., reforms of capital and energy markets)

Behavior, social norms, information asymmetry (e.g., norms and labels)

Source: Original analysis for this publication.

most vulnerable. A growing number of countries are developing just transition frameworks, helping them establish a social mandate and guiding principles for action based on equity and fairness. These frameworks offer a people-first approach that considers how to include and support people and societies to enhance the equity and fairness of climate policy decisions and outcomes.

To explore the range of policies needed to ensure efficient and fair decarbonization, this report proposes a simple typology with five categories. It builds on the framework proposed in the *Decarbonizing Development: Three Steps to a Zero-Carbon Future* report (Fay et al. 2015), which explores the alignment of development and decarbonization for LMICs and identifies the types of climate policy packages needed to achieve complete decarbonization of our economies by 2100, considering the many market failures, imperfections, risks, undesired distributional effects, and political economy obstacles that such a deep transition entails. Building on this report, we classify policies in five categories:

- Planning for a future with zero net emissions
- Getting the prices right
- Facilitating, enabling, and triggering sectoral transitions
- Getting the finance flowing
- Ensuring a just transition

Planning for a Future with Zero Net Emissions

Having a common vision of how to achieve climate objectives will help countries design appropriate policy packages. Developing a long-term strategy (LTS) for low-carbon, climate-resilient development can help countries do this. An LTS provides a realistic pathway toward long-term objectives and helps identify useful milestones for shorter-term strategies and plans. Although it is possible to reduce emissions by 10 or 20 percent by acting only on the emissions that are cheapest to abate, a transition to net zero requires action on all emissions sources, transformational actions in many sectors, and a very different approach to sequencing and prioritization. Rather than identifying the lowest-cost abatements, it is important to design the least-cost transition with the right sequencing and timing of actions in each sector. LTSs can be the basis for developing short-term climate plans or strategies, including nationally determined contributions (NDCs).

Implementing long-term climate strategies requires a comprehensive and coordinated effort involving multiple sectors and stakeholders. There is no one-size-fits-all approach. Governments need to prioritize actions and establish a clear roadmap while considering various challenges, including financial and technical constraints. The process should consider the country's long-term vision, sustainable development, political economy, societal impacts, stakeholder engagement, governance, environmental impacts and trade-offs, adaptation elements, sectoral strategies, implementation approaches, monitoring plans, and revision processes.

With an ambitious long-term target, countries can benefit from investing early in relatively expensive emissions-reduction options that help make technologies cheaper or ease costs by distributing them over a longer period. Many RE technologies have become more affordable today due to successive rounds of government investment and policy support in earlier periods. For example, the German government's policy support in 2000 allowed people who installed solar panels to earn a premium on the energy they generated, driving a huge boost in demand for solar panels when they were still very expensive. With demand soon outpacing supply from German manufacturers, China saw an opening and began exporting solar panels to Europe. Over the next two decades, China continued to support solar panel manufacturing with policies, such as subsidies and feed-in tariffs (FiTs), and rapidly became the world's largest and lowest-cost solar panel producer (De La Tour, Glachant, and Ménière 2011).

Acting early is important in sectors that are difficult to decarbonize or where technological tipping points or social norms are serious barriers. In most sectors, an abrupt transformation would be more expensive than a smooth shift toward zero net emissions. In sectors that are particularly expensive and difficult to decarbonize, such as transportation, starting early makes the transformation as progressive and smooth as possible, minimizing costs in the long term. Transitions can be impaired by complementarities in demand (peer effects), increasing returns to scale, or learning by doing. For example, more people will buy EVs if they see others buy them; a large share of EVs will create incentives for denser charging stations, which will in turn make EVs more attractive. Such big shifts to move from a carbon-intensive to a low-carbon equilibrium require a large initial effort.

The Climate Policy Database shows that countries have been developing long- or short-term climate strategies and targets, but they are more likely to be political and nonbinding. Most formal and legally binding policies occurred in the earlier days of climate policy making (2000–10), particularly when it came to GHG reductions and RE targets. Since then, there has been a proliferation of nonbinding policies, particularly around the time of the Paris Agreement, when more than 100 countries announced nonbinding targets (see figure 2.6).

Two countries that are pioneering economy-wide low-carbon strategies are Costa Rica and Indonesia. Costa Rica first highlighted its strategy for a low-carbon economy (Case Study 1) to the UNFCCC in 2000, and for the last two decades has built its technical expertise with international partners to develop models and policy analysis for decarbonization. The result is a net zero national decarbonization plan, submitted as its LTS to the UNFCCC in 2019, which includes stakeholder engagement and considers climate justice and a just transition (Government of Costa Rica 2020). The LTS was the

FIGURE 2.6   Total Number of Formal or Legally Binding and Political or Nonbinding Climate Policies Announced, 1990–2020

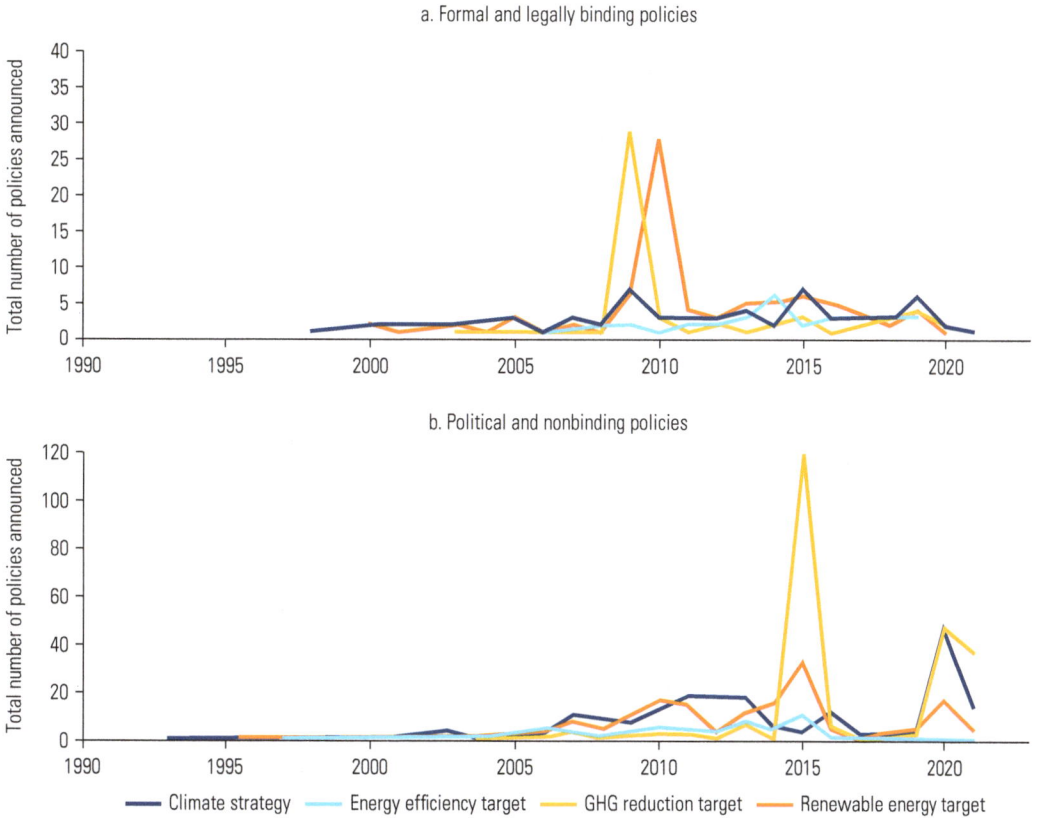

a. Formal and legally binding policies

b. Political and nonbinding policies

Climate strategy — Energy efficiency target — GHG reduction target — Renewable energy target

Source: World Bank calculation based on data from the Climate Policy Database 2022.
Note: GHG = greenhouse gas.

basis for its 2020 NDC update. Costa Rica also institutionalized measures into law and integrated low-carbon development into governmental processes. Key lessons from its success include a clear transformation pathway, stakeholder buy-in, political sponsorship, and adequate institutional arrangements for financing, monitoring, and ensuring accountability.

At COP15, Indonesia (Case Study 2) pledged to reduce its GHG emissions by 41 percent by 2030 with international assistance and set a net zero target for 2060. Its LTS presents a low-carbon trajectory that would reach 1.6 metric tons of CO_2 equivalent (tCO_2e) per capita emissions by 2050. To achieve its goal of reducing over 60 percent of emissions by forestry and land use and making them a net carbon sink by 2030, the government has placed a moratorium on new licenses for forest conversion and peatlands, established two new agencies, introduced the Presidential Regulation on the Economic Valuation of Carbon, and implemented a jurisdictional emission reductions program in East Kalimantan. It has also signed agreements with the Forest Carbon Partnership Facility's (FCPF) Carbon Fund, Green Climate Fund, and Norway to access results-based payments to advance the implementation of REDD+ (for Reducing Emissions from Deforestation and forest Degradation, conservation of forest carbon stocks, sustainable forest management, and enhancement of forest carbon stocks in developing countries). It has also set up the Indonesia Environment Fund to channel future climate finance and develop a pipeline of projects and programs.

Information-gathering and feedback processes are key to successfully implementing climate policies and should be part of the planning process. A repeated theme across almost all the case studies in this report is the importance of effective monitoring, reporting, verification, and information sharing. In some cases, effective monitoring requires specific technologies, such as the Deforestation Detection in Real Time (DETER) satellite technology that helped monitor deforestation in Brazil (Case Study 10). In other cases, countries can support monitoring and evaluation by strengthening institutional capacity and training relevant personnel. Guangdong Province in China (Case Study 20), for example, reduced agricultural pollution by training agricultural officers, farmers, and enterprises in improved livestock waste management practices and helping them develop certification standards and regulations for safe, green agricultural products.

As climate policies are introduced in dynamic and adaptive settings, ensuring continual learning and feedback is crucial for ensuring the desired effect of a specific policy. Policy implementation also involves a degree of learning by doing. Even though much can be learned from other countries' experiences, building learning and feedback mechanisms into the implementation process allows countries to quickly identify and respond to issues as they come up.

Getting the Prices Right

Global momentum on carbon pricing is building, but policies do not go far enough. In the past three decades, the share of global GHG emissions covered by carbon pricing and Emissions Trading System (ETS) mechanisms has risen from 0.15 percent in 1990 to 23 percent in 2022 (figure 2.7; World Bank 2022a). At the time of the first *Decarbonizing Development Report* in 2015, 39 national and 23 subnational jurisdictions had implemented or scheduled the implementation of carbon pricing instruments such as carbon taxes or ETS. Eight years later, these numbers stand at 46 and 36, respectively (World Bank 2022b).

The momentum is clearly building, but a lot more needs to be done. Despite encouraging progress, in 2022, less than 4 percent of global GHG emissions were covered by a carbon price at or above the range needed to meet the Paris Agreement's goals.

FIGURE 2.7 Share of Global GHG Emissions Covered by Carbon Pricing and ETS Mechanisms, 1990–2022

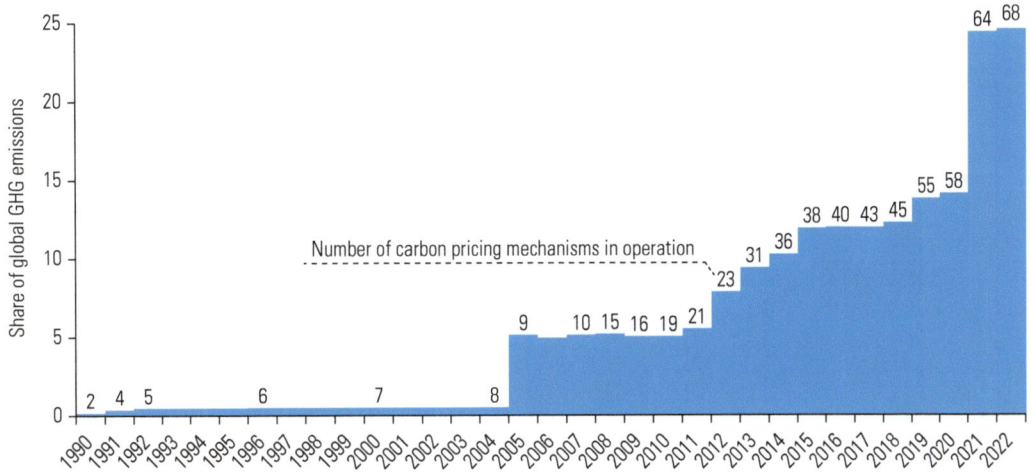

Source: World Bank 2022b.

Note: ETS = Emissions Trading System; GHG = greenhouse gas.

For countries looking to introduce carbon pricing mechanisms, British Columbia's carbon tax (Case Study 4) stands out as a helpful model. Introduced in 2008, this policy has resulted in increased economic growth, decreased inequality, and significantly reduced GHG emissions. Design was a critical element of this policy's success. It was broad in nature, applying to all fuels purchased in the country, and revenues were used to reduce other taxes in a way that narrowed the gap between rich and poor households.

China's experience implementing a national ETS (Case Study 5) provides further lessons on how policy design can influence feasibility and outcomes, and the trade-off between the two. Specific design choices have led the policy to function differently from a traditional cap-and-trade system, limiting its ability to drive least-cost abatement. However, it has delivered benefits in terms of redistributing resources across provinces. Limitations in capacity; training for enterprises in ETS rules and procedures; and the implementation of an effective monitoring, reporting, and verification system have also resulted in delays, concerns related to data transparency and accuracy, and low emissions allowance prices.

Reforming fossil fuel subsidies is another important element in getting the prices right but continues to be politically challenging. Following a temporary decline in 2020 due to the pandemic-driven fall in demand and price, global fossil fuel subsidies shot up to almost US$700 billion in 2021 (figure 2.8). Although many countries have pledged to reduce inefficient subsidies, governments have felt compelled to shield households from rising energy prices as the global economy rebounded and the Russian Federation's

FIGURE 2.8   Fossil Fuel Subsidies by Fuel over Time

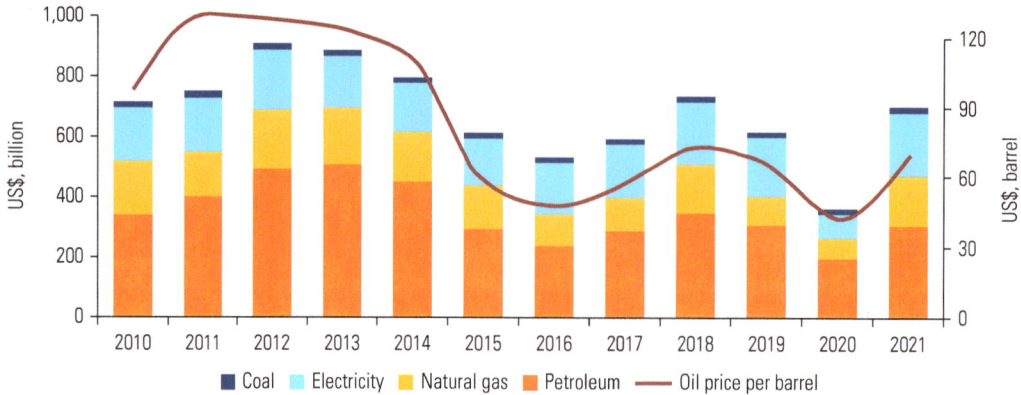

Source: OECD 2022.

war on Ukraine led to a global energy crisis. These outlays are principally concentrated in oil and power, but some countries also have large natural gas subsidies (figure 2.9).

Reforming such subsidies is widely advocated to help address the funding challenges of most LMICs, but if poorly implemented, the reforms can disproportionately impact the poorest in society. In recent years, efforts to reform fossil fuel subsidies in France, Chile, and Iran have met with protests and social resistance. Yet more than 40 countries had implemented subsidy reforms by 2020 (IEA 2021b). One such country is the Arab Republic of Egypt (Case Study 6), which implemented energy subsidy reforms to help reduce its budget deficit and create the fiscal space to strengthen social assistance, health, and education. Effective and proactive communication was key: the government's public multimedia campaign, launched alongside its tariff reform, encouraged the use of energy efficiency measures to reduce impacts from higher energy prices. The government also shielded the most vulnerable from price increases by increasing the social protection budget by around 60 percent and introducing more targeted support mechanisms with cash transfers.

Facilitating, Enabling, and Triggering Sectoral Transitions

As highlighted in Figure 2.5, the transition toward zero net emissions faces multiple barriers, and providing the right incentives with the right prices is often not a sufficient policy. Additional policies will be required when it is impossible to get the optimal prices, for instance due to political economy challenges, or when the right prices do not translate into the right incentives or the expected changes in behavior. This can happen for multiple reasons, such as the following:

- **Investments with long lifetimes:** in the absence of perfect predictability and credibility of future carbon prices, investors may not internalize the expected growth in carbon price over time and make suboptimal decisions.

FIGURE 2.9   Fossil Fuel Subsidies by Fuel for the Top 25 Countries in 2020

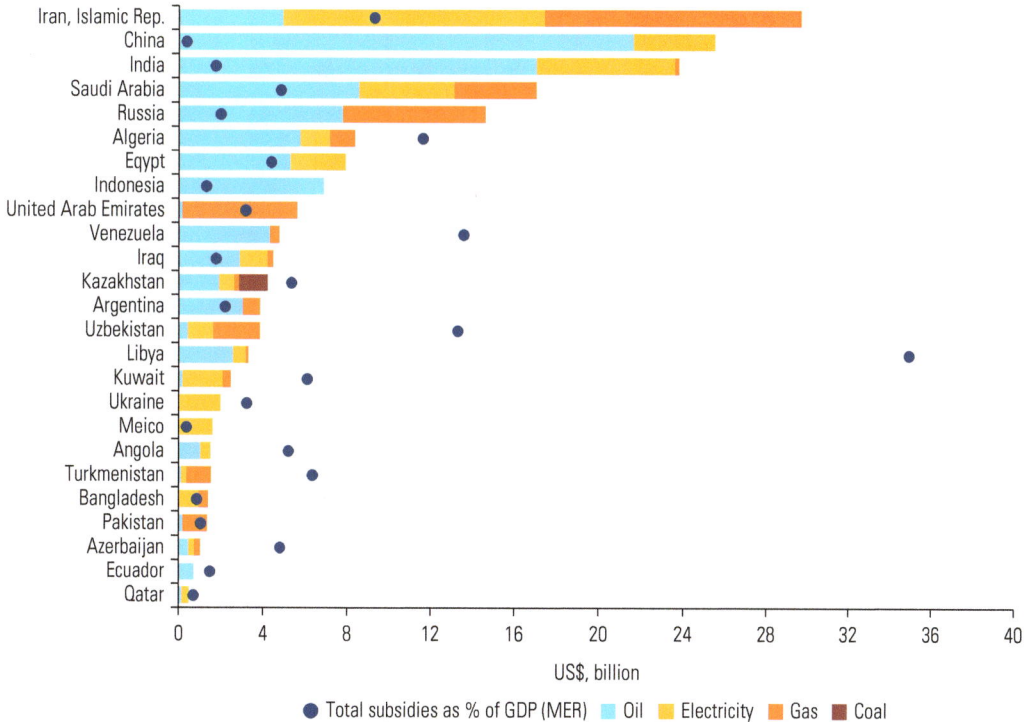

Source: IEA 2023a.

Note: GDP = gross domestic product; MER = Market Exchange Rate.

- **Market imperfections:** some sectors are heavily regulated and do not necessarily respond to a change in prices, for instance, when investment and dispatch decisions in a power system are not driven by prices but through other mechanisms.
- **Technology lock-ins and learning by doing:** for instance, when established fossil-fuel-based technologies compete with early-stage clean alternatives that need investments to catch up.
- **Network effects:** when infrastructure systems need to be transformed, for instance, to shift transportation from individual vehicles toward public transit and rail transport, or to make sure there is a charging network in place to allow the transition to EVs.
- **Behaviors:** people often do not make a full cost-benefit analysis to inform their decisions (for instance, when buying appliances), or sometimes the performance of a product is difficult to observe (for instance, the energy efficiency of a building).

In such cases, there is a potential justification for overlapping policies, with specific sector-targeted policies that can range from labels and regulations to targeted subsidies and direct investment in infrastructure. When the prices can be adjusted and provide the right incentive, the objective of complementary policies will be to ensure that the prices translate into a change in incentives and behaviors. When the prices cannot be adjusted, at least temporarily, then policies can substitute the price change, and ideally transform the economic system and political context enough to make the price change more politically and socially acceptable. In all cases, policies will also ensure that the right technologies and infrastructure systems are available to allow people, firms, and investors to change their behaviors and reduce their emissions.

As a result of decarbonization policies and market developments, many low-carbon technologies have become more cost-competitive. Solar power, onshore wind, and EVs are now competitive in sectors representing around 25 percent of global GHG emissions. By 2030, this could rise to 70 percent (figure 2.10).

Further cost reductions in low-carbon technologies and infrastructure are fundamental to the transition to a low-carbon economy, but barriers remain. In the energy sector, the world has seen tremendous progress in RE technologies. The levelized cost of solar energy has fallen by around 90 percent over the past decade, and wind power costs have dropped by around 72 percent. Although the cost of RE is now cheaper than fossil-fueled energy in many parts of the world, LMICs still face significant barriers in transitioning to clean energy. Obstacles include significant upfront investment costs—although savings accrue over longer time periods—and high borrowing costs, which can increase the cost of decarbonizing a power system by more than 30 percent (SystemIQ 2020). In the transport sector, EVs have made rapid cost improvements and are close to passing the tipping point in which they are cheaper than their internal combustion engine equivalents (SystemIQ 2020). However, similar barriers exist in installing the necessary charging infrastructure and providing adequate financing for households and industries to upgrade vehicle fleets.

Although today's technologies are enough to enable countries to make meaningful emissions reductions by 2030, reaching zero net emissions by 2050 will require significant innovation and development of technologies that are not yet market ready. The International Energy Agency's Net Zero by 2050 roadmap assumes that most global CO_2 emissions reductions through to 2030 can be achieved using technologies that are already available. But reaching net zero by 2050 in the energy sector requires substantial innovation in batteries, hydrogen electrolyzers, and direct air capture and storage (IEA 2021a). Technological innovation will also be required in hard-to-abate sectors such as steel, cement, chemicals, shipping, and aviation, and both increased research and development funding and well-targeted policies supporting technological demonstration and deployment are crucial to ensure technological solutions come online in time.

For some technologies, success is not going to be easy; nor is it always possible to replicate success in other technologies. The costs of many technologies—such as wind turbines, batteries, and electrolyzers—are declining with increased policy support and market penetration, but all technologies do not show the same degree of promise.

FIGURE 2.10 **Low-Carbon Solutions by Sector: Progress Since Paris Agreement and a Look Forward to 2030**

Low-carbon solution maturity

Increasing share of new sales/build

■ Concept ■ Solution development ■ Niche market ■ Mass market ■ Late market

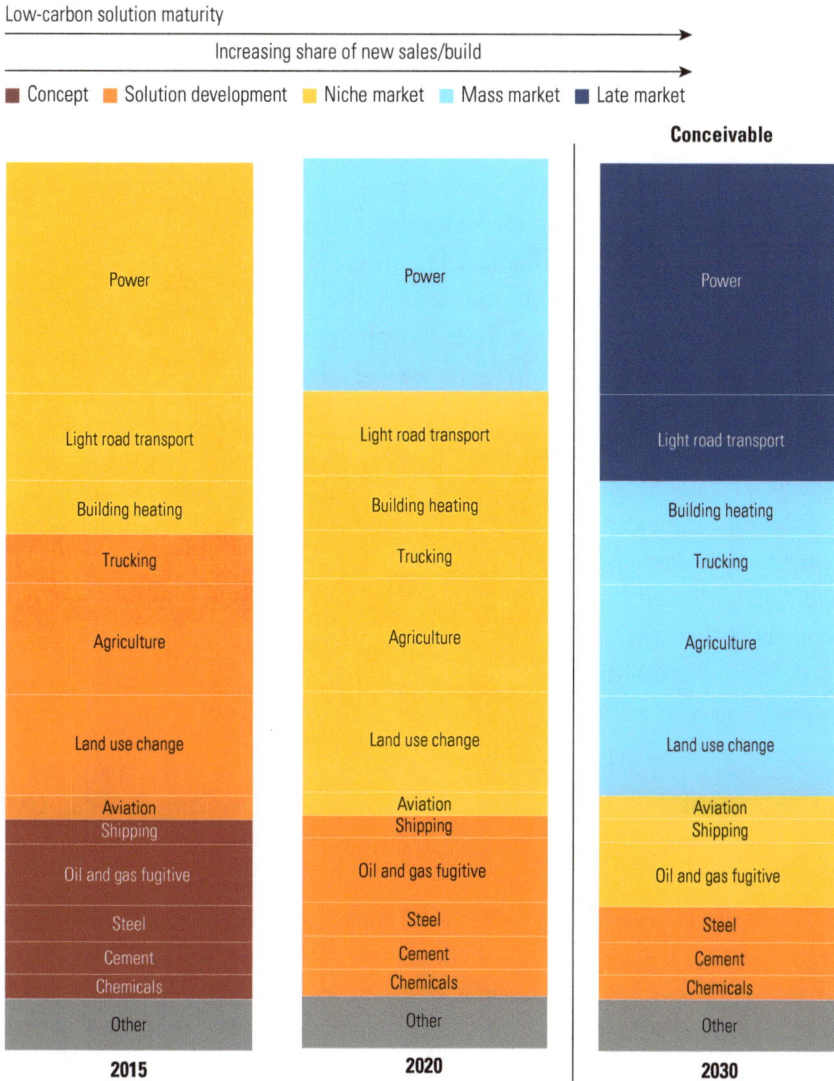

Conceivable

2015 | **2020** | **2030**

Source: SystemIQ 2020.

Due to greater project complexity and public resistance, longer times between technological upgrades, and more limited historical investment, nuclear energy and carbon capture and storage technologies have greater levels of uncertainty around their cost improvement curves, and policy makers should account for these higher risks when considering investment and policy support (Way et al. 2022).

To ensure that the needed technologies and infrastructure are available and affordable, countries can use technology support and demand support policies. The former aims to enhance the supply of technologies and infrastructure by providing incentives that reduce the cost of their development, such as funding for research and development activities. The latter aims to accelerate progress by stimulating demand for innovative solutions and technologies, such as financial incentives for adopters, or the development and enforcing of codes and standards. Here, we consider trends and country experiences in both policy categories.

Technology support policies

Historically, HICs have tended to play a leading role in research, technology development, and deployment policies (figure 2.11). As green innovation faces both environmental and knowledge externality market failures, there has always been a strong rationale for technology support policies to help ensure progress in research, knowledge production, and technology. With their more advanced technological capabilities, HICs have tended to be frontrunners in introducing policies relating to research, technological development, and deployment. The United States was an early mover in this space, with several policies designed to promote innovation in RE technologies in the 1970s. Primarily motivated by energy security and affordability concerns following the 1973 energy crisis, these policies played a crucial role in driving early progress in solar and wind energy. Brazil stands out as a middle-income that introduced a research and development policy early on, in 1985. Its National Electric Energy Conservation Program, PROCEL, designed to promote efficient electricity use, has generated 92.2 terawatt hours of energy savings over 30 years, with significant cost savings (IEA 2023b).

More recently, technological demonstration, development, and deployment have been critical for the successful implementation of decarbonization policies in UMICs, LMICs, and LICs. For example, under partnerships with the Global Environment Facility (GEF) and the World Bank, the Monterrey waste-to-energy project (Case Study 9) generated 17 megawatts of electricity and reduced emissions by 5.7 metric megatons of CO_2 equivalent ($MtCO_2e$)—of which 262,000 tons was methane—from 2004 to 2020. The project is an early example of a circular economy solution that provided a clean and cheaper source of electricity for the Monterrey metropolitan area. Its success was facilitated by political will, local capacity building, supportive regulations, verification of landfill gas impact, and other factors that created a foundation for an integrated waste management system. Another example is Brazil's DETER satellite system that uses georeferenced imagery to identify deforestation hotspots needing urgent attention (Case Study 10). Research shows it has been successful; deforestation and land-use change emissions were reduced by 82 percent and 65 percent, respectively, from 2004 to 2012. However, to ensure effectiveness, enforcing penalties for violating laws related to deforestation is vital, as there are many political economy challenges here.

Technological demonstration, development, and deployment can be as effective and, in many cases, more effective when using low-cost technologies and indigenous practices. In the Sahel, farmers are using traditional practices such as agroforestry and

FIGURE 2.11 **Announcement of Policies Relating to Technology Development, Deployment, Research, and Infrastructure Investments**

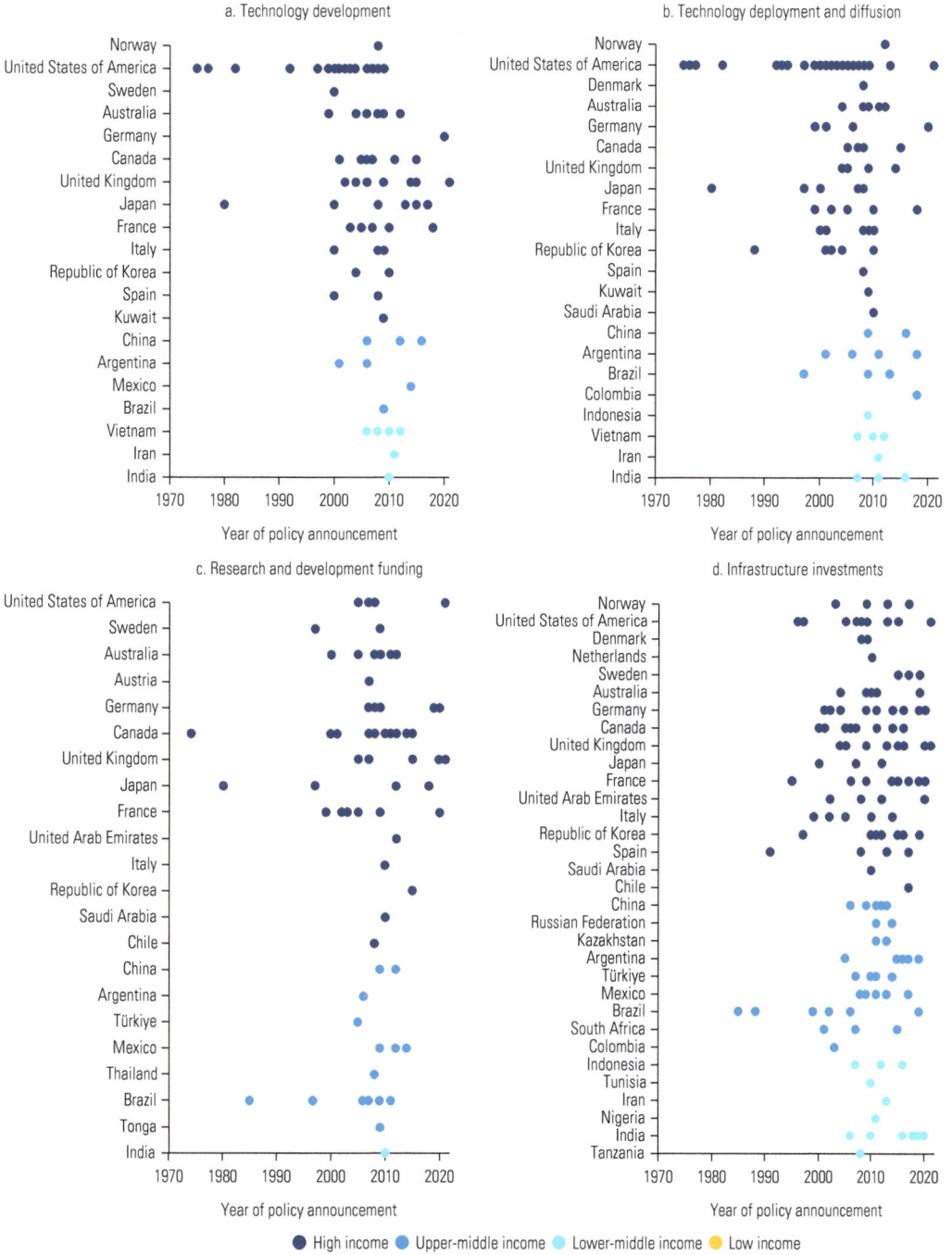

a. Technology development

b. Technology deployment and diffusion

c. Research and development funding

d. Infrastructure investments

● High income ● Upper-middle income ● Lower-middle income ● Low income

Source: World Bank calculations based on data from the Climate Policy Database 2022.

rainwater harvesting to restore soil and capture rainfall (Case Study 11). Information and training are critical to increasing the adoption of these practices, as evidenced by successful initiatives such as "zaï schools" in Burkina Faso and training programs in Niger that resulted in a 90 percent increase in adoption rates. Trained farmers continue to transmit knowledge to their neighbors up to three years after training, making information campaigns and training cost-effective ways of boosting the adoption of profitable and accessible technologies.

Infrastructure investments are crucial for all countries, but the nature of investment and associated policy challenges will differ across different country types. As HICs and middle-income countries (MICs) generally already have energy, buildings, and transport systems in place, they will need to upgrade or replace much of their infrastructure. Many countries face significant inertia, as the path dependency of previous infrastructure and energy systems often constrains future infrastructure developments. In contrast, LICs with relatively undeveloped energy, transport, and building infrastructure can leapfrog emissions-intensive infrastructure systems of the past and design and deploy completely new systems from scratch. With affordable access to capital and the appropriate skills and regulatory frameworks in place to develop such infrastructure, these countries could make such infrastructure investments at the accelerated pace required for meeting decarbonization goals, rapidly improving their development outcomes.

Several case studies in this report highlight countries' experiences in upgrading and investing in infrastructure to reduce emissions. For example, in Türkiye, more than 175,000 public buildings have been estimated to have an annual technical energy efficiency potential of more than 10,000 gigawatt hours, requiring a US$18 billion investment (Econoler International 2016). Working with the World Bank, the Ministry of Energy and Natural Resources has developed an Energy Efficiency in Public Buildings Project (Case Study 15) to renovate 400 to 500 central government buildings and spur the market for a national public building renovation program. So far, the project has completed 30 building renovations, reducing energy use by 22 to 74 percent. It also funded the development of a national program for energy efficiency in public buildings, which aims to introduce consistency and predictability to the market, attract new suppliers, drive down costs, and allow for scale-up. In Latin America, Lima's Bicycle Infrastructure Plan (Case Study 13) aims to leapfrog previous emissions-intensive infrastructure systems by developing a connected cycle network of almost 1,400 kilometers by 2040, with a proposal to adopt a bicycle strategy to promote cycling, particularly among women. The World Bank's Lima Traffic Management project will finance selected road safety interventions to address funding, technical capacity, and political pushback challenges. Lima's officials also participated in the Latin America Cycles (Latinoamérica Pedalea) knowledge exchange program to learn from regional cycling project leaders and form cross-sectoral alliances to promote cycling projects.

While policies to facilitate and encourage the development of low-carbon infrastructure often take the form of direct investment, often "softer" institutional and operational interventions can be equally important in improving the performance of existing infrastructure systems. A key example is South Africa's efforts to improve its bus rapid transport (BRT) system (Case Study 14). Originally developed to support the 2010 football World Cup, South Africa's BRT system had become financially unsustainable. Poor access and lack of integration with other transport systems also meant that the service was not meeting user needs. In response, the city of Cape Town launched a pilot project to improve business and operational efficiency, including pooling vehicles with centralized dispatch, centralized revenue and cost management, vehicle tracking and fleet management systems, and improved salary structures for drivers. Impressively, the pilot did not require additional public investment in vehicles or companies; it was supported completely by the city's business and consulting services. At negligible cost (and without job losses), the pilot reduced fleet size from 78 minibuses to 40 well-maintained vehicles and expanded service coverage from three to five licensed routes. It also improved working conditions for drivers and reduced fuel consumption and emissions by around 45 percent, transporting the same volume of passengers with fewer kilometers driven.

Demand support policies

Policies incentivizing the adoption and scaling up of low-carbon technologies have been more widely introduced across countries of different income groups. While technology support policies are important for developing new technologies and bringing them to market, demand support policies—which incentivize the adoption of low-carbon technologies—also play a crucial role in driving greater access and affordability. Many countries across all income groups introduced FiTs and policies encouraging grid access and greater priority for renewables to incentivize RE uptake when it was more costly than fossil fuels (figure 2.12). A key example is India (Case Study 16), which has set ambitious RE targets and implemented government programs and policies to support the growth of solar energy. This includes the National Solar Mission and incentives such as state-dependent FiTs, renewable purchase obligations, reverse auctions to encourage competitive bidding, reduced solar energy tariffs, and net metering that credits solar energy owners based on the surplus energy they export to the grid. The government has also worked with development finance institutions and the private sector to encourage investment.

Many countries have also introduced emissions or efficiency standards, which aim to reduce the carbon content or emissions intensity of products, buildings, and vehicles (figure 2.12). A particularly successful example is the International Finance Corporation's EDGE certification efforts in Colombia (Case Study 19). The EDGE platform enables the design, costing, and certification of green building space and has been used to certify 25 percent of new buildings in the country over 2021–22. Effective training and government support to provide appropriate tax incentives have been key to the success of this project.

FIGURE 2.12 Demand Support Policy Announcements

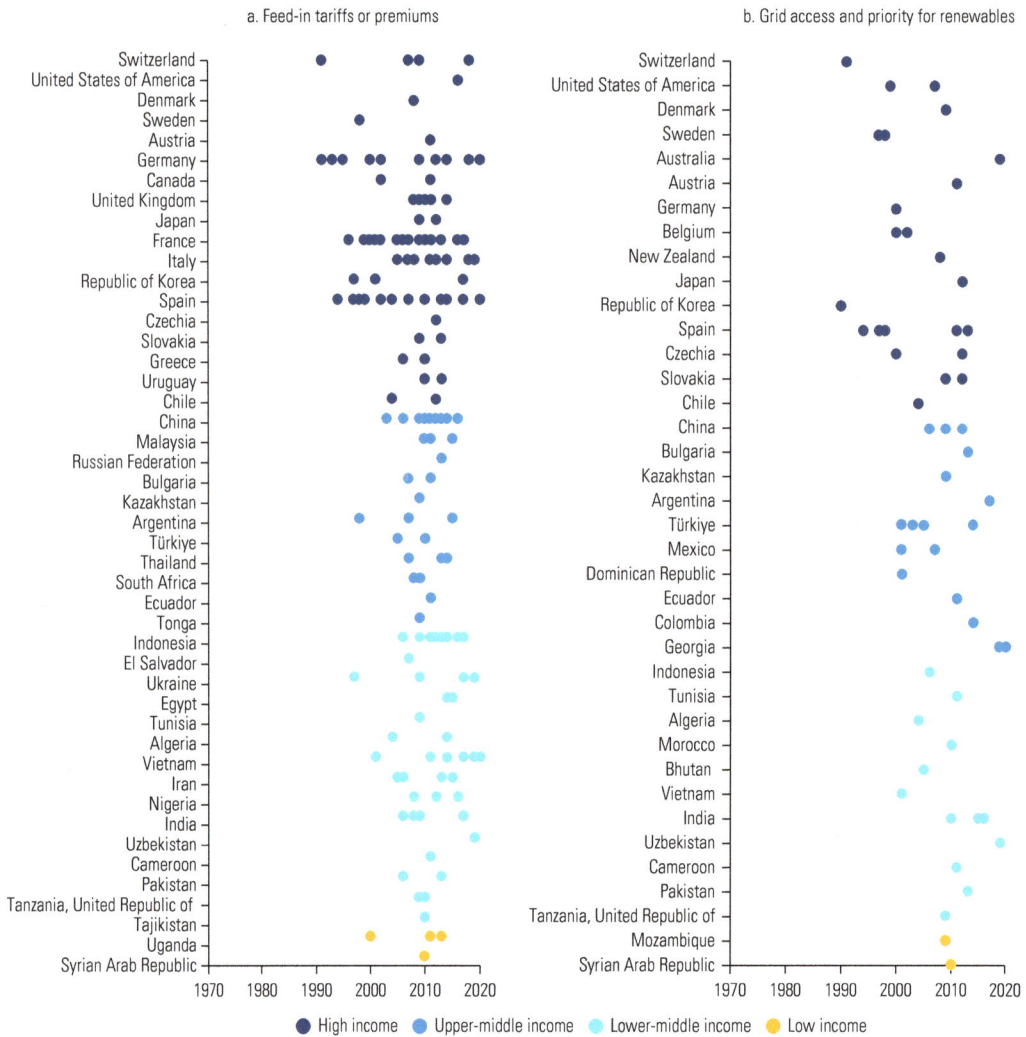

a. Feed-in tariffs or premiums

b. Grid access and priority for renewables

● High income ● Upper-middle income ● Lower-middle income ● Low income

Continued

Getting the Finance Flowing

Despite significant growth in climate finance over the past few decades, current levels of finance flowing to LICs and MICs still need to quadruple by 2030. In response to policies, climate investments have increased significantly over 2011–21, with public and private climate finance nearly doubling each year. Between this period, governments and businesses committed a cumulative US$4.8 trillion (figure 2.13, CPI 2022), more than 85 percent of which was directed to mitigation efforts, particularly solar photovoltaic and onshore wind power. Although annual average

FIGURE 2.12 *continued*

c. Vehicle fuel-economy and emissions standards

d. Product standards

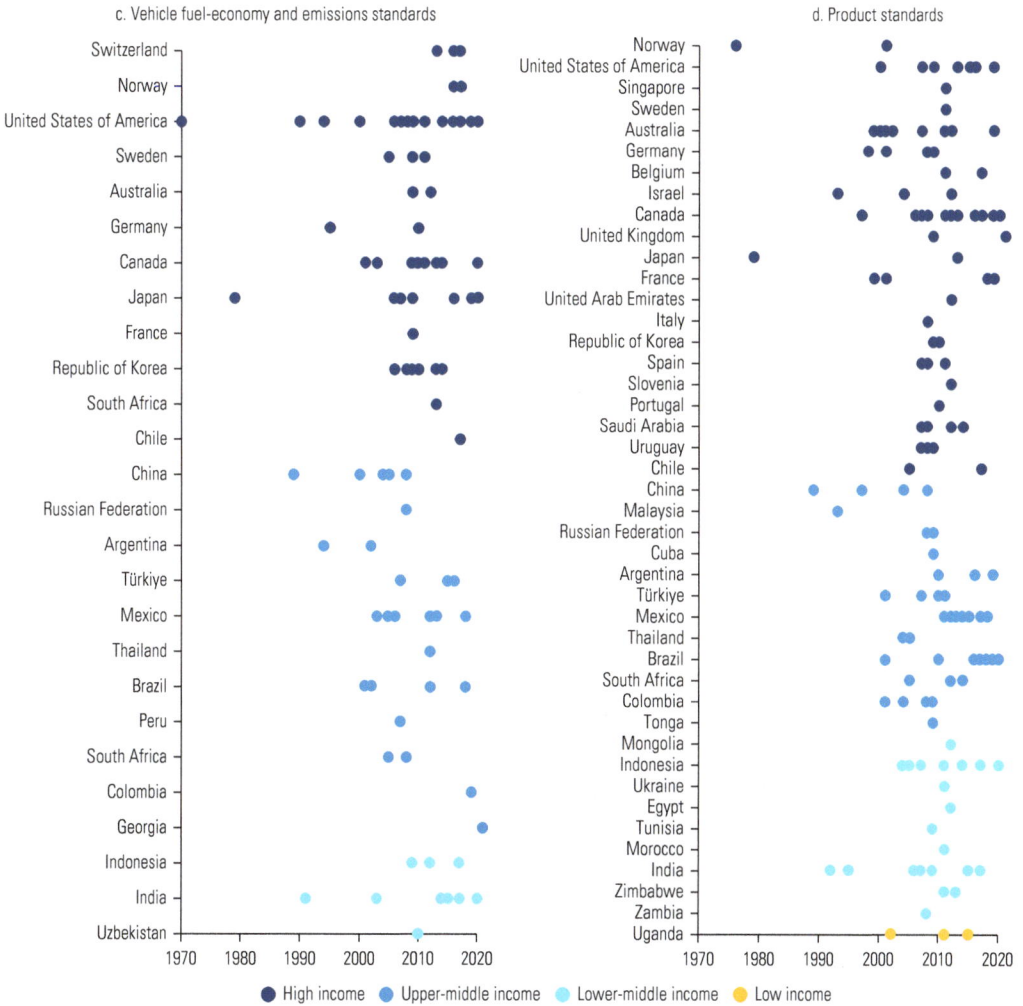

● High income　● Upper-middle income　● Lower-middle income　● Low income

Source: World Bank calculations based on data from the Climate Policy Database 2022.

climate finance flows in LICs and MICs reached nearly US$425 billion in 2020, this is still nowhere near enough to support total global needs for mitigation and adaptation. Annual climate finance to all sectors in LICs and MICs needs to quadruple to around US$1.7 trillion by 2030.

Public actors have historically accounted for the majority of climate finance; going forward, scaling up private finance will be critical. In 2020, public sources provided almost 60 percent of mitigation finance to LICs and MICs, led by national development finance institutions (27 percent), state-owned financial institutions (12 percent), and multilateral development banks (8 percent) (figure 2.14). However, with governments

FIGURE 2.13 **Global Climate Finance, 2011–21 (US$ billion)**

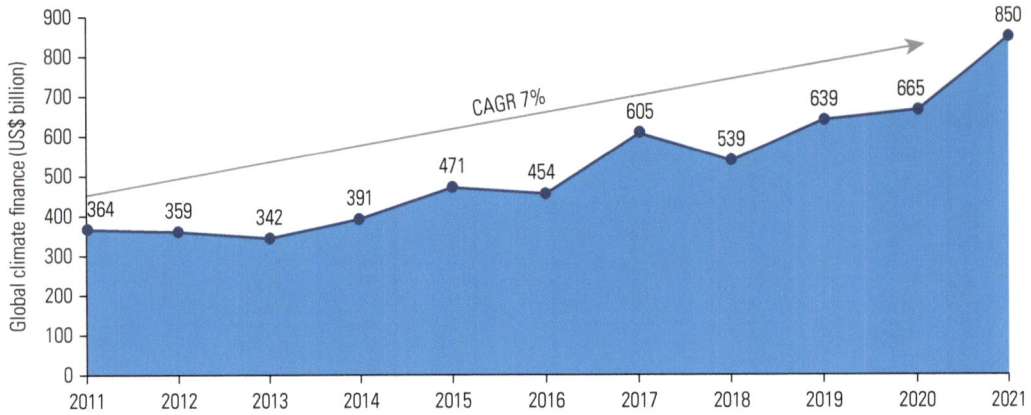

Source: CPI 2022.

Note: US$850 billion in 2021 is an estimate that will be confirmed in the Climate Policy Initiative's forthcoming *2023 Global Landscape of Climate Finance*; CAGR = compound annual growth rate.

FIGURE 2.14 **Climate Finance Flows to LICs and MICs, 2019–20 Average (US$ billion)**

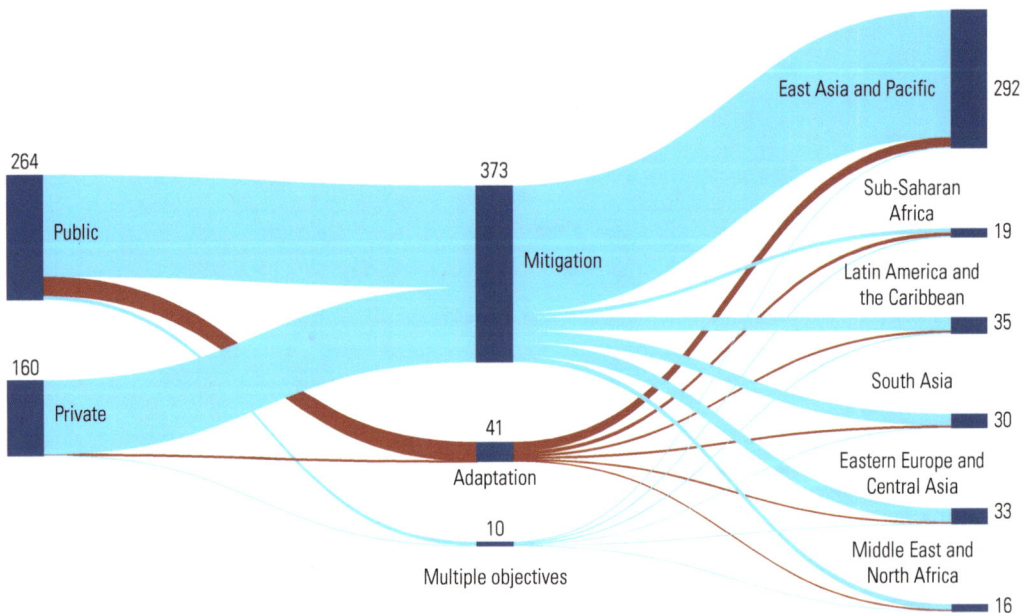

Source: World Bank calculations using rounded data from CPI 2021.

Note: LICs = low-income countries; MICs = middle-income countries.

facing highly constrained fiscal spaces following the pandemic, and LICs and MICs having higher government borrowing costs, it has become difficult for public finance to meet pressing investment needs. Mobilizing and scaling up finance from the private sector is therefore key to helping countries access the capital they need to achieve climate objectives.

Policies to incentivize private sector participation and improve the attractiveness of the investment climate are critical. The private sector often finds it unattractive to invest in countries facing higher investment risk. Combining public and private capital can help address these risks and attract greater funding for climate investments. Development finance institutions—including the World Bank—can play an important role in creating blended financing structures to improve the risk-return profile of specific projects. Improving the regulatory and investment environment can also help attract private sector participation. The case of Kenya's power sector (Case Study 23) provides a helpful example. Through a series of regulatory reforms, Kenya was able to attract the necessary private capital and incentivize almost 30 independent power producers to help triple generation capacity, improve system reliability, and reduce carbon intensity by around 60 percent.

In addition to attracting new finance, we need to green existing flows by taking into account climate-related risks and opportunities. Greening the financial system creates an opportunity to mobilize new investment and lending in sectors and activities that contribute to climate objectives. Greening the financial system also means managing climate-related risks that could adversely impact the financial sector (World Bank 2021). Case Study 22 provides a key example. As well as being the first Latin American country to issue local currency green bonds in its domestic market, Colombia has initiated several actions to green its financial sector. These include requiring a climate risk stress test that assesses the impact of different climate scenarios on the banking sector, implementing regulatory reforms for banks and investors to help integrate climate risks into risk management, increasing governance and disclosure practices, and developing a green taxonomy to facilitate green investment classification. Although it is still too early to evaluate their success, these initiatives are considered important building blocks that will encourage a more sustainable financial system in Colombia going forward.

Ensuring a Just Transition

To implement increasingly ambitious climate policies, governments need to protect the most vulnerable populations and manage distributional impacts (box 2.1). Reducing distributional impacts and ensuring that the most vulnerable are not harmed by policy design and implementation are crucial for building social acceptance and support.

Some policies—such as carbon taxes or fossil fuel subsidy reform—can generate resources that countries can use to redistribute benefits and mitigate negative effects. Social protection, active labor policy, and other approaches can also help ensure that decarbonization policies are progressive and support the transition.

A just transition approach involves enhancing the equity and fairness of policy decisions and outcomes. This means sharing the costs and benefits fairly, distributing risks and capacities to respond (distributional justice), and ensuring transparent and inclusive decision-making with equal accessibility that compensates for structural exclusion (procedural justice).

Governments are already using a just transition approach to help smooth the transition away from coal power. It is important to manage the social impacts associated with decommissioning coal-fired power plants. This includes early retirement or retraining the work force and investing in affected communities. Experience from the European Union shows that a successful and smooth transition out of coal is more likely when supported by community engagement and investment in public infrastructure to attract alternative activities and jobs.

Other sectors could also benefit from a just transition approach. For example, the shift to EVs will transform the car industry's global value chain and, while there will be winners and losers, the overall number of jobs will decline, as EVs have a simpler and more efficient design. In parallel, if the workforce has appropriate skills and mobility, green activities, such as afforestation, can be major job creators.

Policy communication and engagement can also help build support for decarbonization policies. In Indonesia, where backlash to fossil fuel subsidy reforms contributed to the downfall of the Suharto regime in the 1990s, the 2005 reform success was built on a wide-scale, well-prepared communication campaign highlighting that savings would be recycled through a cash transfer to compensate for the impact of reforms. The importance of civic engagement and communication is being applied in sector and economy-wide decarbonization planning in various forms, including citizens' assemblies like Costa Rica's Citizen's Climate Change Advisor Council.

Policies that create winners also help build a support base for decarbonization (Global Commission on the Economy and Climate 2018). For example, people are more likely to support and implement policies that use demand support instruments, such as subsidies and incentives, than those that use technology support instruments, such as taxes and fines. The same applies to nonmarket and market instruments (OECD 2018). Many governments favor demand support instruments for decarbonization. The 2022 US Inflation Reduction Act is the largest ever fiscal package for decarbonization, almost completely composed of demand support instruments, including public investment and tax credits for clean energy, fuel, and vehicles; conservation; and reducing air pollution.[1] Over time, these public investments can create coalitions that support decarbonization.

Sometimes compensation and other approaches are needed to ease opposition of those industries that could incur costs. Governments can accommodate those groups that are negatively affected through direct compensation, as Germany did with its Coal Phase-Out Law, which allots considerable public resources to coal power companies and coal mining regions. Case Studies 24 and 25 focus on lessons from coal mine closures in South Africa and Europe.

BOX 2.1 **Using Ex Ante and Ex Post Assessments to Understand Distributional Employment Effects**

Concern about the employment impact of policies can be a contentious and politicized issue. Decarbonization will involve shifts in labor demand away from fossil fuels and emissions-intensive industries. With the right information, policy design can help mitigate negative impacts and support job transitions.

Ex ante assessments of the employment impacts of decarbonization help policy makers better understand aggregate outcomes and basic distributional effects. Ex ante or prospective studies tend to project modest, often positive, aggregate employment impacts globally and in most countries at the national level. They also suggest that employment impacts are likely to be concentrated spatially and in specific sectors. Low-skilled workers, particularly those in energy supply or energy-intensive industries, will generally be more affected. Advanced ex ante tools also show that there is often a mismatch between the location, requirements, and quality of employment alternatives in sectors or regions where job losses are projected to take place.

Ex post assessments help add more granularity and context-specific information about distributional impacts that can help design more progressive and just policies. While the aggregate employment impacts of climate policies tend to be modest and net positive at a macro or project level, distributional effects can lead to uneven or unfair outcomes, with impacts often concentrated in a specific sector, region, or socioeconomic or cultural group. The impacts of job losses can also be compounded when people lose benefits—such as pension, health care, social standing, or identity—from their previous job, or where lower-quality jobs or weak labor market regulations decrease the attractiveness of jobs created or increase job transition costs. Although ex post studies provide some justification for increased focus on how climate policies can ensure the just transition of the workforce and creation of decent work and quality jobs stipulated in the Paris Agreement, they also suggest that the fear of widespread negative employment impacts should not cause countries to delay climate action.

Source: Godinho 2021.

Note

1. A summary of the Inflation Reduction Act is available at https://www.congress.gov/bill/117th-congress/house-bill/5376.

References

CPI (Climate Policy Initiative). 2021. "Global Landscape of Climate Finance 2021."

CPI (Climate Policy Initiative). 2022. "Global Landscape of Climate Finance: A Decade of Data." https://www.climatepolicyinitiative.org/wp-content/uploads/2022/10/Global-Landscape-of-Climate-Finance-A-Decade-of-Data.pdf.

De La Tour, A., M. Glachant, and Y. Ménière. 2011. "Innovation and International Technology Transfer: The Case of the Chinese Photovoltaic Industry." *Energy Policy* 39 (2): 761–70.

Econoler International. 2016. *Market Assessment Report for Energy Efficiency in Public Buildings.* Prepared by Econoler International on behalf of the Turkish Ministry of Energy and Natural Resources under the World Bank–GEF Small and Medium Enterprise Energy Efficiency Project.

Eskander, S., S. Fankhauser, and J. Setzer. 2020. "Global Lessons from Climate Change Legislation and Litigation." Working Paper 27365, National Bureau of Economic Research, Cambridge, MA. https://doi.org/10.3386/w27365.

Fay, M., S. Hallegatte, A. Vogt-Schilb, J. Rozenberg, U. Narloch, and T. Kerr. 2015. *Decarbonizing Development: Three Steps to a Zero-Carbon Future. Climate Change and Development.* Washington, DC: World Bank. http://hdl.handle.net/10986/21842 License: CC BY 3.0 IGO.

Global Commission on the Economy and Climate. 2018. *Unlocking the Inclusive Growth Story of the 21st Century: Accelerating Climate Action in Urgent Times.* Washington, DC: New Climate Economy. https://newclimateeconomy.report/2018.

Godinho, C. 2021. "What Do We Know about the Employment Impacts of Climate Policies? A Review of the Ex Post Literature." *Wiley Interdisciplinary Reviews: Climate Change* 13 (6): e794.

Government of Costa Rica. 2020. "Contribución Nacionalmente Determinada 2020." https://unfccc.int.

IEA (International Energy Agency). 2021a. "Net Zero by 2050: A Roadmap for the Global Energy Sector." International Energy Agency. https://www.iea.org/events/net-zero-by-2050-a-roadmap-for-the-global-energy-system.

IEA (International Energy Agency). 2021b. *World Energy Outlook 2021.* Paris: IEA. https://www.iea.org/reports/world-energy-outlook-2021.

IEA (International Energy Agency). 2023a. Fossil Fuels Consumption Subsidies 2022. Paris. https://www.iea.org/reports/fossil-fuels-consumption-subsidies-2022, License: CC BY 4.0.

IEA (International Energy Agency). 2023b. Policies and Measures Database. https://www.iea.org/policies.

OECD (Organisation for Economic Co-operation and Development). 2018. "Making Carbon Pricing Work for All: Experiences and Insights." OECD Publishing.

OECD (Organisation for Economic Co-operation and Development). 2022. "Support for Fossil Fuels Almost Doubled in 2021, Slowing Progress Toward International Climate Goals, According to New Analysis from OECD and IEA." https://www.oecd.org/newsroom/support-for-fossil-fuels-almost-doubled-in-2021-slowing-progress-toward-international-climate-goals-according-to-new-analysis-from-oecd-and-iea.htm.

SystemIQ. 2020. "The Paris Effect: How the Climate Agreement Is Reshaping the Global Economy." https://www.systemiq.earth/wp-content/uploads/2020/12/The-Paris-Effect_SYSTEMIQ_Full-Report_December-2020.pdf.

Way, R., M. Ives, P. Mealy, and D. Farmer. 2022. "Empirically Grounded Technology Forecasts and the Energy Transition." *Joule* 6 (9): 2057–82.

World Bank. 2021. "Toolkits for Policymakers to Green the Financial System." World Bank, Washington, DC.

World Bank. 2022a. Carbon Pricing Dashboard. https://carbonpricingdashboard.worldbank.org/.

World Bank. 2022b. "State and Trends of Carbon Pricing 2022." https://openknowledge.worldbank.org/handle/10986/37455.

3. Decarbonization Policy Implementation: Illustrative Case Studies

The case studies in this chapter provide examples of decarbonization policy implementation, providing country context and policy details, examining results where possible, and outlining key takeaways and lessons learned. The case studies cover a wide range of sectors and geographic settings to provide a diversity of experiences for policy makers to learn from. Countries are taking many different approaches; this is an illustrative list and does not attempt to cover the full landscape of decarbonization policy making.

These real-world policies are far from the first-best recommendation—indeed, many would not be considered best practice—but their implementation highlights important lessons on how to design and execute low-carbon policies. In most cases, there is no ex post assessment of their performance, outcomes, or economic costs and benefits. Such assessments are difficult, especially in the context of multiple policies that are implemented in parallel and rapid changes in the cost and availability of technologies. Identifying a causal link between a policy and changes in greenhouse gas (GHG) emissions often remains out of reach, with a few exceptions highlighted in the case studies. This report, therefore, cannot conclude on the efficacy or efficiency of these policies, and its value added is in the description of the process and design of policies that have been implemented.

We have classified the case studies using the typology outlined in chapter 2, but most policies combine different dimensions of climate action and do not cleanly belong in a single category. For example, we have classified Case Studies 4 and 6 under "Getting the Prices Right," but they both combine pricing policies with demand support policies to facilitate the shift of households and firms toward more efficient low-carbon policies and with interventions to navigate the political economy of the reform and ensure a just transition.

Planning for a Future with Zero Net Emissions: Costa Rica

Case Study 1. Developing and Implementing a Net Zero Development Pathway in a Middle-Income Country: Costa Rica's National Decarbonization Plan

Contributors: David Groves, Felipe DeLeon, and World Bank staff

Context

Building on its long tradition of sustainable development and strong focus on ecotourism, Costa Rica became an early champion of global decarbonization to limit global warming.[1] Its first national communication to the United Nations Framework Convention on Climate Change (UNFCCC) in 2000 highlights its early strategy for a low-carbon economy, beginning with developing a national GHG inventory in 1995 and implementing renewable hydropower and wind projects to expand access to electricity and eliminate fossil fuel power generation (Government of Costa Rica 2000). In 2007, the government expanded its commitment by announcing its goal to become carbon neutral. By 2011, Costa Rica had become one of the first countries to participate in the UN's Nationally Appropriate Mitigation Actions program, which provided financial support to reduce GHG emissions from its coffee supply chain.

In 2015, Costa Rica submitted its intended nationally determined contribution (NDC), which quantified near-term and intermediate targets and actions for reducing emissions in accordance with the Paris Agreement. This effort brought together a national team led by the Costa Rica Climate Change Directorate (Dirección de Cambio Climático de Costa Rica), known as the DCC team, with support from national and international sector experts, including the World Bank (PMR 2015). The NDC articulated an initial set of targets and approaches for reducing net GHG emissions, with a goal of reducing net emissions to 9.37 MtCO$_2$e, or 25 percent by 2030, compared with 2012 (World Bank 2016a). The NDC process also revealed a need for more comprehensive modeling of economic development and emissions pathways to formulate a complete long-term decarbonization strategy.

Costa Rica's government accelerated efforts to decarbonize in 2018. At this time, the president appointed the Climate Change Directorate within the Ministry of the Environment and Energy to lead the development of a new national decarbonization strategy. The Office of the President and First Lady became directly involved in designing, monitoring, and coordinating the plan (Calfucoy et al. 2022). This commitment to climate action helped bring not only the Ministry of the Environment but also the Ministry of Finance and other line ministries—such as energy, transport, and housing—into strategic decarbonization planning. This, in turn, attracted international support, particularly from the multilateral development bank (MDB) community, for building in-country analytical capacity to drive the complex planning processes to come.

Policy

With international support, Costa Rica built internal technical capacity within its government and national universities. Through partnerships with the University of Costa Rica, the Inter-American Development Bank (IDB), the United Nations Development Programme, and others, Costa Rica was able to garner resources to develop technoeconomic models and capabilities for advanced policy analysis to support dialogues on plausible and beneficial decarbonization pathways (Bataille, Waisman, and Vogt-Schib 2021). By developing strong technical capabilities in the central DCC team, they successfully argued for ambitious climate action with diverse stakeholders, some of whom did not originally share that ambition.

Using this new capability and with international assistance, Costa Rica developed a whole-of-economy net zero national decarbonization plan (NDP), which it submitted as its long-term strategy (LTS) to the UNFCCC at the end of 2019. Importantly, this NDP set the ambitious goal of net zero GHG emissions by 2050—consistent with the more aggressive 1.5°C global warming limit. Taking advantage of its extensive renewable hydropower resources, Costa Rica's NDP called for the electrification of its transport sector, increases in energy efficiency and electrification of buildings and many industries, and investments to promote a more circular economy by collecting and recycling material and fully treating wastewater. Remaining emissions, particularly from agriculture and livestock, are to be completely offset through increased carbon sequestration from forests (Government of Costa Rica 2019). To achieve these outcomes, the NDP defined a framework with more than 70 targets and specific near-term actions for 35 agencies and line ministries, which served as the basis for several large policy-based loans (Jaramillo et al. 2023).

The LTS team formulated and evaluated development pathways that would lead to net zero emissions by mid-century while providing tangible benefits to the country. Costa Rica followed a "deliberation with analysis" approach in which models and quantitative analysis of emissions pathways, costs, and benefits under uncertainty support intense stakeholder engagements and discussions around the analytical results and revealed trade-offs (Groves and Lempert 2007). Developing whole-of-economy pathways and presenting targets and timelines to all emitting sectors enabled technical discussions with different sectors to explore the necessary changes and identify barriers and needed enabling conditions.

Costa Rica's climate policy development process strongly engaged technical and nontechnical stakeholders. The LTS explicitly served as the basis for developing Costa Rica's NDC update in 2020. It used an extensive stakeholder engagement process using a locally developed method called "Climate Conversations" to ensure that it properly considered climate justice and a just transition and that it accounted for the interests of a broad range of Costa Ricans, including those from marginalized communities (Government of Costa Rica 2020). During the process of updating the NDC, the DCC team held nine decarbonization workshops with some 350 sectoral participants to explore the NDP's benefits and costs (Groves et al. 2020).

The Costa Rican government has taken the lead on institutionalizing measures into law and integrating low-carbon development into governmental processes. Presidential support was crucial in driving the Climate Change Law through congress. Several ministers, including the ministers of finance and planning, attended meetings convened by the president and first lady to agree on how they could support the LTS effort. This high-level engagement was also instrumental in developing and agreeing to the terms of the policy-based loans, which provided concessionary funding for NDP-aligned national development.

Costa Rica has taken important steps to operationalize its NDP, pursuing a wide range of activities to shift its economy toward carbon neutrality. According to its fourth national communication to the UNFCCC, it implemented 17 policy actions and 17 specific mitigation programs between 2015 and 2020. Its NDP lays out 23 projects and programs and 20 policies that would need to be implemented going forward.

Results and Impacts

Costa Rica's NDP represents one of the most ambitious strategies for low-carbon development for a middle-income country. The NDP covers all major emissive sectors and would lead to net zero by 2050 under baseline assumptions. A follow-on study, supported by the IDB, evaluated the NDP under thousands of plausible futures, reflective of different assumptions, and found that the country would achieve close to zero emissions in most futures (figure 3.1) and that the net benefits of implementing the NDP would likely be highly positive, estimated at $41 billion through 2050 under baseline assumptions.

Analysis of the NDP suggests that its implementation would have highly positive macroeconomic benefits. Evaluations show positive effects on economic growth, employment, and poverty. One study finds that decarbonization and digitization investments could result in 135,000 net new jobs by 2050. Another shows that implementing the NDP could offset longer-term gross domestic product (GDP) and job losses from COVID-19 (Groves et al. 2022). A macroeconomic study, focused on the agriculture, forestry, and other land use sectors, finds cumulative positive wealth impacts in these sectors of about US$9 billion by 2050, and estimates that investments could lift over 4,500 people out of poverty by 2050 (Banerjee et al. 2022).

Articulating a strong decarbonization plan has helped Costa Rica mobilize at least $2.4 billion in international concessional finance. According to a review of the effects of the NDP on financial resource mobilization, Costa Rica has received funds

FIGURE 3.1   Costa Rican GHG Emissions over Time, without Decarbonization and with the NDP

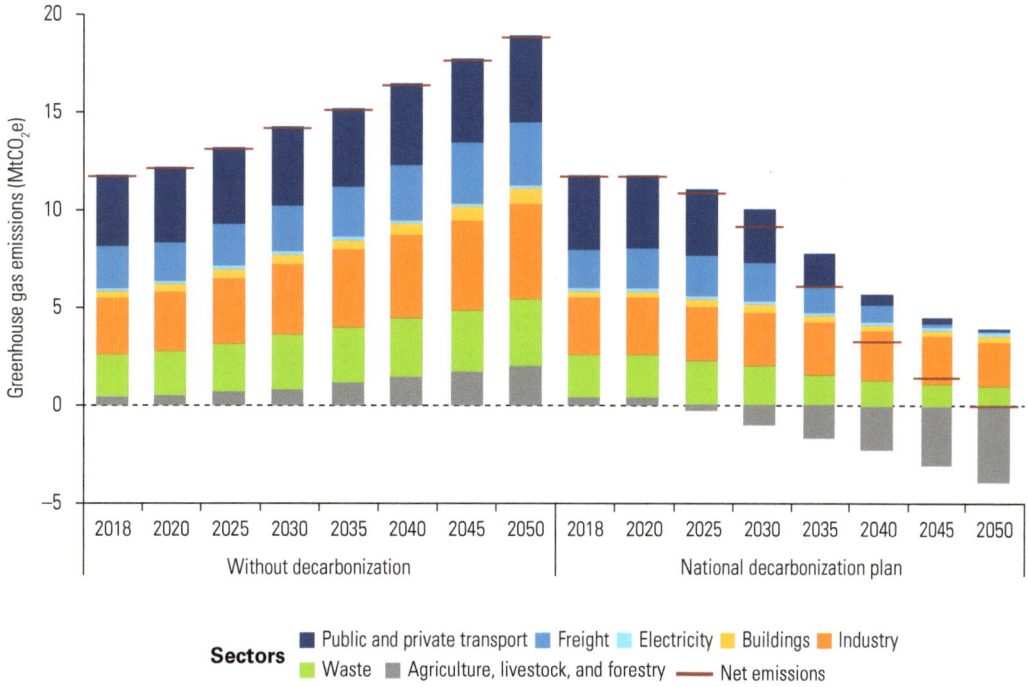

Source: Groves et al. 2020.

Note: Emissions from the electricity sector are negligible in Costa Rica under baseline assumptions. GHG = greenhouse gas; $MtCO_2e$ = metric megatons of CO_2 equivalent (million tons); NDP = national decarbonization plan.

from 13 different sources, including several MDBs and other development partners, in the form of grants, policy-based loans, and dedicated external funding (Jaramillo et al. 2023).

Through governmental leadership, Costa Rica was able to drive agreement on aggressive climate action. The multiprong approach to stakeholder engagement, with workshops across different sectors and groups as well as meetings with larger emitting businesses and state-owned enterprises, was essential. The close links between the central technical and stakeholder engagement teams strengthened their ability to encourage diverse interest groups to consider options of far more ambitious emissions reductions than they had initially thought viable. The high-level political backing also played an important role in reaching an agreement from the state-owned petroleum importer and refiner to the LTS plans for transport electrification.

Key Takeaways

The Costa Rican experience developing and starting to implement its NDP provides several key takeaways on how a middle-income country can build the necessary technical capacity and political and public support to move toward net zero. It further highlights some key challenges to the full implementation and achievement of a net zero.

- Successful LTS implementation must be guided by a clear transformation pathway that identifies and enables the many targets and changes required to achieve its goals. The concept of a whole-of-economy low-emissions development pathway must be the technical core of an LTS, and its elaboration should be a central aspect of its development process.

- There must be widespread stakeholder buy-in of targets, processes, and narratives of change over the short, medium, and long terms. Stakeholders must understand and agree on the importance of their roles, as this helps ensure that most of their decisions are aligned with the Paris goals. Costa Rica used international expertise and resources to empower and strengthen the national team and help it develop and run a series of sectoral workshops, with the Ministry of Environment and Energy maintaining control and full visibility of the work. This approach allowed the national team to use and defend the analysis throughout the iterative stakeholder engagement process, which would not have been possible with purely outsourced analysis.

- Full political sponsorship at the head-of-government level can ensure the appropriate buy-in and governance to enable LTS implementation. The unprecedented changes implied by the LTS will be disruptive for important sectors, resulting in shifts of activity and investment away from old modalities and into new ones. This can lead key groups to challenge the feasibility of such rapid change and not align with the minister or agency charged with coordinating LTS work. Only clear and constant support from the highest political figures can counter this.

- LTS implementation requires adequate institutional arrangements for financing, monitoring, and ensuring accountability. The mechanisms and institutions responsible for ongoing independent auditing and advice on LTS progress should be made clear and codified in law. Findings and recommendations should be reported at the highest level of government and widely publicized to encourage country leaders to take full responsibility for successful implementation. The challenge of financing decarbonization actions is also an important obstacle. While the central government successfully secured policy-based loans from development banks to support climate action, much more funding will be needed, particularly from the private sector. Finally, local and household actions will drive much of the country's shift to low-carbon development, but municipal authorities often have limited technical and planning capabilities, which can make it difficult to identify and scope specific projects that are in line with LTS requirements and can enhance local conditions. New partnerships between local universities, technical groups, and local governments can help overcome this challenge.

Planning for a Future with Zero Net Emissions: Indonesia

Case Study 2. Reducing Deforestation in Indonesia

Contributor: Alexander Lotsch

Context

Indonesia is an economic powerhouse in Southeast Asia. This archipelago nation has benefited from solid economic growth in recent decades. It is the 10th largest global economy in terms of purchasing power parity, is the only Southeast Asian member of the Group of 20 (G20), and has made significant gains in poverty reduction. It is also endowed with remarkable natural resources; as home to the world's third-largest tropical forest, it is a globally significant carbon sink.

Its economic success was at times accompanied by one of the world's highest rates of forest loss. Primarily driven by the production of agricultural commodities, notably palm oil and pulp and paper plantations, deforestation rates within the country's forest area (*kawasan hutan*) peaked in the late 1990s, and the country lost 8.49 million hectares of forest cover between 2000 and 2020 (Ministry of Environment and Forestry 2021). During those two decades, deforestation, land use, and peat fires contributed about 42 percent to Indonesia's overall GHG emissions. This land transformation heavily impacted Indonesia's peatlands—the partially flooded lowland areas of Kalimantan, Sumatra, and Papua—which have one of the world's largest biological carbon stocks, estimated at 13.6–40.5 Gt (Warren et al. 2017). Mangrove conversion for agriculture and aquaculture in coastal areas similarly contributed to high emissions (World Bank 2021b). (At 3.31 million hectares, Indonesia has around 20 percent of the world's total mangrove stock and, at times, the fastest absolute rate of loss [Arifanti 2020].) Recurring seasonal fires amplified during the dry El Niño years, including on peatlands, have significantly contributed to Indonesia's emissions. In 2015, fires burned 2.6 million hectares of Indonesian land, with daily emissions greater than those of the entire European Union (EU) economy (World Bank 2016b).

The effective protection of carbon-rich ecosystems has been stacked against the economics of land use in Indonesia. High opportunity costs have been a main barrier to counter the industrial-scale land use conversion for high-value agricultural commodity production. In the absence of a market value for standing forests and a valuation of the services they provide, economic forces are a principal driver of forest conversion, including for smallholders (Acosta and Curt 2019). These are compounded by inadequate management, weak governance, and limited enforcement capacity, especially at the subnational level, which are key underlying challenges for better land management and more effective protection of ecosystems. Despite these significant challenges,

Indonesia has started to reverse the historically negative patterns of forest loss in recent years through policy, regulations, and leveraging results-based payments.

Policy

Institutional reforms have aligned responsibilities for forests and climate, but challenges remain. In 2015, the government merged the environment and forestry ministries and mandated the new Ministry of Environment and Forestry (MoEF) to lead the country's climate commitment and oversee legally designated forest areas. Yet the Ministry of Agrarian and Spatial Planning retained responsibility for other forest lands (those designated within other-use areas), which complicates land administration and governance. At the same time, the Ministry of Agriculture implements land-relevant, demand-side policies, such as agricultural targets, often without full coordination with the MoEF. Other land-related decisions, such as issuing permits, are the responsibility of the local government, whose incentives do not align with national commitments, and revenue-raising options are limited. Between 2016 and 2019, the national government also established two new agencies, the Peat and Mangrove Restoration Agency (Badan Restorasi Gambut dan Mangrove, BRGM), responsible for delivering peatland restoration targets and expanded to include mangrove in 2021, and the Indonesia Environment Fund (Badan Pengelola Dana Lingkungan Hidup), a unit under the Ministry of Finance responsible for channeling financing for climate and environmental projects. These two new agencies have mandates that cut across sectors and provide models for how to align policy targets and coordination.

The government of Indonesia has made significant international commitments under the 2015 Paris Agreement to reduce the country's GHG emissions, with a focus on REDD+ (Reducing Emissions from Deforestation and forest Degradation, conservation of forest carbon stocks, sustainable forest management, and enhancement of forest carbon stocks in developing countries)(Government of Indonesia 2016). In the enhanced NDC submitted in 2022, the government pledged to reduce GHG emissions by 43.2 percent by 2030 with international assistance (31.9 percent with its own resources unconditionally) relative to a business-as-usual (BAU) scenario. Indonesia aims to meet more than 60 percent of the emissions reduction target through actions in forestry and land use (FOLU). These are projected to reduce emissions from a BAU projection of 714 $MtCO_2e$ to 214 $MtCO_2e$ in 2030 under the NDC's unconditional target (UNFCCC 2022). Going even further, Indonesia's FOLU Net Sink 2030 plan also outlines the government's aim to make forestry and land use a net carbon sink (that is, zero or negative net emissions) by 2030 by restoring 2.7 million hectares of peatlands, rehabilitating 5.3 million hectares of degraded forestlands, and further reducing deforestation and forest degradation (Ministry of Environment and Forestry 2022a).

These commitments draw on a series of policy reforms over the past decade. In 2011, the government placed a moratorium on new licenses for forest conversion in primary forests (a measure made permanent in 2019); in 2016, it placed a moratorium on licenses in peatlands. These measures were complemented by major land rights programs, helping address incentives for land clearing. In 2021, it introduced a Presidential Regulation on the Economic Valuation of Carbon to support result-based payments that incentivize conservation and restoration activities.[2] To complement the moratoria through command-and-control measures, the MoEF revoked 3.1 million hectares of forest concession licenses in 2022 and required concession holders to protect high conservation value forest areas. Some level of restoration of 1.3 million hectares of peatlands has been undertaken by BRGM to date, with a further 3.6 million hectares undertaken by the private sector within concessions under the government's peatland management regulations (Ministry of Environment and Forestry 2022b).

Indonesia has also mapped out its longer-term emissions trajectories toward a net-zero target in 2060. Its LTS demonstrated the technical feasibility of a low-carbon trajectory, reaching 1.61 tCO_2e per capita emissions by 2050 under its low-carbon strategy scenario, aligned with the Paris Agreement. The LTS does not provide a pathway to achieve the 2060 net zero target, but instead relies on unidentified measures or new technologies to fill the gap (Chrysolite et al. 2020).

The recognition of indigenous people's forest rights was a significant step forward in forest policy in Indonesia. In 2013, the Constitutional Court of Indonesia gave indigenous people the right to manage the forests in which they live, which led to a revision of the 1999 Forest Law. The National People's Organization (Aliansi Masyarakat Adat Nusantara, AMAN) filed the case and objected on the basis that government could grant permits for companies to exploit customary land for mining and palm oil, paper, and timber production (Johnson 2013). AMAN estimates that 40 million hectares of Indonesia's state forest should be under customary control, but only a fraction has been mapped or handed back to date. The process has been hampered by overlapping land claims, challenges in demonstrating indigenous occupation, and a slow bureaucracy (Jong 2022; Sari et al. 2018).

In addition, the government improved the enabling environment for REDD+. Actions included formulation of an enabling policy framework for REDD+ at national level and broad-based implementation plans at subnational level. Other activities include developing measurement, reporting, and verification systems; benefit-sharing arrangements for the proceeds of results-based payments; and a feedback and grievance redress mechanism.[3] International support contributed to these efforts, including through activities funded by the Forest Carbon Partnership Facility (FCPF) Readiness Fund implemented by the World Bank.

With key building blocks in place and experience of REDD+ pilots and initiatives, the government was in a position to access results-based payment to advance REDD+ implementation. It has been implementing a jurisdictional Emission Reductions Program in East Kalimantan since 2016, and it signed a $110 million Emission

Reduction Payment Agreement with the FCPF Carbon Fund in 2019 (a first payment of $20.9 million was made in November 2022).[4] It has also attracted support and finance through results-based emissions reduction payments from the Green Climate Fund ($103.8 million for early REDD+ results achieved at national level from 2014 to 2016) and through bilateral cooperation, most notably with Norway. More recently, the BioCarbon Fund Initiative for Sustainable Forest Landscapes has indicated to pay for future emission reductions generated in the Jambi and support the province's long-term low-emission economic growth strategy.

Results and Impacts

Indonesia's actions to reduce forest conversion have significantly lowered its annual GHG emissions in recent years. Between 2000 and 2006, an average of 1.13 million hectares of forests were converted to other land use annually. After a peak in 2015 (1.09 million hectares), the annual conversion rate came down to 0.11 million hectares for 2020–21. Accordingly, emissions from forests and land use gradually decreased from 743 $MtCO_2e$ in 2015 to an annual average of 490 $MtCO_2e$ for 2016–19 and reached 165 $MtCO_2e$ in 2020.[5] In contrast to earlier years (2001–15), the rise in oil palm prices since 2016 does not appear to have led to an upswing in forest clearing (Kiely et al. 2021). With these trends, Indonesia has outperformed Brazil and the Democratic Republic of Congo with respect to reducing forest-related emissions. National actions, such as the revoking of forest concession licenses, have been further complemented by and expanded in several provinces. East Kalimantan, for instance, has imposed a moratorium on new licenses for mining, forestry, and estate crops and developed policies to accelerate social forestry licensing and fire prevention. The effective implementation of these and other policies will be critical to sustain this trend at national and subnational levels.

To sustain the progress, it is important to further deepen and strengthen the policy framework for net zero emission from forests and land use. This includes the expansion for protection for forest and peatland areas not yet covered by current moratoria, as well as for subnational plans to extend protections to areas designated as nonforest areas (which often have important carbon-rich ecosystems, such as mangroves). It will be necessary to continue clarifying land tenure status to allow for stronger enforcement by responsible agencies. There is further scope to use fiscal incentives (including intergovernmental transfers) to protect carbon-rich ecosystems—forests, peatland, mangroves—and to develop a financing strategy for the implementation of actions set out in the FOLU Net Sink 2030 roadmap.

Key Takeaways

Indonesia was one of many countries to have advanced national REDD+ policies since the concept became a formal part of the UNFCCC negotiations in 2007 and was eventually enshrined in Article 5 of the Paris Agreement. The government has taken regulatory actions (moratoria, revoking licenses) and enhanced capacity for land use decision-making (including new institutions) that have reduced deforestation and promoted restoration and conservation. Major initiatives—including the World Bank's FCPF—have contributed to the development of the following: technical standards for jurisdictional REDD+ (such as for the definition of baselines and protocols for measuring, reporting, and verification); robust frameworks for social and environmental safeguards; benefit–sharing; and legal and transactional modalities that need to be in place to transfer emission reductions internationally. Most countries have pursued jurisdictional implementation, building on experience from earlier, smaller-scale REDD+ projects, and expect to use the emission reductions achieved in recent years to meet their stated NDC targets.

The successful implementation of REDD+ across a number of large jurisdictions globally using rigorous technical, legal, and safeguards standards is also now attracting demand from the private sector and allows governments to leverage additional finance for implementation—for example, through the Carbon Offsetting and Reduction Scheme for International Aviation. Yet, while efforts over the past decade have demonstrated that REDD+ can be implemented at scale and deliver viable emissions reductions that meet market demand and requirements, a significant scale-up of land-based mitigation actions, including REDD+, continues to be critical to meet the temperature targets of the Paris Agreement (Roe et al. 2021; Smith et al. 2019). Also, a key issue in Indonesia, and elsewhere, remains that there is currently no clarity on longer-term sources for future REDD+ payments, including from voluntary and compliance carbon markets.

Planning for a Future with Zero Net Emissions: United Kingdom

Case Study 3. The United Kingdom Climate Change Act: A Climate Change Framework Law

Contributors: Thomas Kerr and Grace Henry

The United Kingdom (UK) Climate Change Act has led the way for the development of climate legislation around the world. A world-first national "framework" legislation, the Climate Change Act created a comprehensive and overarching law that set out the United Kingdom's approach to reducing emissions and preparing for the impacts of climate change. Passed in 2008, it initially included a legally binding emission reduction goal of 80 percent below 1990 levels by 2050 (CCC 2020). In 2019, this was updated to require net zero emissions by 2050, making the United Kingdom the first Group of Seven country to enshrine such a target into law (Evans 2019). The act requires the UK government to undertake climate change risk assessments (CCRAs) and develop adaptation plans that respond to these risks.[6]

National framework legislation can provide stability and direction to achieve climate goals. This form of legislation can help create the institutions required to plan, implement, and sustain credible commitments on climate policies that last beyond political cycles (World Bank 2020e). Legislation can enshrine stable and ambitious targets into law, create mechanisms for realizing them, and ensure proper oversight and accountability. Many other nations have since adopted similar legislation, including Denmark, France, Germany, Ireland, Mexico, New Zealand, and Sweden; this case study analyzes the features of the UK Climate Change Act and evaluates its impact on the United Kingdom's decarbonization and adaptation pathways.

Context

The United Kingdom has the world's fifth largest GDP, and this advanced economic development has allowed it to take progressive action on climate change. Since 1990, the country has been transitioning away from the energy sources that previously fueled its economic growth, decreasing its coal use by over 90 percent from 2.6 million terajoules in 1990 to 218,000 terajoules in 2020 (IEA 2022h). Both absolute and per capita emissions peaked in the 1970s and then declined, largely assisted by the transition away from coal and deindustrialization (Ritchie, Roser, and Rosado 2020).

Public pressure and political consensus supported the creation and implementation of the Climate Change Act, which was adopted in 2008 with support across party lines and strong civil society engagement (CCC 2020; IPAC 2021). Before this, scientific evidence on the effects of climate change had been mounting (IPCC 2007). In 2005, the UK government commissioned the Stern Review on the Economics of Climate Change, which concluded that "the benefits of strong and early action far outweigh the economic costs of not acting" (Stern 2006). At the same time, environmental nongovernmental organizations were increasing pressure on the government to give statutory force to emission reduction targets (Centre for Public Impact 2016). Together, these factors contributed to the adoption of the UK Climate Change Act 2008 (figure 3.2).

Policy

The Climate Change Act provides an overarching framework and governance structure for climate mitigation and adaptation in the United Kingdom, with the key features set out here (CCC 2020).

Long-term goal: The act contains a legally binding goal for reducing the United Kingdom's GHG emissions by 2050 (Provision 1), initially by at least 80 percent below 1990 levels, updated in 2019 to reflect the Paris Agreement and require net zero emissions (Government of the United Kingdom 2019). The 2050 goal signals the government's long-term commitment to a low-carbon economy.

FIGURE 3.2   Key Milestones of the UK Climate Change Act 2008

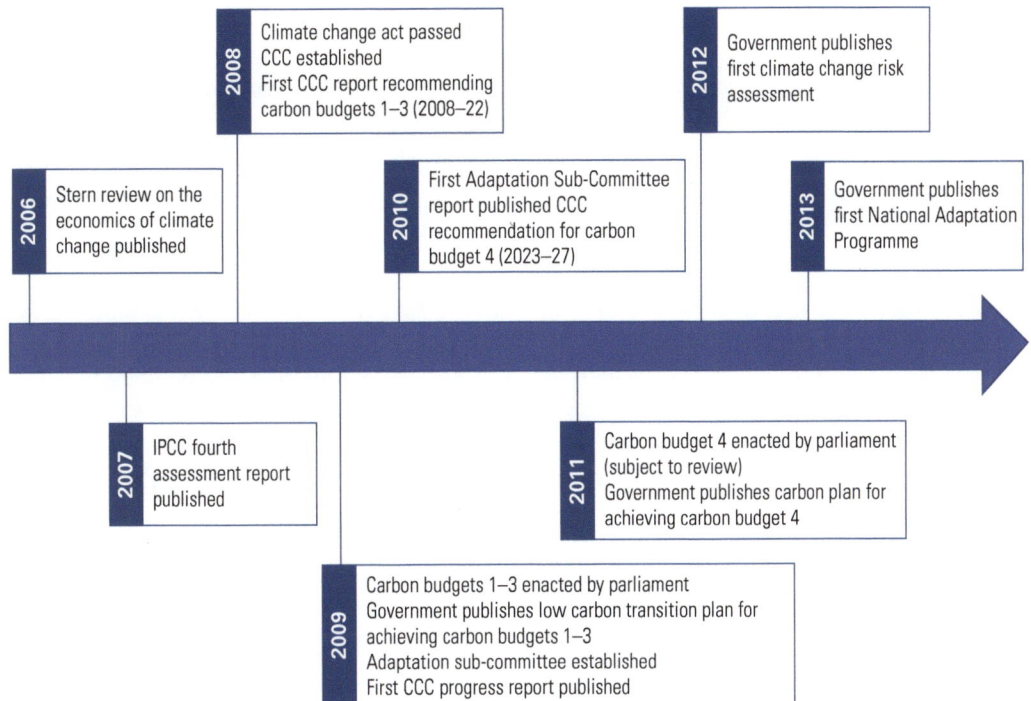

Source: Adapted from Fankhauser, Averchenkova, and Finnegan 2018.

Note: CCC = Climate Change Committee; IPCC = Intergovernmental Panel on Climate Change.

Intermediary short-term targets: The act contains interim targets called carbon budgets that are designed to provide a pathway toward the long-term goal. These carbon budgets are legally binding limits for GHG emissions over five-year periods (Provision 4). The budgets are legislated 12 years in advance to enable government and business planning to occur. The government has a legal duty to meet both the short- and long-term targets, but the act does not spell out penalties for noncompliance. In the event of noncompliance with these legal duties, members of the public and organizations with appropriate legal standing can bring judicial review cases.

Continual process of adaptation planning: The act prescribes an iterative approach to adaptation planning (Provision 56), involving mandated five-year CCRA cycles, followed by updated risk management responses published in the National Adaptation Programme.

Independent advisory body: The act created the Climate Change Committee (CCC) as an independent statutory adviser (Provision 32). The CCC has two committees with politically impartial experts: the Mitigation Committee, which provides recommendations on the carbon budgets and monitors annual performance on reducing emissions, and the Adaptation Sub-Committee (ASC), which advises the government on key climate risks facing the United Kingdom and reviews adaptation progress every two years. It may also provide additional advice on request. Although the CCC has no formal decision-making powers, the government is obliged to respond to its assessments and provide explanations where deviations from recommendations occur.

Regular government reporting: The act assigns clear duties and responsibilities to the government. Once a carbon budget has been adopted, the government must put forward its policies that will enable legislated targets to be met. This mechanism enables public scrutiny and judicial review to occur if the government's responses appear non-compliant.

Results and Impacts

The United Kingdom has achieved significant reductions in GHG emissions while continuing to grow its economy (figure 3.3). In 2020, these totaled 429 $MtCO_2e$, 31 percent below 2008 levels and 42 percent below 1990 levels (CCC 2022; ClimateWatch n.d.). This is the largest reduction in GHG emissions by any G20 country since 1990 (CCC 2021).

Greater emission cuts have occurred from sources that the act covers. The United Kingdom's GHG emission reduction targets only account for *territorial emissions*—that is, those that occur within the national boundaries, plus its share of international aviation and shipping emissions. The United Kingdom's carbon budgets and the Paris Agreement do not account for *consumption emissions*, which are adjusted for international trade and include emissions associated with the production, transportation, use, and disposal of imported products and services. Territorial emissions

FIGURE 3.3   The United Kingdom's Emission Reductions and GDP Growth

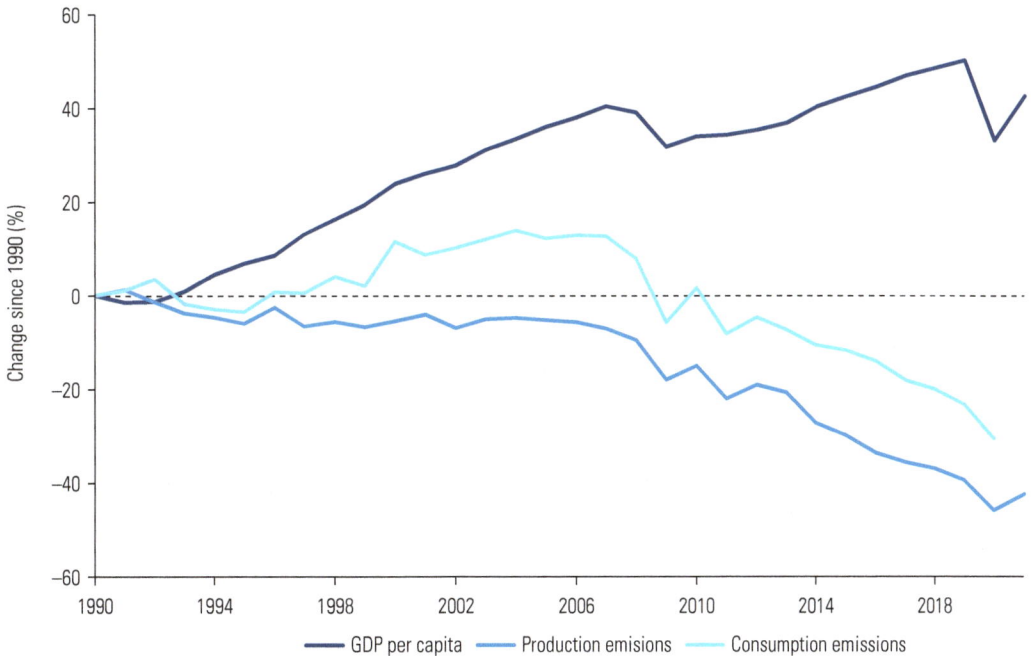

Source: CCC 2022.
Note: GDP = gross domestic product.

have decreased 47 percent below 1990 levels, compared with 29 percent for consumption emissions. Reductions in consumption emissions have also occurred, but to a lesser extent.

The Climate Change Act has facilitated structured and science-based political debates. The reporting procedures, progress reports, five-yearly carbon budgets, and risk assessments provide structure to the frequency and content of climate debates. This ensures that important climate issues get regularly addressed and updated. CCC findings and recommendations have also helped politicians hold the government to account and argue for more ambitious policy measures. In the first 10 years of operation, the CCC and ASC were referenced in 856 parliamentary interventions. Additionally, the proportion of parliamentary speeches related to climate change that referenced the CCC almost doubled from 2010 to 2017 (figure 3.4). This demonstrates that the CCC has functioned as a knowledge broker for many UK parliamentarians.

The United Kingdom is the only G20 country that has aligned its 2030 emission reduction targets with a 1.5°C pathway (Srouji et al. 2021). Each year, the United Nations Environment Programme's Emissions Gap Report publishes the difference between country emission targets and targets that are compatible with 1.5°C levels (UNEP 2021). Through the Climate Change Act, the UK government's target setting

FIGURE 3.4   CCC Mentions by UK Parliamentarians

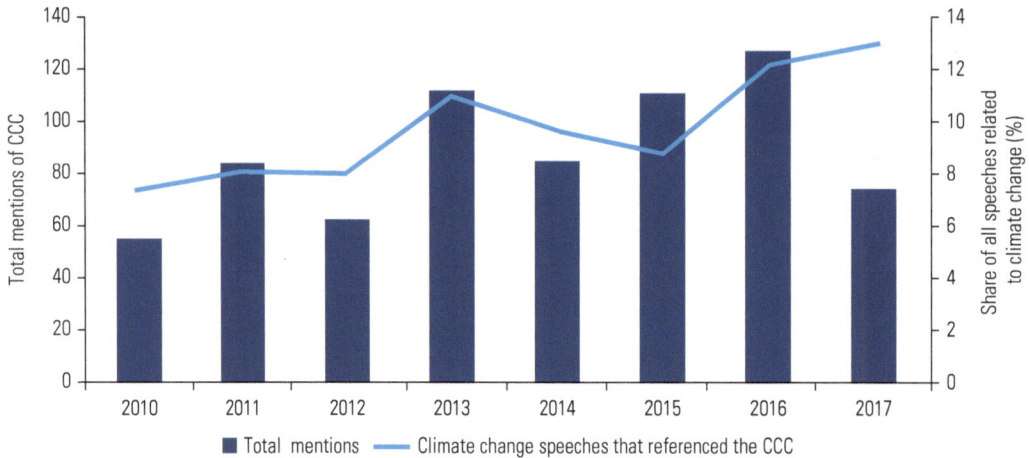

Source: Fankhauser, Averchenkova, and Finnegan 2018.
Note: CCC = Climate Change Committee; UK = United Kingdom.

has been based on the scientific carbon budget recommendations of the CCC. This has helped eliminate gaps between the United Kingdom's ambition to limit global warming to 1.5°C and its corresponding territorial emissions reduction targets.

Although the United Kingdom has made progress in identifying and creating awareness of climate risks, its responses to these risks require further work. Since introducing the Climate Change Act, the UK government has published three comprehensive CCRAs, increasing the country's ability to identify and raise awareness of the climate risks it faces. Although the government has made some improvements in adaptation plans for flood and erosion management, water scarcity, and extreme weather impacts on business, progress in other areas—such as agricultural productivity, pathogen risks, health impacts from temperature extremes, air quality, and digital infrastructure—is lagging. The 2021 CCC assessment highlights that the government has yet to demonstrate strong progress in climate risk adaptation in any of the 34 priority areas assessed. Overall, the gap between future levels of risk and planned adaptation is widening.

The Climate Change Act has proven to be an accountability mechanism for when the government's actions fall short of its targets. In 2022, three climate organizations jointly took the UK government to the high court to argue that it had failed to show how its policies would sufficiently reduce emissions to meet its legally binding carbon budgets (Client Earth 2022). In a landmark hearing, the court found that the government had failed to meet its obligations under the Climate Change Act and ordered it to undertake additional measures and provide an updated climate strategy with quantified figures on how its policies would achieve the required targets. Several other applications for judicial review have been refused.

Key Takeaways

The UK Climate Change Act has highlighted how national climate framework legislation can help improve the stability and accountability of domestic climate goals. The design and implementation of framework legislation can vary, resulting in different outcomes.

- *Independent expert climate committees can be useful:* The CCC has helped UK politicians make more scientifically informed decisions that take a long-term view. This technical approach to decision-making is similar to how many countries deal with monetary policy.
- *Political and public buy-in are required:* The Climate Change Act alone does not achieve emissions reductions. Its success depends on political parties respecting the requirements of the act and implementing the recommendations of the CCC. This requires strong public institutions, cross-party support, and ongoing public engagement.
- *Both long-term targets and short-term milestones are necessary*: The Climate Change Act has demonstrated that long-term targets can help set the trajectory and short-term milestones are needed to keep governments on track. These targets can integrate and complement NDCs to make the NDCs legally binding in national law.
- *Addressing climate risks can be complex:* Since introducing the Climate Change Act, the United Kingdom has made significant advancements in climate mitigation but progress on adaptation has been limited. The quantifiable metrics of mitigation targets make it easier for governments to be held accountable for mitigation than for adaptation planning.

Looking to the Future

Wider adoption of evidence-led climate governance and policy making is possible. The UK Climate Change Act and CCC have demonstrated the benefits of facilitating science-based climate debates and target setting. It is possible to draw further lessons from other countries' climate framework legislation to improve climate governance around the world. The newly formed International Climate Councils Network is one possible forum for such collaboration and knowledge-sharing (ICCN 2021).

Governments should consider how they can reduce consumption emissions. National carbon accounting frameworks and GHG emission targets generally focus on production emissions and do not consider consumption emissions (IPCC 2019). For the world to limit global warming to 1.5°C, a more holistic and less nationalistic view of emissions is required. Although the UK government initially excluded international shipping and aviation emissions from its carbon budgets, its sixth carbon budget (2033–37) will incorporate its share of these emissions, demonstrating progress in accounting for emissions outside of national boundaries (Government of the United Kingdom 2021). Further work is required on consumption emissions.

Adaptation planning also requires greater attention. As global temperatures rise, the risks of climate change become greater. The UK Climate Change Act shows how national framework legislation can improve climate risk identification and reporting; it also shows that additional work is required to translate these findings into action. Governments should look to incorporate adaptation planning across all sectors of the economy to safeguard the continued potential of sustainable development. The World Bank report *Adaptation Principles: A Guide for Designing Strategies for Climate Change Adaptation and Resilience* (Hallegatte, Rentschler, and Rozenberg 2020) is a useful guide to assist governments with effective adaptation planning.

Getting the Prices Right: Economy-wide Policies to Promote Structural Change: British Columbia

Case Study 4. Taxing Carbon for Development: Lessons from British Columbia

Contributors: Dirk Heine and Mariza Montes de Oca Leon

Context

Since Finland announced the first carbon tax in 1990, more than 37 countries have introduced carbon taxes (World Bank 2022m). As of 2022, nine more were scheduled or in consideration, including in Botswana, Côte d'Ivoire, Indonesia, and Morocco. A carbon tax applies a price incentive directly in proportion to the GHG emissions generated by a given product or activity. By applying the same price per $MtCO_2e$ across multiple sources or goods, carbon taxes contribute to cost-efficient climate change mitigation (Pryor et al. 2023).

Several carbon tax designs have been tried in practice, but 30 years of academic literature have focused on one design option that has a good chance of aligning climate mitigation with economic development. That design introduces carbon taxes "upstream," on the carbon content of fuels, at the same tax rate across all emissions sources, and uses revenues to substitute conventional taxes, especially on labor. The real-world carbon tax closest to this design is the carbon tax reform introduced in Canada's British Columbia (BC) province in 2008.

The BC carbon tax stands out as a model for decarbonizing development because the policy design led to several positive outcomes, including: a net increase in economic growth; a decrease in income inequality and improvement of the rural-urban divide; a significant reduction in GHG emissions; and increased public support of the carbon tax reform over time. These positive economic and environmental impacts are key expectations of climate policy in lower-middle-income countries (LMICs). The features that made this policy successful in North America may generate even greater outcomes in LMICs.

Policy

The first carbon tax in the Americas, the BC example, applies two fundamental carbon tax reform ideas. In 1992, all countries agreed on the Polluter Pays Principle (Rio Declaration, Principle 16) of charging polluters in proportion to damages caused to society. The BC carbon tax implements this idea, with a uniform tax applied to a broad tax base. The exemptions are for fuel exported from BC, fuel used in select industrial processes, and marine diesel used in interjurisdictional transportation, among others.

The second fundamental idea underlying carbon taxation is the principle of shifting the tax burden away from taxing "goods," such as labor and income, and instead taxing "bads," such as emissions. Economists have argued that shifting tax burdens away from distortionary tax bases—such as labor effort and profits from innovation—toward emissions can help accelerate economic growth, while also reducing emissions and raising much needed resources.[7] For example, Sweden introduced its carbon tax in 1991 to help shift taxes away from labor during its largest macro crisis since World War II. During the 2001 crisis, Germany introduced a form of carbon taxation, raising electricity taxes while raising feed-in tariffs (FiTs) for renewable energies, to help finance a reduction in social security contributions. Türkiye raised fuel taxes to substitute conventional macrofiscal tightening. The BC government clearly communicated its commitment at the start of the reform that the tax would not raise the overall fiscal burden on firms and households; rather, revenues would substitute other, more distortionary, taxes.

The BC government introduced its carbon tax directly after the financial crisis in 2008, enabling it to reduce conventional taxes and support the economy by reducing the tax burden on labor. It clearly communicated this fiscal shift, committing from the start that its carbon tax reform would not lead to an overall increase in overall taxation. In 2017, BC returned 35 percent of the revenues to individuals and 65 percent to businesses. Tax cuts included the general corporate income tax from 12 percent to 11 percent, and the two lowest personal income tax rates by 5 percent (table 3.1; see also Heine and Black 2019).

Applied to all fuels purchased in BC, the tax's broad base covers approximately 70 percent of the province's GHG emissions and offers long-term predictability (Murray and Rivers 2015). The tax rate started at Can\$10/tCO$_2$e in 2008 and gradually increased to Can\$50/tCO$_2$e in 2022. Signaling future carbon prices long in advance was a key component of BC's reform, giving the private market long-term price signals to avoid stranding assets. A tax rate increase schedule served as a commitment device to help shield carbon taxes from fluctuations in political attitudes (Carattini, Carvahlo, and Fankhauser 2018). From the outset, BC's tax was designed to increase by Can\$5 annually until 2012. Evidence from BC household surveys shows that this strategy was eventually successful: at the time of the tax reform, slightly less than half the population supported the reform, but as time passed and knowledge of the workings of the reform became more widespread, support rose to more than half. There may also have been positive spillovers: Washington State is considering its own carbon tax reform, modeled on the BC example.

TABLE 3.1   Revenue Neutrality in British Columbia: Tax Cuts and Carbon Tax Revenue

Revenue/tax category	2016/2017 (million Can$)
Carbon tax revenue	**1,220**
Personal tax measures	
Low-income climate action tax credit of $115.50 per adult plus $34.50 per child	(195)
Reduction of 5% in the first two personal income tax rates	(309)
Northern and rural homeowner benefit up to $200	(84)
Children's fitness credit and children's arts credit	(8)
Other	(11)
Total personal tax measures	**(607)**
Business tax measures	
Production services tax credit	(340)
General corporate income tax rate reduced from 12% to 11%	(232)
Small business corporate income tax rate reduced from 4.5% to 2.5%	(230)
Scientific research and experimental development tax credit	(148)
Other	(159)
Total business tax measures	**(1,120)**
Total revenue measures	**1,727**

Source: British Columbia Budget and Fiscal Plan 2017.

Note: Several measures are aggregated into "other" for summarizing purposes. Can$ = Canadian dollars.

Results and Impacts

The significant academic literature that has evolved evaluating the BC example broadly finds that it achieved a combination of emissions reductions with improved socio-economic outcomes. Extensive empirical evidence confirms that the tax reduced emissions and inequality, raised growth and employment, and over time, received majority support from citizens.

The BC carbon tax has reduced GHG emissions and fuel consumption. There is evidence of a reduction in fuel demand from the tax as well as a reduction in GHG emissions (Ahmadi and Yamazaki 2020; Metcalf 2019; Murray and Rivers 2015). Some analysis has found insignificant results, pointing at the size of the rate (too low) or the time frame (Pretis 2022).

The carbon tax had benign impacts on economic output. Studies find evidence of no adverse economic effect and some indication of a positive impact (Metcalf 2019), including increased output by 0.8 percent, largely due to the reduction of corporate income taxes encouraging energy savings and productivity-enhancing investments (Ahmadi and Yamazaki 2020).

Aggregate employment has increased, albeit with different responses across industries. Although the carbon tax is found to have a positive effect on employment of 0.75 percent annually (Yamazaki 2017), there is also evidence of differing impacts on specific industries as they shift from carbon-intensive to clean sectors (Azevedo, Wolff, and Yamazaki, forthcoming). This finding suggests that protecting workers, rather than jobs in carbon-intensive sectors, through the transition is a good way to complement carbon taxation.

The BC carbon tax is progressive, narrowing the gap between poor and rich households (Beck et al. 2015). This is due to the revenue recycling scheme (figure 3.5), showing that the distributional implications of such a tax reform cannot be estimated without a precise understanding of the use of the revenues. The study also highlights the importance of income sources in driving distributional impacts: the difference between poorer and richer individuals arises more from differences in income sources (for example, sector of employment) than from differences in what they consume. This is relevant because most studies of distributional impacts of carbon pricing have focused on impacts through consumption, as assessing impacts through incomes is methodologically challenging.

Key Takeaways

BC's carbon tax reform provides crucial lessons for LMICs considering carbon taxes, showing that it is possible to enhance development and decarbonize. Numerous empirical studies point to positive impacts on economic output, aggregate employment, and

FIGURE 3.5 Distributional Impacts of British Columbia's Carbon Tax

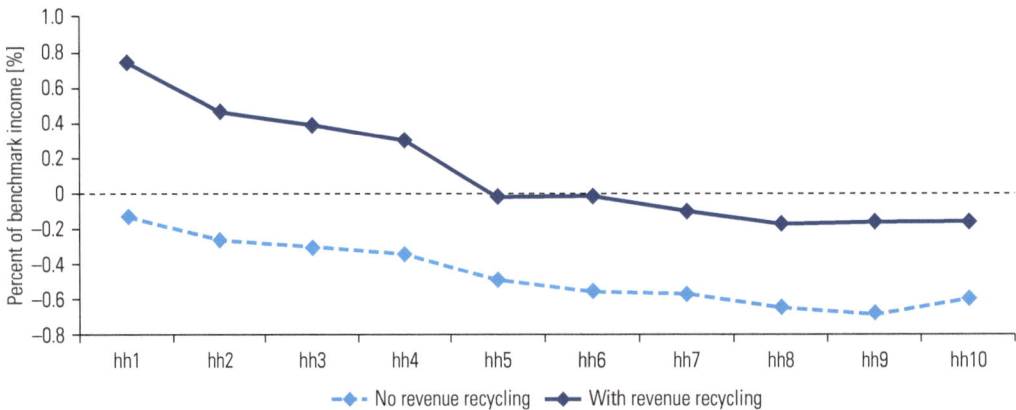

Source: Beck et al. 2015.
Note: hh = household.

tax progressivity resulting from the carbon tax reform. Yet, design matters, and not all carbon taxes are equal. BC's reform provides real-life lessons of how a well-communicated, well-designed tax-burden-shifting strategy can allow countries to implement high carbon tax rates up front while improving political support. The development gains observed in the literature materialized quickly for the citizens in the form of lower personal and corporate tax burdens and higher labor opportunities, increasing public support over time.

How do the lessons learned from this Canadian province translate to the world? The global picture is mixed. The number of jurisdictions applying carbon taxes has risen, from two in 1991 to 37 in 2022, with nine more scheduled or under consideration (World Bank 2022a). The average carbon tax rate has also risen but remains low, at $3/tCO$_2$ in 2021 (weighted for emissions). Despite this progress, most countries, especially in the developing world, continue to use energy excise taxes and subsidies, with an important impact on carbon intensity. The impact would be even greater if they were extended to all fuels and applied a rate aligned to fuel carbon content.

Getting the Prices Right: Economy-wide Policies to Promote Structural Change: China

Case Study 5. Emissions Trading Systems in China

Contributors: Samuel Jovan Okullo, Joseph Dixon Callisto Pryor, and Harikumar Gadde

As of April 1, 2022, there were 32 emissions trading systems (ETSs) in operation globally, covering nearly one-fifth of global GHG emissions. Economists point out that ETSs and carbon taxes can both achieve mitigation at least cost with a preference for one policy instrument over the other emerging when accommodating for some real-world attributes.

ETSs are premised on tradable pollution rights, also referred to as allowances or permits. In a traditional ETS, governments institute a cap on the volume of emissions for one or more sectors of the economy and distribute allowances via free allocations or auctioning. In contrast to carbon taxes, ETSs deliver greater certainty over the degree of emissions reductions, but less certainty over the carbon price. Whereas free allocation enables ETSs to achieve greater political buy-in without undermining mitigation ambition, they are relatively more complex and costly to administer than carbon tax systems. For example, ETSs generally require a more comprehensive monitoring, reporting, and verification framework; a liquid market; and a credible price signal.

This case study explores how an ETS operates, through the lens of the China National ETS. Officially launched in 2017, its first compliance period covered the years 2019 and 2020, and the first trading of allowances started in July 2021. China's ETS differs from other major "cap-and-trade" schemes, like the EU ETS, in that it caps the emissions intensity of output rather than the absolute quantity of emissions. This means that compared with a traditional cap-based approach, emissions can continue to rise with output, creating an additional challenge for emission reduction objectives. Currently, all allowances in China's ETS are allocated free to regulated entities based on technology and fuel benchmarks. Although this has been done to help address regional redistribution objectives, it likely distorts emission reduction incentives and lowers the scheme's overall cost-effectiveness. The evolving design of China's national ETS—including from an intensity-based to an absolute cap-based scheme—provides the opportunity to address and improve several design elements.

Context

China's CO_2 emissions rose to 11.9 $GtCO_2$ in 2021, amounting to about one-third of the global total (IEA 2022c; Ritchie and Roser 2020). To decarbonize, China's strategy is premised on the dual goals of peaking emissions before 2030 and achieving carbon neutrality by 2060. These goals, reaffirmed in October 2021 as part of the 1+N policy framework, underpin China's NDC and emphasize the crucial role that China's national ETS will play in supporting their realization.

China first announced its decision to use a national ETS in 2011 and has built crucial hands-on experience through its eight regional pilots, most of which have been operational since 2013. China's short-term ambition for its national ETS is to help accelerate energy efficiency, with a target of reducing carbon intensity by 18 percent by 2025 compared with 2020. In the long term, the ETS (combined with renewable energy mandates) aims to support achieving carbon neutrality targets, as stipulated in China's series of five-year plans.

Like most other developing economies, China's key challenge is how to reduce emissions without hampering economic growth. One key design decision, therefore, was launching the national ETS functionally as a tradable performance standard, meaning the regulation targets intensity benchmarks, and any compliance obligations begin to surface only when exceeding those benchmarks. A second design element was to adopt an ETS for the power sector initially, before expanding it to trade-exposed sectors, several of which are still selectively regulated under the various regional pilots (Yin 2021). Third, regulators opted to initially allocate free allowances rather than auction them. Fourth, compliance for gas-fired power plants is capped to only their freely allocated allowances, while that for coal-fired power plants is capped to their free allowance allocation plus up to a 20 percent maximum of their verified emissions (ICAP 2021; Ministry of Ecology and Environment 2020). For the second compliance period (calendar years 2021 and 2022), regulated entities are permitted to borrow against their 2023 allowance budget to help offset financing hardships stemming from disruptions to global fuel supply. Intensity benchmarks have also been tightened for the second compliance cycle relative to the first (Yin 2023a).

Policy

The national ETS scheme covers coal- and gas-fired power plants that emitted more than 26 metric kilotons of carbon dioxide in any one year between 2013 and 2019. This comes to just over 2,100 power plants. These power plants are responsible for approximately 4.5 $GtCO_2$ or just over 40 percent of China's CO_2 emissions. It is projected that at full scale, the scheme will cover close to 80 percent of China's emissions and span multiple sectors, including iron and steel, chemicals, and building and materials, several of which are currently still regulated under the various regional pilots.

The Ministry of Ecology and Environment (MEE) oversees the administration and implementation of the national ETS, and in some cases, gives local government ministries the authority to supervise major emitters within their jurisdictions. Despite free allocations and limited compliance, power generators with above-average intensities generally need to purchase allowances to be able to meet their compliance require-ments. To support the development of domestic carbon offsets, ETS participants can use China's certified emissions reductions (Xue 2022), that is, emission reduction activ-ities implemented by companies outside the ETS on a voluntary basis and the resulting emission reductions certified by the government, to meet up to 5 percent of their ETS compliance requirements.

The rollout of the national ETS and its several components continues to experience some delays. Its initial launch experienced multiple delays as the government remained concerned about several issues, including inequality impacts across provinces, down-stream impacts of higher prices, and the complexity of the scheme itself (Yin 2021). Although such delays are not atypical for new policy rollouts, in China's case these were compounded by evolving administrative arrangements that included the transfer of oversight from the National Development and Reform Commission—China's main economic planning body—to the MEE; concerns about the accuracy of emission data; the unfamiliarity of establishments, especially those that had no prior ETS experience with their compliance obligations and reporting requirements; the COVID-19 (coronavirus) pandemic; and the setting up of a robust and trusted trading platform (Singh, Stanway, and Xu 2021).

Results and Impacts

The national ETS completed its first trading period in December 2021, covering the compliance years 2019 and 2020. The second compliance cycle covers emissions from 2021 and 2022, and all entities will need to surrender allowances and have their emis-sions validated by the end of 2023 (Yin 2023b). A total of 179 $MtCO_2$ of allowances were traded between July 14 and December 31, 2021, with prices closing that year at ¥54.2, or US$8.5, per metric ton CO_2. This represented a cumulative turnover of close to ¥7.7 billion, or US$1.3 billion (Ministry of Ecology and Environment 2022). Allowance trading was sparse, with bunching taking place toward the December 31 deadline. Compliance was reported at 99.5 percent, but issues with the accuracy of emissions data surfaced (Xu and Stanway 2022). Since January 2022, prices have been mostly stable, fluctuating between US$8–9/$MtCO_2$. While there is some oversupply of allowances, which can undermine allowance prices, authorities are yet to decide whether allowances from the first compliance cycle are bankable to the second cycle (ICAP 2023).

China aims to raise the effectiveness of its ETS through design improvements. Substantial design flexibility has enabled it to manage price volatility over the second compliance cycle. To inform these design improvements, authorities are maintaining a consultative approach where various stakeholders have windows for public review and comment on proposals. Trust and inclusivity in the government's decision-making process, combined with the inclusion of state-owned enterprises in China's national

ETS are likely to ensure that the national ETS's complete rollout continues to face little resistance. Stakeholder engagement and capacity building to better understand reporting requirements and compliance obligations, especially in regions that were not covered by regional pilots, also continue to be crucial for confidence building and will continue to be necessary as the national ETS expands.

Although it is too early to empirically assess the effectiveness of the national ETS, empirical assessment based on the regional pilots can be helpful for understanding possible impacts. These assessments, which are based on data prior to 2020, in general point toward a greater than 10 percent reduction in enterprises' emissions due to ETS operation (Cui et al. 2020; Cao et al. 2021). The reductions were achieved both through energy conservation measures and fuel-switching activity. The consequences of the Chinese power market structure—where electricity prices are regulated and power markets nonliberalized—are understood to have lowered the effectiveness of ETS operations, mainly by interfering with the capacity to fully pass-through allowance costs. This, combined with the low allowance prices that were observed in the regional pilots, has curbed the capacity for even greater emission reductions. Reported economic consequences of the regional pilots include negative impacts on employment and improvements in total factor productivity.

The current design of the national ETS potentially limits its ability to drive least-cost abatement. Technology-specific intensity benchmarks can distort incentives for emission reduction across power stations of different sizes or those using different fuels and technologies, limiting the potential for the ETS to deliver additional emissions reductions. In particular, the use of intensity benchmarks could potentially incentivize power production from more emissive units—for example, by shifting investment and power generation to less efficient smaller coal-fired generators or unconventional coal units with less stringent benchmarks (Yin 2023a). The economics is clear that a cap-based scheme is more cost-effective than an intensity-based system and the technology-fuel benchmarks distorting incentives, but an inspection of plant-level data is required to provide clarity on the empirical magnitude of the inefficiencies.

Key Takeaways

China's experience with designing and implementing an ETS, as well as the implementation experience from other jurisdictions, offers some important takeaways. Ultimately, China's nascent national ETS represents a compromise between ambition and pragmatism, recognizing the need to address many technical, regulatory, distributional, economic, and political issues in a phased manner. Design features—including the coverage and technology-specific benchmarks—have facilitated implementation and operability—but may have reduced effectiveness. The country can address these issues as it reviews and refines the ETS over time. In this regard, efforts have already been made to strengthen third-party verification, and there are now penalties for submitting fabricated or false reports. To increase liquidity, China also intends to allow financial traders into the market.

China's experience with ETS implementation and administration has highlighted several challenges, not all unique to this market. These including enterprises' unfamiliarity with the ETS rules, concerns related to data transparency and accuracy, implementation delays, and low allowance prices and trade volumes. As China continues to learn and improve the design, implementation, and administration of its national ETS, there are several lessons that can be looked at and considered.

- Establishing and fully enforcing a robust monitoring, reporting, and verification system early is crucial not only to ensure smooth implementation but also to avoid the potential for data manipulation and fraud.
- It will also be important to identify policy changes and reforms early, harmonize them with the need for increased effectiveness of ETS implementation, and communicate them clearly to support regulated entities' compliance. Capacity building and continuous training for enterprises are also key.
- Adjusting the ETS's design and implementation modalities to align with the rapidly changing global and national policy environments as well as international commitments can bring additional challenges for its full and timely implementation, but it is necessary to foster an economy-wide decarbonization.
- Opening up markets to more actors such as the financial sector can increase liquidity, which can in turn facilitate a transparent price signal. But it can also increase the risk of market manipulation, which could exacerbate underpinning issues in a nascent ETS market.
- It is important to define upfront the role of offsets, including sources and reliance on existing crediting mechanisms. There must also be clarity on the potential for domestic credits to be used as a vehicle to attract international investments in non-ETS sectors. The linkages between the domestic and international carbon markets must be determined at the earliest possible date.
- Translating and transitioning subnational instruments into a national framework poses challenges and complexities, including in relation to governance and institutional responsibilities. This may be more challenging in jurisdictions where subnational governments have greater levels of autonomy.

Getting the Prices Right: Economy-wide Policies to Promote Structural Change: Egypt

Case Study 6. Energy Subsidy Reform in Egypt

Contributors: Defne Gencer, Min A Lee, and Tom Moerenhout

Context

In the aftermath of the Arab Spring, Egypt faced both political and economic challenges, affected by a growing fiscal deficit, economic slowdown, increasing poverty, socioeconomic transition, and energy shortages. In 2013, Egypt's power sector was recovering only about 30 percent of its operational and capital costs, while government expenditure on energy subsidies had reached an estimated 22 percent of the budget and 7 percent of GDP, exceeding combined expenditure on education, health, and infrastructure (ESMAP 2017). Electricity supply was unreliable, with frequent outages that affected both consumer welfare and manufacturing output. At the same time, substantial liquid fuel subsidies incentivized excessive production and consumption of fossil fuels, and therefore GHG emissions, harming the environment and the climate and discouraging investment in energy efficiency and cleaner power generation alternatives. This case study provides an overview of the government's efforts to reform energy subsidies between 2013 and 2017 and discusses main challenges, implementation approaches, and outcomes.

Policy

In 2014, Egypt embarked on an ambitious and comprehensive effort to reform energy subsidies as part of a broader effort to tackle long-standing structural constraints to inclusive growth and macroeconomic stability. Egypt's development partners supported the energy subsidy reforms, which were part of the government's broader macrofiscal reform efforts. The three-year Development Policy Financing (DPF) series, supported by the African Development Bank, the Agence Française de Développement, and the World Bank, provided a total of $3.15 billion in financing in support of the government's program that focused on fiscal consolidation, sustainable energy, and competitiveness. In addition, a three-year, $12 billion International Monetary Fund (IMF) program approved in 2016 featured energy subsidy reform as a main pillar. In the context of the broader program, the government requested technical and advisory support from the World Bank, part of which was funded by a series of technical assistance grants from the Energy Subsidy Reform Facility within the Energy Sector Management Assistance Program (ESMAP 2017), provided between 2014 and 2020.

The stated goal of the reform effort was to reduce energy subsidies to 0.5 percent of GDP by 2019 by imposing gradual increases in fuel and electricity prices and maintaining limited support for liquefied petroleum gas (LPG) and electricity for poor and vulnerable households. The government took decisive action from the outset and gradually implemented the planned reforms. In July 2014, the government implemented the first annual electricity tariff adjustment, raising electricity tariffs by 31 percent on average and petroleum and natural gas prices by 40 to 78 percent (World Bank 2016c). Implementation of the first annual electricity tariff adjustment was achieved as part of a five-year tariff reform plan outlined in Prime Ministerial Decree No. 1257 of 2014 to reform gas and electricity subsidies. The second annual electricity tariff adjustment in 2015 increased average electricity tariffs by another 19 percent (World Bank 2016c).

The government implemented an annual electricity tariff adjustment in 2017, raising tariffs by 33 percent on average, at a much higher rate than the planned 17 percent increase over the previous five-year tariff adjustment plan. Specifically, diesel and gasoline prices increased by 40 to 55 percent and electricity tariffs by 40 percent on average. LPG cost recovery was estimated at only 35 percent, even after the tariff adjustment (World Bank 2017). This time, LPG prices were also included, doubling to bring prices closer to costs, with the last price increase announced in October 2021, bringing it to its current price of LE 70 per cylinder.

In view of challenging macroeconomic circumstances, in 2017 the cabinet approved the deferral of the deadline for the power sector to reach full cost recovery. Starting in 2016, instead of announcing an electricity tariff trajectory, the government set a subsidy target in its Medium-Term Fiscal Framework as part of the broader set of steps agreed with the IMF, and adjusted tariffs annually to achieve the then-target of full cost recovery by FY2018–19. Although projected at 2.5 percent of GDP for FY2016–17, energy subsidies reached 3.9 percent (2.9 percent for fuels and 1 percent for electricity). Due to the devaluation of the currency, even with the retail tariffs for consumers in FY2017–18 already higher than originally targeted for FY2018–19, the original objective of full cost recovery by FY2018–19 could not be reached, and the cabinet approved a new subsidy trajectory targeting FY2021–22. The current five-year plan extends from FY2021 to FY2025.

To mitigate the potential adverse impacts from energy price increases, along with broader macroeconomic pressures and inflation, the reforms were accompanied by action in multiple domains. To facilitate the acceptance of the reforms, the government launched a proactive communications effort to explain the rationale of the reforms and inform the public about what the reforms entailed. Among other important communication elements, the efforts included a public multimedia campaign emphasizing the importance of energy efficiency measures to mitigate the impact of the price increases.

Most importantly, the government also took concrete action to strengthen the country's social protection mechanisms. The main element of the effort was to move away from broad-based price subsidies toward targeted support, including through cash transfers. The government increased the social protection budget allocation by about LE 85 billion (approximately $5 billion) in FY2017–18, or by 60 percent compared with the previous period. The government also took critical action to broaden the coverage of the social protection system, while providing broader support through skill enhancement and youth employment programs, along with improved service delivery.

The government of Egypt continues to strengthen the country's social protection mechanisms, including through efforts supported by complementary World Bank operations to develop, fund, and strengthen the Takaful and Karama cash transfer program. *Takaful* ("dignity" in Arabic) is a cash transfer program that is conditional on school attendance and the use of maternal and child health care services to promote the accumulation of human capital among children. *Karama* ("solidarity" in Arabic) provides a monthly income to poor people over the age of 65 and people with severe disabilities who are unable to work. These programs are based on a proxy means-testing questionnaire cross-checked with a unified national registry, linked with a unique identification number. Throughout their lifetime, the programs have reached approximately 31 million registered applicants in the database; about 3.11 million households are currently enrolled, three-quarters headed by females.

Results and Impacts

Implemented alongside crucial macrofiscal reforms, Egypt's energy subsidy reform efforts contributed to the government's efforts to ease fiscal pressures, with the budget deficit falling from 12.9 to 8.1 percent of GDP between 2013 and 2019 (World Bank 2020b). Energy subsidies declined from 6.9 percent of GDP in FY2013 to 1.9 percent in FY2019 (figure 3.6). While the share of energy subsidies stood at 1.9 percent in

FIGURE 3.6   Evolution of Egypt's Energy Subsidies, FY2010–19

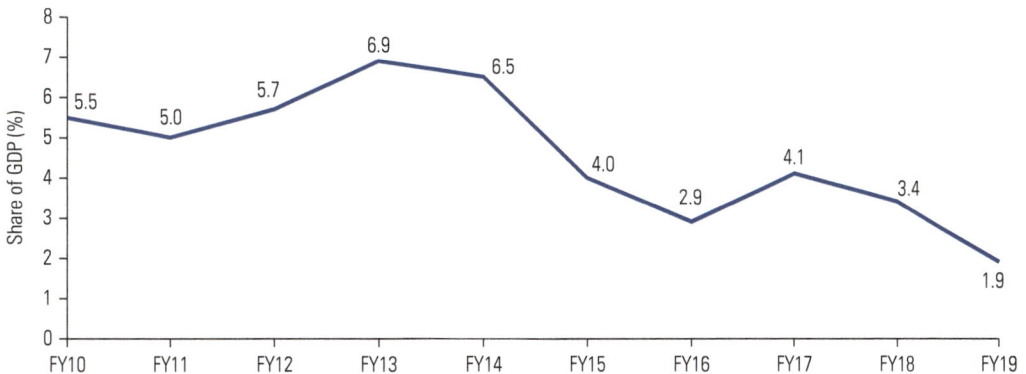

Source: World Bank 2020b.

Note: FY = fiscal year; GDP = gross domestic product.

FY2019—above the government's original target of 0.5 percent set in 2014—the electricity and fuel pricing reforms, together with other macroeconomic reforms and strengthened social assistance programs and accompanying delivery mechanisms, strengthened Egypt's macroeconomic resilience to face shocks, including the impacts of the COVID-19 crisis.

Even though challenges posed by the COVID-19 pandemic affected reform implementation, the government remains committed to tackling energy subsidies through gradual increases in electricity tariffs over the medium term. For example, in July 2020, it announced a new electricity tariff in the midst of the pandemic. For liquid fuels, it implemented an automatic fuel price–indexation mechanism for 95-octane gasoline in April 2019 and approved a new price mechanism for all petroleum products in June 2019 (OECD 2021). As a result, fuel subsidies declined by approximately 65 percent from July 2019 to March 2020.

Egypt's 2014–17 energy subsidy reforms and accompanying government policies created the fiscal space to strengthen social assistance, health, and education. Before the reform, energy subsidies had exceeded key social spending categories for many years. Consistent adjustments in energy prices and energy subsidy reductions have yielded significant fiscal savings, which the government redirected toward social protection and human development spending. Starting in FY2015, health and education expenditure exceeded energy subsidies (figure 3.7).

Together with broader energy sector reforms by the government, these subsidy reforms have helped to encourage private investment, thereby enabling increased electricity generation over the past five years. In addition to improved sector

FIGURE 3.7 **Energy Subsidy and Health, Education, Social Protection Expenditure in Egypt, FY2014–18**

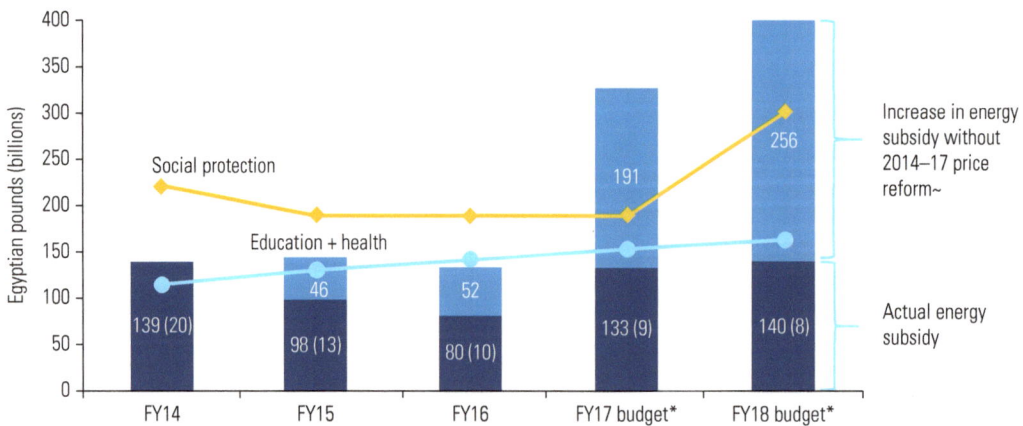

Source: World Bank 2017.

Note: ~ = World Bank estimate; * = Ministry of Finance budget for energy subsidy. Numbers in parentheses are in $, billions.

performance, the government's reforms, including electricity tariff reforms, FiTs, and broader regulatory framework encouraging privately developed renewables-based power generation, can be credited with two important environmental achievements. The share of oil-fired power generation went down from more than 34,000 gigawatt hours (GWh) in 2014 to 7,145 GWh in 2019 (IEA 2022b), while wind and solar power generation output increased rapidly. In 2014, solar power generation stood at 244 GWh and wind power generation at 1,444 GWh—a sixfold growth for solar and almost threefold for wind. The reforms and subsequent renewable energy (RE) scale-up allowed the government to increase its targets for the share of renewables-based generation capacity to 42 percent of total installed capacity by 2035. Reaching this target and consistently increasing RE generation output would yield substantive emissions reductions.

Key Takeaways

Through comprehensive and gradual reforms undertaken over a series of years, the government of Egypt managed to significantly reduce the fiscal burden from energy subsidies and improve energy sector financial viability, consumer welfare, and economic productivity, while attracting significant private investment in cleaner alternatives. The World Bank's Implementation Completion and Results (ICR) report for the Egypt DPF series noted the following key features of the country's energy subsidy reform experience:

- *Strong government ownership of the reform program and close cross-sectoral coordination:* The government initiated and led the reforms, mobilized the required resources, and remained committed throughout the reforms, taking strong action when required based on thorough analytical work—for example, surrounding the currency devaluation and COVID-19. It also organized an instrumental group for coordination and knowledge sharing between key agencies, to keep the reform effort moving forward smoothly and addressing issues.
- *Transparent and timely government communication with the general public regarding the reform program and associated support from international donors:* The government proactively engaged with the public and key stakeholders to raise awareness of the financial and opportunity costs of energy subsidies and supported evidence-based public debate. Through carefully designed messaging and innovative communication approaches, it has supported behavior change and facilitated acceptance of the energy price reforms.
- *Strengthened social assistance measures and delivery mechanisms helped mitigate impacts on vulnerable households:* The government adopted social protection measures throughout the reform process, redirecting fiscal savings from the energy subsidy reform to strengthen social programs.

The government expanded the food subsidy system while also doubling the maximum benefit under the Social Solidarity Pension, the country's largest social safety program. These measures are credited with preventing further deterioration of household welfare amid challenging circumstances.

- *Broader energy sector policy was a key enabler of improved outcomes:* The energy subsidy reforms were part of a much broader effort by the government to improve the energy sector's policy framework and its operational, technical, and financial performance. These include:
  - The new sector design stipulated by issuance of the 2015 Electricity Law and 2017 Gas Law
  - Fuel switching from highly subsidized and inefficient sources (for example, from heavy fuel oil to gas in power generation, from heavy fuel oil and diesel to gas in industry and transport, and from LPG to gas in households)
  - Resolving of cross-sectoral debts/receivables between petroleum and electricity, and between railways, aviation, and petroleum, which helped improve the energy sector's fiscal situation and encouraged demand control in indebted sectors
  - Improved energy supply efficiency
  - Improved billing systems via prepaid meters for electricity and gas and digital tracking of fuel transport
  - Better control of unauthorized sales of LPG and liquid fuels.

Getting the Prices Right: Economy-wide Policies to Promote Structural Change: European Union

Case Study 7. European Union: Carbon Border Adjustment Mechanism

Contributors: Alexandru Cosmin Buteică and Eliza Barnea

Context

A border carbon adjustment mechanism (BCA) is a policy instrument whereby a government imposes a carbon price on certain carbon-intensive goods that are imported from other jurisdictions at the border. The main objective is to adjust the carbon price levied on those imported goods with the carbon price charged on domestically produced goods, for example through a carbon tax or an ETS covering domestic industry. In this sense, a BCA is an extension of a direct carbon pricing instrument like a carbon tax or an ETS to goods imported from other jurisdictions to provide a level playing field and prevent carbon leakage.

With the introduction of the European Green Deal and the adoption of a 2050 net-zero target, the EU has increased its efforts to level the playing field of climate ambition around the world and minimize the risk of carbon leakage. One element of the EU strategy is the Carbon Border Adjustment Mechanism (CBAM), which was adopted in April 2023, with implementation starting in a staged approach from October 1, 2023.

Policy

In its initial phase, the CBAM will set a price on carbon-intensive goods imported by the EU in five sectors: cement, iron and steel, aluminum, fertilizers, electricity, and hydrogen. The mechanism will function as a carbon price levied on imports to the EU that have industrial emissions, with obligations for importers to submit CBAM certificates priced in line with EU ETS allowances from 2026.

The CBAM includes provision for imports to the EU to be granted reduced charges if they have already paid a direct carbon price in their country of origin. For countries that export to the EU, this creates an incentive to introduce a carbon price to capture the revenues domestically. This argument is stronger for countries that have close trade ties with Europe. For instance, Türkiye's Medium Term Programme (2023–25) explicitly connects its plans for introducing a national ETS in Türkiye to the EU CBAM.

The adopted regulation envisages that CBAM should only cover direct emissions produced during the manufacturing process of the included goods. To maintain administrative simplicity, indirect emissions, such as those resulting from electricity consumption for manufacturing, heating, or cooling, will not form the basis of the CBAM charge. The CBAM could be expanded in the future to incorporate indirect emissions from purchased energy and the Commission has the option to establish calculation methods and system boundaries for embedded emissions at a later point through delegated acts (European Parliamentary Research Service 2023).

The phase-in of the CBAM will be accompanied by the gradual reduction of free allocations under the EU ETS between 2026 and 2034. In 2034, sectors covered by the CBAM will stop receiving free allocations. This phased implementation will allow producers, importers, and traders in EU member states to adjust to the new regulation.

Results and Impacts

The policy has yet to enter into force. In December 2022, the Council and the European Parliament reached a political agreement on the implementation of the mechanism and in April 2023 the Council of the EU adopted the regulation, which is set to enter a transitional phase on October 1, 2023.

The CBAM proposal is likely to affect EU industry in various ways. EU manufacturers of the five product categories could see increased output and FDI inflows as third-country imports become less competitive under CBAM, while phasing out free allowances under the EU ETS may decrease exports. EU downstream producers using these categories as inputs in their supply chains may face higher costs and reduced competitiveness, possibly prompting them to seek less carbon-intensive suppliers to avoid financial adjustments. Nevertheless, the European Parliament expects the CBAM to incentivize third-party producers to implement more efficient processes, while the phaseout of free allocations is expected to increase the ambition of EU producers to decarbonize. The European Parliamentary Research Service estimated in 2023 that the CBAM would reduce carbon leakage by 29 percent by 2030, with limited negative impact on GDP.

LMICs with manufacturing sector exports to the EU would most likely be affected by rising import costs and increasing prices on intermediate inputs. This could lead to a decline in output and employment, which is expected to be very small at the macroeconomic level but could be significant for the most exposed and carbon-intensive sectors (such as steel or chemistry) and in the locations in which these industries are concentrated. While the CBAM would have an important role in countering carbon leakage and fostering competitiveness, academic research shows that the impact on global emissions will be limited (Fischer and Fox 2012).

Facilitating, Enabling, and Triggering Sectoral Transitions: Japan

Technology Support Policies

Case Study 8. Industrial Energy Efficiency in Japan

Contributors: Grace Henry and Thomas Kerr

Decarbonizing the industrial sector (steel, cement, chemicals, aluminum, and other manufacturing) is vital for achieving net zero emissions. In 2019, the industrial sector accounted for 38 percent of global final energy use and 26 percent of global GHG emissions (IEA 2021a). To date, there has been limited progress in reducing emissions from the sector, which is considered hard to abate due to the cost and complexity of delivering decarbonized high-temperature process heat and capturing process emissions. Fossil fuels still account for 68 percent of the sector's energy mix, and there has been limited adoption of low carbon technologies such as green hydrogen and carbon capture and sequestration. Most industrial decarbonization progress has been made through energy efficiency measures such as waste heat recovery, combined heat and power, and process optimization. In the years ahead, the demand for industrial goods is projected to rise, largely driven by population growth and urban development (Bocca and Ashraf 2022). As a result, industrial emissions create a pressing challenge to global warming, creating a pressing challenge for governments to develop and implement policies that can support and advance industrial decarbonization.

Japan, the world's third-largest producer of industrial goods, is implementing plans and policies for industrial decarbonization. In 2019, industry added $1.46 trillion to Japan's economy (World Bank 2022e) as well as 189 tCO_2e (IEA 2020c). The country has made progress in reducing these emissions by 28 percent since 1990, largely through energy efficiency improvements, which led to an 18 percent decrease in final energy consumption between 2000 and 2019. Further reductions are in the pipeline: as the government has announced its aim to achieve net zero emissions by 2050 and released the "Green Growth Strategy through Achieving Carbon Neutrality in 2050" (IEA 2021c).

Context

Due to its advanced economic development and limited natural resource endowments, Japan has had to develop innovative decarbonization strategies. With the world's third-largest GDP and the fifth-largest volume of GHG emissions (ClimateWatch 2022; World Bank 2022e), it is a densely populated island nation with minimal domestic reserves of conventional energy sources, such as coal, oil, and gas (Cheng et al. 2022). It has no international gas pipelines or electricity connections and has been troubled by natural disasters affecting domestic energy supplies, creating challenges to both energy security and sufficiency. This has led Japan's Ministry of Economy, Trade and Industry to create innovative energy efficiency policies that have provided emissions reduction cobenefits to the industrial sector.

Policy

The country's domestic energy challenges have catalyzed widespread energy efficiency measures. The 1979 Act on the Rational Use of Energy laid the groundwork for Japan to become one of the world's most energy-efficient economies. Implemented in response to the 1979 energy crisis and oil shock, the act has undergone seven major revisions, allowing it to expand and improve over time (figure 3.8; IEA 2017). It sets energy performance standards and energy reporting and management requirements for factories and workplaces that consume more than 1,500 kiloliters of oil equivalent energy each year (IEA 2021c; LSE 2022), representing approximately 70 percent of energy consumption across the industrial sector. The act also sets out energy efficiency benchmarking indicators, which companies are obliged to submit progress reports on, and a nonbinding 1 percent reduction target. In 2018, the government boosted support through a new tax system that allows energy-efficient companies to benefit from accelerated depreciation of their energy efficiency investments.

Results and Impacts

Japan has achieved one of the world's highest energy efficiency levels, but the pace of improvement is slowing. The Act on the Rational Use of Energy and other government incentives have helped some industrial subsectors stimulate energy efficiency improvements of more than 1 percent per year. However, a combination of a modest

FIGURE 3.8 Timeline of Japan's 1979 Act on the Rational Use of Energy

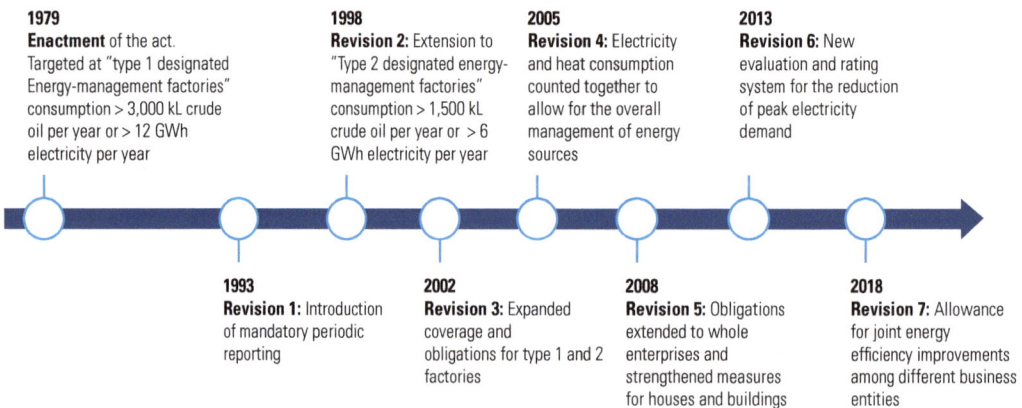

1979
Enactment of the act. Targeted at "type 1 designated Energy-management factories" consumption > 3,000 kL crude oil per year or > 12 GWh electricity per year

1998
Revision 2: Extension to "Type 2 designated energy-management factories" consumption > 1,500 kL crude oil per year or > 6 GWh electricity per year

2005
Revision 4: Electricity and heat consumption counted together to allow for the overall management of energy sources

2013
Revision 6: New evaluation and rating system for the reduction of peak electricity demand

1993
Revision 1: Introduction of mandatory periodic reporting

2002
Revision 3: Expanded coverage and obligations for type 1 and 2 factories

2008
Revision 5: Obligations extended to whole enterprises and strengthened measures for houses and buildings

2018
Revision 7: Allowance for joint energy efficiency improvements among different business entities

Source: Adapted from International Energy Agency 2017.

Note: The figure only includes the updates that are most relevant to industrial energy consumption. GWh = gigawatt hours; kL = kiloliter.

benchmarking target and voluntary compliance has stalled recent progress. In 2019, no more than 38 percent of companies in any single industrial subsector were reaching the government's energy efficiency benchmarks (Ezawa 2021). Improvements in steel production have notably plateaued (figure 3.9), with only 16 percent of electric furnace steel producers meeting the benchmarks. The energy intensity benchmarks are comparable to the EU's ETS, indicating that increased enforcement and compliance of existing policies could bring about further improvements (IEA 2021c).

Energy efficiency measures have helped cut energy intensity (figure 3.10), but further measures are needed for deep decarbonization. Japan's industrial emissions have decreased by 28 percent since 1990, despite the carbon intensity of its industrial energy consumption decreasing by only 4 percent. Although energy efficiency measures have

FIGURE 3.9 **Energy Intensity Index in Japan, by Industrial Subsector, 1973–2018**

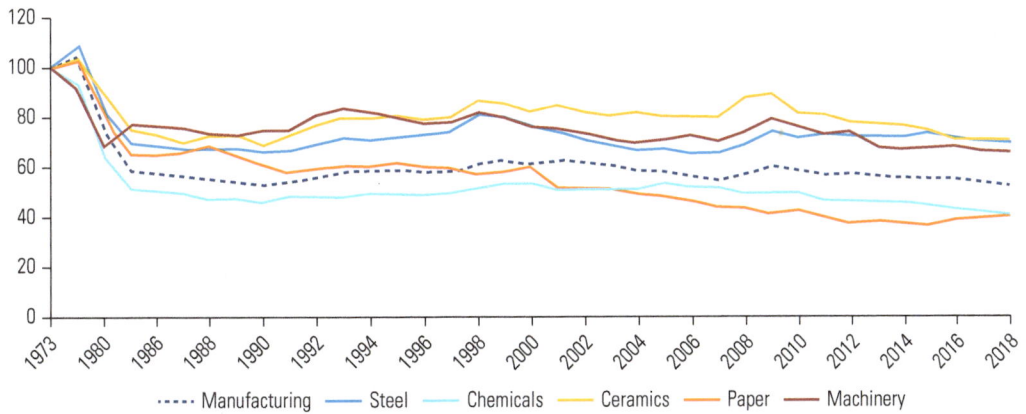

Source: Ezawa 2021.

FIGURE 3.10 **Total Final Consumption in Japanese Industry, by Source, 2000–18**

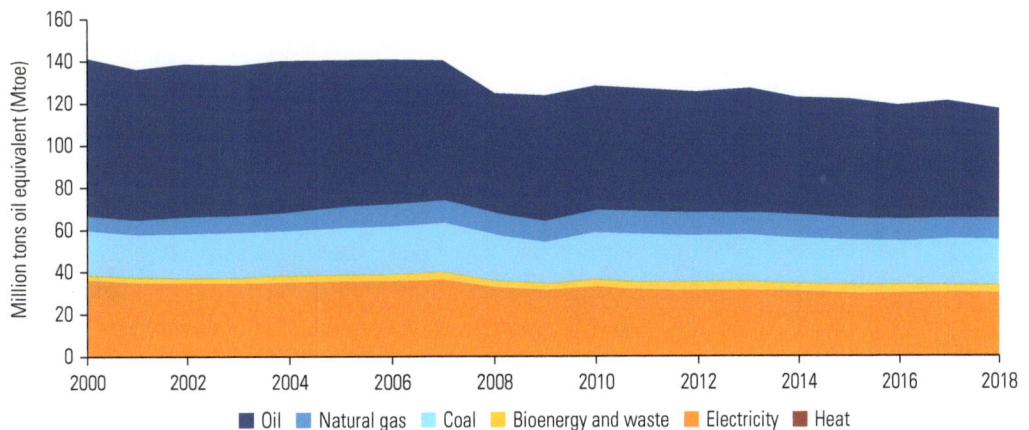

Source: International Energy Agency 2021c.
Note: Includes nonenergy consumption.

helped Japan decrease industrial energy consumption by 18 percent since 2000, the country will need to go beyond energy efficiency measures to transition to cleaner fuels, decarbonizing power-sector emissions fuels, and upscaling carbon capture and sequestration projects. It is making progress in these areas through targeted research and development spending, the world's first basic hydrogen strategy, and green public procurement initiatives. These initiatives benefit from Japan's strong institutional arrangements, including the New Energy and Industrial Technology Development Organization, which helps optimize the results of research and development spending by fostering collaboration between the private sector, academia, and government.

Key Takeaways

Energy efficiency measures can help decrease energy consumption, operating costs, and emissions. Although Japan's energy-saving initiatives were originally targeted toward energy security challenges, they have also provided cobenefits in emission reductions and resource productivity.

Energy efficiency policies may need to adapt as technologies evolve and ambitions increase. Japan's Act on the Rational Use of Energy has had seven major revisions, expanding its coverage and improving the methodology standards used. Despite these revisions, energy efficiency improvements in some industrial subsectors have declined over time. This may be the result of diminishing marginal returns, highlighting the need for additional support or compliance measures once results begin to plateau.

Deep decarbonization requires wide policy support. Japan's example has shown that no single policy is enough on its own to achieve complete industrial decarbonization. Rather, a range of policy measures is needed to support the supply of low-carbon technologies and the demand for low-carbon industrial goods.

Looking to the Future

Improvements in industrial energy efficiency could help address global energy security concerns. The Russian invasion of Ukraine has sparked a global energy crisis (IEA 2022f). Decreasing energy consumption in the industrial sector could help decrease the severity of this crisis and provide long-term benefits through continued emissions savings.

International collaboration could help accelerate industrial decarbonization. Global cooperation and best practice sharing could drastically reduce the time required to implement decarbonized industrial supply chains. Japan has demonstrated international leadership in low-carbon cooperation, through its international research and development advancements, contributions to multilateral climate funds, and international partnerships, such as the Joint Crediting Mechanism. Addressing the energy and climate crises will require further international collaboration.

Facilitating, Enabling, and Triggering Sectoral Transitions: Mexico

Case Study 9. Climate-Smart Solid Waste Management in Mexico

Contributor: Silpa Kaza

Improvements in solid waste management are vital to limiting global warming. Municipal solid waste contributes to the generation of GHGs, mainly methane and CO_2. The quantities of waste generated globally have increased at an alarming pace over the past decades and are anticipated to increase by 73 percent by 2050 from current levels, more than double estimated population growth (Kaza, Shrikanth, and Chaudhary 2021). At the same time, the state of waste management continues to lag in both capacity and effectiveness.

Reducing and managing methane from waste can be a win-win for climate and municipalities. It is estimated that up to 20 percent of human-induced methane emissions stem from the anaerobic arising from the anaerobic decomposition of organic waste (CCAC Secretariat 2021). It is possible to avoid the release of these emissions through improved management or capture of methane, which can then be used to produce thermal energy, gas, or electricity. This can provide environmental and economic cobenefits, particularly when used to increase energy access or displace more polluting forms of energy, such as coal.

Mexico has been a leader in Latin America by demonstrating how landfill gas (LFG) management systems can improve environmental and community outcomes. Between 2004 and 2020, an LFG collection and power plant in the city of Monterrey, Nuevo León, reduced CO_2 emissions by 5.7 $MtCO_2e$ and delivered millions of dollars in municipality savings by providing low-cost electricity to power the metro system and public lighting, with revenues supporting a "proof of concept" solar energy supply to public schools in a low-income community in the Monterrey metropolitan area (SIMEPRODE 2020). The project, supported by the Global Environment Facility (GEF) and the World Bank, has served as a pilot to systematically build capacity, test operating models, and understand regulatory needs for widespread replication.

Context

Like many countries, Mexico has faced challenges with its solid waste management practices. In 2001, it only collected 77 percent of solid waste and disposed of less than 35 percent sanitarily (World Bank 2001). Most of the collected waste ended up in open dumps, contributing to almost one-quarter of the country's total methane emissions and global warming, contaminating aquifers and surface waters, providing a breeding ground for disease vectors, and exacerbating urban flooding.

Population growth, industrialization, urbanization, and economic growth have increased the generation and concentration of solid waste, particularly in metropolitan areas (figure 3.11). This has put a strain on Mexico's waste management systems. Without any formal waste minimization or recycling programs, additional challenges were created for collecting, transporting, disposing of, and managing solid waste (Castrejón-Godínez et al. 2015). Municipalities, which were responsible for addressing these challenges and delivering adequate waste management services, lacked the technical, institutional, and financial resources to make such improvements.

In the early 2000s, Monterrey was facing rising electricity prices and growing demand for public services. Mexico faced a countrywide electricity shortage, prompting regulatory changes in support of public-private partnerships (PPPs). High electricity prices increased the economic outlook for private sector investments in alternative energy sources (ELLA 2011). At the time, the only way to employ independent RE was by establishing a partnership between electricity producers and consumers at a lower cost than the national grid (World Bank 2007). Consumers with a large and stable demand for electricity were ideal customers in such arrangements. Together, these factors created ideal conditions for an integrated solution to Monterrey's waste management, electricity, and public service provisions.

Policy

Under its National Development Plan 1995–2000, the government developed a strategy to improve and strengthen solid waste management at municipal and state levels by

FIGURE 3.11 **Mexico Municipal Solid Waste Trends, 1997–2012**

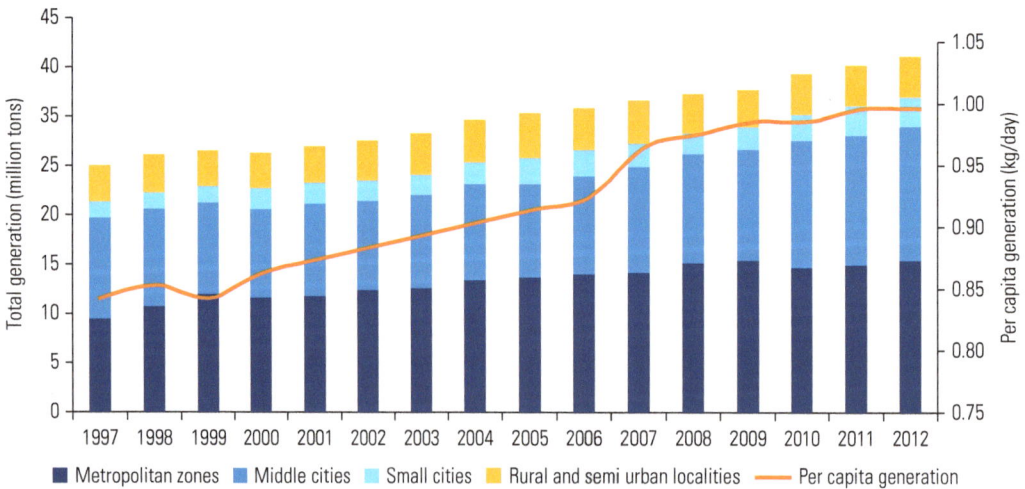

Source: Castrejón-Godínez et al. 2015.

Note: A *small city* is one with fewer than 100,000 people; a *middle city* has 100,000 to 500,000 people. kg = kilogram.

strengthening regulations and institutions, expanding service provision, and managing GHG emissions. In 1997, Mexico developed its First National Communication and Climate Change Action Plan, prioritizing the prevention of uncontrolled LFG release from landfills. In 2000, it approved the Kyoto Protocol, making a national commitment to promote climate mitigation.

International support helped deliver the additional resources needed for Latin America's first waste-to-energy landfill project. In the 1990s, Mexico had no LFG management projects and lacked the institutional capacity and technical knowledge to implement them. The GEF (2001) provided the initial resources to start the Monterrey project (2001–06), and the World Bank built on this until 2017. The support aimed to:

- Introduce cost-effective, demonstrated technology to collect and use LFG
- Develop municipal capacity for LFG collection and use
- Demonstrate an institutional and management framework for LFG capture and use at an existing facility in Mexico
- Design a replication strategy for comparable cities in Mexico and disseminate lessons from the Mexican experience to other interested parties regionally

A strategic PPP was created to align incentives, with the public sector partner managing the landfill and receiving lower-cost electricity from the plant operator, SIMEPRODE. The latter was an autonomous, state-controlled institution, which enabled full coverage of the metropolitan area and avoided the need to engage with individual entities. SIMEPRODE had six-year state-administration terms instead of three-year municipal terms, allowing for continuity, institutional memory, and better coordination between public entities (World Bank 2014a).

Participation in international carbon markets helped provide additional revenue streams. Mexico had ratified the Kyoto Protocol in September 2000, making emissions reduction projects—including Monterrey's waste-to-energy landfill initiative—eligible for funding through the Clean Development Mechanism (CDM). In 2009, the country developed guidance for quantifying, reporting, and verifying GHG emissions reductions associated with LFG under the organization of Climate Action Reserve, a North American carbon offset registry. This established standards for the waste management sector and strengthened participation in carbon markets.

Results and Impacts

The Monterrey waste-to-energy project has had widespread community benefits. After three years of operating, the plant had delivered 181 GWh of electricity and prevented 700 ktCO$_2$e in methane emissions. Approximately 730,000 citizens in seven municipalities benefited from reduced methane emissions and a clean and cheaper source of electricity. With the extended World Bank project, SIMEPRODE and Bioeléctrica expanded capacity to 17 megawatts (MW), reducing emissions by another 5.7 $MtCO_2e$ in 2004–20, of which 262,000 tons was methane.

The project was an early example of a circular economy solution that used waste from urban areas to generate clean, affordable electricity in the Monterrey Metropolitan Area at a cost that was 10 to 20 percent lower than national utility rates. This powered half of the city's public lighting, all of the local metro system (Metrorrey), and public institutions such as the Water and Sewerage Service Department, the National System for Integral Family Development, Sistema de Desarrollo Integral de la Familia or DIF, and the Nuevo León state government. By 2020, the municipality of Monterrey had saved $20 million pesos in public lighting, the municipalities of San Pedro and Apodaca had saved $11.5 million pesos, and Metrorrey had saved $35 million pesos, equivalent to 32 percent of its profits.

The project also generated carbon credits, providing additional benefits. The project received CDM funding in multiple phases for 1 $MtCO_2e$ in 2007, and 835 $ktCO_2e$ in 2011, demonstrating how carbon credits can make projects profitable and providing a model for replication across Mexico and Latin America (SIMEPRODE 2020). Between 2007 and 2012, the CDM helped reduce emissions from waste-to-energy landfills by more than 19 $MtCO_2e$ across Latin America.

Key Takeaways

The government of Mexico, CDM stakeholders, and the private sector all had environmental and financial incentives to improve waste management, reduce emissions, and provide electricity. This alignment of incentives allowed them to successfully implement an integrated waste management solution and sustain it for many years.

Blending finance between GEF, World Bank, the private sector, and carbon markets enabled the advancement of climate goals, but early-moving projects need additional assistance to prove their concept. As the first waste-to-energy project of its kind in Latin America, external financing, technical expertise, and institutional support from GEF and the World Bank were crucial to the project's success. To address uncertainty in the initial gas estimations, the project conducted field measurements and used conservative models. The Monterrey project and World Bank support have helped reduce investment risks and uncertainties in subsequent projects.

Although improving solid waste management can be an expensive undertaking for municipal governments, integrated solutions have their benefits and are a public good. The Monterrey project has demonstrated that waste can generate value in the form of electricity and carbon credits. But this was only made possible with political will, local capacity building, a supportive regulatory environment, verification of the impact of the LFG generated, and other necessary aspects that helped build the foundation for an integrated waste management system to thrive.

Looking to the Future

Further work and an integrated approach are needed to improve global solid waste management. At current rates, global improvements in waste management practices are not enough to offset the adverse impacts of poorly managed waste, and investments need to extend beyond infrastructure (UNEP 2022). In a business-as-usual (BAU) scenario, the gap between waste generated and waste that is managed properly will widen further.

Managing solid waste streams is becoming more complex. Waste from electrical and electronic equipment containing new and complex hazardous substances presents the fastest-growing challenge in both high-income countries and LMICs.

Minimizing waste production and diverting waste for productive use are key. Advancing circular economy initiatives that aim to reduce, reuse, and recycle waste streams will be vital in reducing the economic, social, and environmental impacts of the rising volumes of global solid waste.

Facilitating, Enabling, and Triggering Sectoral Transitions: Brazil

Case Study 10. Reducing Deforestation in Brazil

Contributor: Diji Chandrasekharan Behr

Context

Brazil is an upper-middle-income country that aspires to high-income status and joining the Organisation for Economic Co-operation and Development. In 2021, approximately 87 percent of its 214 million population lived in urban areas (World Bank 2018b). It is also home to one of the world's most unique and precious ecosystems, the Amazon biome, a significant global carbon sink that influences regional precipitation patterns. The country's current export basket is heavily dominated by agricultural commodities such as soya beans (10 percent) and nonrenewable resources such as iron ore (10 percent) and petroleum oils (9 percent).[8] This presents challenges, both in terms of the rate of growth and implications for the sustainable management of the country's natural capital and inclusive development in rural landscapes.

As Brazil aims to achieve growth and development, it has the opportunity to do so in a climate-smart manner. Its gross emissions are dominated by agriculture and land use change, especially from deforestation, with a relatively low carbon intensity in the rest of the economy. One of the key issues that it needs to tackle, however, is curbing deforestation. A low-carbon development path supports the country's need to reduce its exposure to climate change risks. Measures to curb deforestation and maintain native vegetation would reduce the agriculture, energy, and other sectors' exposure to the impacts of drought, soil erosion, and heat waves, given the ecosystem services provided by the Amazon and Cerrado biomes.

Tackling deforestation in Brazil requires addressing the key drivers of deforestation, including extensive cattle ranching, land grabbing, and illegal logging. Converting land for crop production is a key driver in the Cerrado. Estimates show that about 70 percent of deforested land in the Amazon is used for cattle ranching, the result of weak law enforcement, poor land governance, and macroeconomic drivers, such as commodity prices and demand, and real exchange rates. Although environmental policies are the responsibility of state and federal governments, municipalities must also be involved in addressing the key drivers of deforestation through their local policies and can influence the extent of land grabbing or illegal logging.

Brazil has successfully curbed deforestation in the past. From 2004 to 2012, during the commodity boom, the country's environmental policies succeeded in curbing deforestation rates by 84 percent (Fearnside 2017). Many researchers credit the Plan for the Prevention and Control of Deforestation in the Legal Amazon (PPCDAm) and enforcement of the Forest Code for the reduction in deforestation.

Policy

Launched in 2004 and overseen by the Environment Ministry, the PPCDAm promoted drastic conservation reform in Brazil. The objective of this plan was to mitigate the trend of increasing deforestation in the Legal Amazon in a coherent, integrated, and effective manner. The PPCDAm had distinct phases, emphasizing aspects of its three axes: land planning, monitoring and control, and promotion of sustainable land use activities (West and Fearnside 2021). A key land use planning action taken in its third phase of (2012–15) was revising the Forest Code in 2012.

Robust monitoring and control are necessary to reverse the weak law enforcement and poor land governance underlying the drivers of deforestation. While the Project to Calculate Deforestation in the Amazon (PRODES) has enabled the use of satellite data to monitor deforestation in the Brazilian Amazon since 1988, the DETER satellite system, launched as part of the PPCDAm, changed the way monitoring was done. Developed by the National Institute for Space Research, DETER is a satellite-based system that captures and processes georeferenced imagery on forest cover in 15-day intervals and uses them to identify deforestation hot spots and areas in need of immediate attention. It then alerts the Brazilian Institute for the Environment and Renewable Natural Resources, which operates as the national environmental police and law enforcement authority, and state environmental agencies on deforestation, allowing for targeted on-the-ground forest law enforcement, inspection, and collection of environmental fines. PRODES provided annual deforestation rates to the public and decision-makers and informed measures such as the Municipality Priority List, which was considered an effective mechanism for tackling deforestation. Established in 2007, the Municipal Priority List singles out municipalities with intense deforestation activity for differential action, including rigorous environmental monitoring and law enforcement, stricter licensing and georeferencing requirements for rural establishments, changes in the approval of subsidized credit contracts, and a refusal by meatpacking plants to buy cattle from embargoed farms.

The 2012 Forest Code, which governs the use and protection of private lands in Brazil, has two types of legally binding protection instruments for conservation on private lands. Permanent preservation areas (PPAs) are areas of vegetation that are critical to the preservation of key ecosystem functions, and legal forest reserves (LFRs) are a percentage of land area that has to be maintained with native vegetation to conserve biodiversity, where clear-cutting is prohibited and sustainable forest management is allowed. The Forest Code also created a new national database, the Rural Environmental Registry (CAR in Portuguese), an online public registry where every landowner must register their rural property, including georeferenced data on all PPAs and LFRs. Registering their property on the CAR also gives landowners access to their rights under the Forest Code, including rural credit from financial institutions (Chiavari and Leme Lopes 2015).

Results and Impacts

Econometric research conducted on the impact of DETER on deforestation reveals positive results. Between 2001–03 and 2015, forest loss decreased by 90 percent in indigenous lands, 64 percent in protected areas, 70 percent in rural settlements, and 78 percent in federal lands. Reduced deforestation also preserved ecosystem services. Studies find that an increase in the number of fines applied in a given year significantly reduced forest clearings the following year, while crop price indices also impact deforestation. When controlling for price effects, municipality-specific fixed characteristics, and time trends, the results show that Brazilian environmental policies had a sizeable direct impact on deforestation levels and helped curb forest clearings (Mullan et al. 2022).

Counterfactual data also reveal that significant areas of deforestation were avoided due to the presence of the combination of policies (Assunçãoa, Gandoura, and Rochad 2019). For example, the Municipality Priority List policy, while effective, was not enough to curb deforestation on its own. Rather, it depended on the presence of other policies. Its effectiveness was enhanced when combined with efforts to designate clear land titling (including protected areas); voluntary supply chain commitments; sectoral agreements involving federal and state governments, companies, banks, and civil society organizations, such as the Soy Moratorium; and the Plan for Accelerated Growth. But without these other policies, the Municipality Priority List did not significantly reduce deforestation. Spatial monitoring systems such as DETER and PRODES were crucial, as they strengthened the implementation of these different policies and contributed to reducing deforestation.

The effectiveness of the PPCDAm declined over time as its implementation budget was significantly reduced. Costing environmental policies is a challenge because of the diverse entities involved and the coding of the budget. A preliminary estimate reveals that the key agencies involved in implementing the PPCDAm and other environmental policies received, at the height of support (2012), an annual amount of approximately $0.64 billion; in 2021, they received $0.38 billion. Compounding the financial challenges are technological limitations associated with implementing DETER, which cannot detect deforestation when there is significant cloud cover. Recent analysis found that deforestation was higher during periods of heavy cloud cover than other times (Sales, Strobl, and Elliott 2022).

The political economy of deforestation undermines the effectiveness of using spatial data-based monitoring and control efforts, such as DETER. Farmers form a strong and powerful special interest group in the Brazilian Amazon that strongly opposes government measures that constrain access to "free" land or increase the cost of agriculture. Analyses have shown the linkage between the presence of municipal-level farmer mayors and deforestation (Braganca and Dahis 2021). One study finds that, between 2019 and 2021, political interference, such as budget cuts, employment freezes, and obstructing decision-making, has weakened monitoring and enforcement and created a big discrepancy between the numbers of deforestation alerts and fines collected (figure 3.12; Werneck, Angelo, and Araújo 2022). At the same time, the number of embargoes and confiscated illegal equipment—two key measures for controlling deforestation—also decreased by 70 percent and 81 percent, respectively. Associated with the weakening of monitoring efforts, mayors who support deforestation are enabling illegal land grabbing and logging. Just 53 of Brazil's 5,570 municipalities were responsible for 66 percent of deforestation in the Amazon between 2012 and 2021.

Complementing monitoring and control with mapping untitled public lands and modernizing the land registration system will also help reduce land grabbing. Mapping untitled public lands would give the government spatial data to facilitate the designation of public lands as protected areas, including sustainable use lands and indigenous territories; form the basis for regularizing private land claims; and help determine which public lands could be designated for private use. Modernizing Brazil's land registration, analysis, and validation practices would be an important complementary action (Stassart et al. 2021). Support to accelerate validation of the CAR would help

FIGURE 3.12 **Deforestation in the Amazon and IBAMA Infraction Notices for Deforestation, 2003–21**

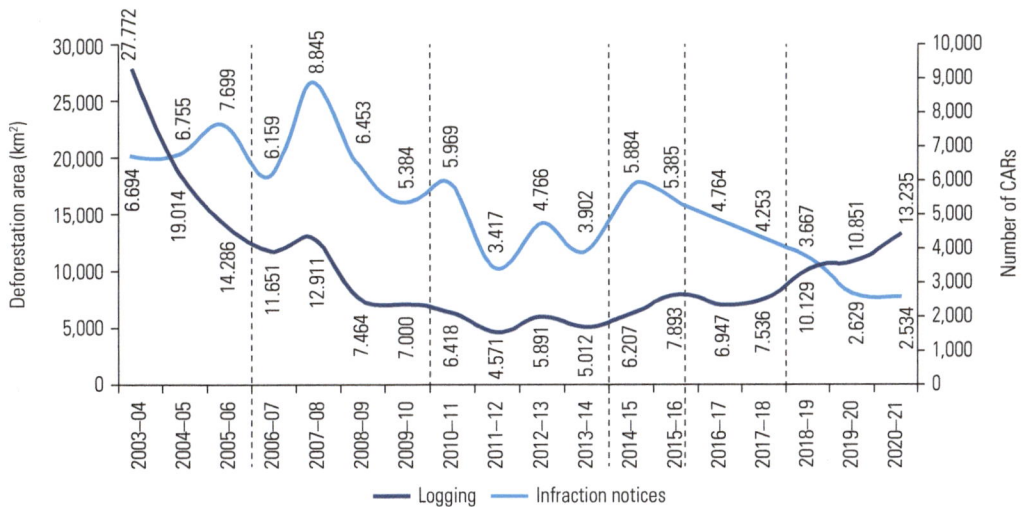

Source: Based on data from INPE 2021.

Note: IBAMA (Instituto Brasileiro do Meio Ambiente e dos Recursos Naturais Renováveis, or Brazilian Institute of the Environment and Renewable Natural Resources) is the national environmental agency. CARs = Rural Environmental Registries (Portuguese); km² = square kilometer.

reinforce this effort, enabling the use of incentives and instruments in the new Forest Code, including the trading forest certificates.

Key Takeaways

While addressing the multiple factors that underlie deforestation in the Legal Amazon is complex and requires a multisectoral approach, there is significant value in having a robust spatial monitoring and control system. Effective implementation of an instrument such as DETER can ensure the effective implementation of the PPCDAm's land use planning, monitoring and control, and sustainable land use axes. Real-time satellite monitoring is an effective tool for implementing policies that can curb deforestation, especially when twinned with enforcing penalties for violating the law. It is therefore important to shield appropriations associated with generating satellite monitoring data, dispatch these data to inspection and law enforcement agencies, and enforce the law without political interference. As the cost of producing and processing high-resolution satellite imagery decreases, linking tools like DETER and PRODES with policy measures such as the PPCDAm and the Municipality Priority List would be more widely replicable.

It would be equally valuable to have a powerful tool to accelerate the process for validating the CAR and removing illegal registrations in the environmental registry system. A way forward would be to have an integrated CAR database and system that is accessible to both the federal and state governments and is based on unique and comprehensive data on, among other things, land tenure, land use changes, and public forests (Moutinho and Azevedo-Ramos 2023). This, along with DETER, will reinforce the implementation of existing policies and regulations, such as the requirement for environmental compliance systems such as CAR to qualify for public loans.

Facilitating, Enabling, and Triggering Sectoral Transitions: the Sahel

Case Study 11. Improving Water Availability and Restoring Soil Fertility in the Sahel

Contributors: Ruth Hill and Sandra Baquié

Context

Soils are the dominant terrestrial sink for carbon, containing three times as much CO_2 as plant biomass above the ground (Manning 2008). They also act as a host for both organic and inorganic CO_2—as soil organic matter and pedogenic carbonates, respectively—by sequestering CO_2 through photosynthesis. As such, soils have an important role to play as passive agents in removing atmospheric CO_2, similar to the role of reed beds in cleaning contaminated waters. Agroecosystems can degrade and deplete soil organic matter levels, but this carbon deficit opens up the opportunity to store carbon through new land management practices, and in turn, mitigate climate change (Lal 2004).

This is particularly important in the Sahel, where agriculture is a large source of employment and economic activity (table 3.2). The sector represents 40 percent of GDP for Burkina Faso, Chad, Mali, Mauritania, and Niger combined, and employs almost three-quarters of the workforce. Many households—particularly poorer ones—depend on farming for their livelihoods and food security. Agriculture is mainly smallholder subsistence dryland farming and is extremely dependent on highly variable seasonal rainfall due to limited irrigation.

TABLE 3.2 **Selected Indicators for Countries in the Sahel, 2021**

	Income classification	GDP per capita (current $)	Population (millions)	Land area (millions km²)	Agriculture employment (% of total employment)	International poverty rate (% living on > $1.90 a day)	Human Development Index (0–1)
Burkina Faso	LIC	953.1	21.5	0.3	76.2	30.8	0.452
Chad	LIC	666.4	16.9	1.3	75.1	37.8	0.398
Mali	LIC	885.2	20.9	1.2	62.4	17.6	0.434
Mauritania	LMIC	1735.8	4.8	1.0	30.8	6.0	0.546
Niger	LIC	569.8	23.3	1.3	72.5	41.8	0.394

Sources: World Bank 2022f; UNDP 2020.

Note: Population and agriculture employment (modeled International Labor Organization estimate) show most recent available values (2018). Estimated poverty rate is based on the most recent value using 2011 purchasing power parity. Human Development Index ranks are from the 2020 Human Development Report with 2019 data from 189 countries. The index is the geometric mean of health, education, and income index with a value between 0 and 1, where a value above 0.800 = very high, 0.700–0.799 = high, 0.550–0.699 = medium, and under 0.550 = low. GDP = gross domestic product; km² = square kilometer; LIC = low-income country; LMIC = lower-middle-income county.

Although structural transformation is required to diversify household income sources, reducing poverty will also require improved agricultural productivity. Due to the dominance of agriculture as a source of income for rural households and the slow pace of structural transformation, short- and medium-term opportunities for growth and poverty alleviation are primarily in the agricultural sector. Yet, productivity in agriculture remains low. For example, in Burkina Faso, where most farmers produce food crops, productivity remains low despite the relatively large average land and livestock holdings. This could be a result of poor access to domestic and international markets, low rates of commercialization, credit and liquidity constraints, frictions in the labor and land markets, or information gaps (De Janvry, Sadoulet, and Suri 2017; Udry 1996).

Access to productive soil and water are two of the main barriers to increasing and ensuring more equal distribution of agricultural productivity in the Sahel. In Burkina Faso, 97 percent of farmers have access to land, and the average size of land holdings is relatively large and equally distributed, although formal ownership is limited. This distribution and the unequal level of agricultural productivity suggest that the size of landholdings is not the primary driver of income inequality. Instead, factors such as soil quality and access to water and markets are more critical. Households have limited access to irrigation, so rainfall conditions are strong predictors of yield, and low and irregular precipitation patterns mean income risk is high (Hill et al. 2019).

Climate change will exacerbate income risk if agricultural productivity does not increase. The latest Intergovernmental Panel on Climate Change (IPCC) report warns that drought frequency, duration, and intensity will likely increase in Africa, particularly in the Sahel (IPCC 2022). In 2030, researchers estimate that 250 million people could live in an African region with high water stress. In turn, climate change will impact yields. One study estimates that sorghum and maize yields in the western Sahel will decline by 1.5 percent on average at 1.5°C global warming and by 4 percent at 2°C global warming (Faye et al. 2018). Although irrigation, which currently represents less than 1 percent of cultivated land, could be a solution, labor market failures may limit adoption in the medium run (Jones et al. 2022), and eventual adoption may increase competition and tensions over scarce water. Indeed, the Sahel is one of the most water-stressed regions in the world, with an unevenly distributed water supply that crosses national boundaries.

Policies

Policies to improve agricultural productivity do not always lead to long-term sustainable solutions to low productivity. For example, current policy mixes often include significant spending on fertilizer subsidies. The impacts of fertilizer subsidies are not straightforward. Indeed, although subsidies are often targeted to poor households, the usual fertilizer mix has negative crop returns if unsubsidized. The benefits of using fertilizer are also compromised by extreme weather conditions, such as floods or droughts, making fertilizer use nonprofitable in bad weather years (Dercon and Christiaensen 2011). As a result, fertilizer subsidies could amplify, rather than reduce, households' income risk. Subsidies also do not address the long-run challenge of poor-quality soils and can lead to emissions of significant amounts of nitrogen dioxide.

To address low agricultural productivity, in the Sahel, farmers use low-cost, efficient traditional practices, such as agroforestry and conventional rainwater harvesting techniques, to capture rainfall, reduce runoff, and restore soils, as well as some of the following interventions.

- Stone bunds: an innovation developed from traditional farming practices. In the late 1970s, farmers in Burkina Faso's Yatenga Province built stone contour bunds following imaginary lines of equal elevation to harvest rainwater. These walls slow water runoff and increase water infiltration in the soil, trapping sediments and organic matter and allowing soils to regenerate. In the 1980s, the development of a simple cost-effective tool to measure water levels made designing the contours accessible to those with no or little education.
- Zaï holes: originating in the same region as stone bunds, farmers traditionally dug a grid of planting pits to reclaim severely degraded land that the water could not penetrate. In the 1980s, farmers perfected this technique by optimizing the depth and diameter of the holes and adding organic matter to the bottom. The resulting planting pits retain water for extended periods and concentrate nutrients where the plants' roots are, allowing crops to survive dry spells and soil quality to improve.
- Half-moon structures: similar to zaï holes, but large and shaped as a semicircle. This shape makes them appropriate for sloped land with severely degraded soil in Niger (Aker and Kelsey 2021).
- Farmer-managed natural regeneration: a low-cost practice for growing trees and shrubs developed in Niger in the 1980s. Tony Rinaudo, a member of an international missionary organization, and local farmers developed an effective way to regenerate selected tree roots that lay underneath cleared fields, selecting the best stems and protecting them by removing competing stems. The resulting trees produce fodder, fuelwood, or food, protect neighboring crops by reducing wind speeds and evaporation, and sometimes enhance soil fertility by adding nitrogen in the soil (Reij, Tappan, and Smale 2009).

Information and training help expand the adoption of low-cost, efficient solutions. Despite the efficiency of the zaï hole and stone bund practices, only one-third of Burkina Faso's farmers practice such anti-erosion measures on their land. Evidence shows that knowledge building is critical to increasing the adoption rate of traditional techniques. In Burkina Faso, the use of zaï holes has expanded thanks to the engagement of a few influential farmers who organized market days, created a "zaï school," or developed a network of trained farmers in their region. A study in Niger using a randomized control trial shows that informational barriers are a major constraint to adopting half-moon techniques, and that training farmers increases the share of adopters by 90 percent on average, with the addition of cash transfers making no difference to the rate of adoption. The study also finds that trained farmers continue to transmit this knowledge to their neighbors up to three years after the initial training and are 50 percent more likely to have neighbors adopting the technique than farmers who were not trained. This evidence suggests that information campaigns and training are cost-effective ways to boost the adoption of profitable and accessible technologies.

Results and Impacts

Not only do traditional agricultural practices significantly increase agricultural productivity, they also improve soil quality. In Niger, farmer-managed natural regeneration increases yields by 16 to 30 percent (Matlon 1985), and adopting this practice increased tree cover by nearly 5 million hectares between 2003 and 2008. Similarly, in Burkina Faso, adopting the zaï holes technique increases yields by 300 to 400 kilograms per hectare in low rainfall years and by up to 1,500 kilograms per hectare in good rainfall years. Over the past three decades, 200,000 to 300,000 hectares of land have been rehabilitated thanks to this technique. Adopting stone bunds also increases yields by around 300 kilograms per hectare, and farmers can get even higher returns by combining zaï holes, stone bunds, and fertilizer use. In Niger, adopting the half-moon techniques has been found to increase yields and reduce land turnover. Trained households cultivated an additional 0.3 hectares of rehabilitated land by the third year after training.

These traditional land management practices contribute to climate change mitigation and improved resilience. Rainwater harvesting, crop rotations, and agroforestry increase soil carbon sequestration at the respective estimated rates of 839, 378, and 1,359 per kilogram per hectare per year in Africa (World Bank 2012). Not only does this mitigate climate change, but the resulting higher soil organic content improves the resilience of crops, which is crucial for climate adaptation and food security. The associated increase in productivity also allows farmers to reduce their use of chemical fertilizers, further contributing to climate mitigation. Indeed, chemical fertilizers are the third most significant contributor to total non-CO_2 agricultural emissions after enteric fermentation and livestock manure (FAO 2018).

Supporting traditional agricultural practices can alleviate poverty, reduce income risk, increase climate resilience, and empower women. Given agriculture is the primary source of income for many poor households, the increased agricultural productivity associated with traditional farming practices could improve welfare and, in turn, lift people out of poverty. For example, a study in Niger estimates that farmer-managed natural regeneration increased cereal production by 500,000 tons a year, covering the needs of 2.5 million people, or 10 percent of the population. Traditional agricultural practices also weaken household reliance on precipitation, allowing them to harvest rainfall and improve soil quality. This reduces their income risk to weather shocks, which is even more critical as climate change and extreme weather events become more severe and frequent. Some agricultural practices can also contribute to women's empowerment—for example, farmer-managed natural regeneration of firewood-producing trees lifts the burden of collecting firewood, which traditionally falls on women.

Key Takeaways

Low-cost technologies and practices can improve soil quality and agricultural household incomes, reduce risk, and contribute to climate change mitigation. Such interventions, which support the productivity of a wide variety of crops, are increasingly used, but a large share of households still do not use them, suggesting there are constraints to adoption that need to be overcome. One of these is the lack of information and knowledge, which appears to be a small constraint to overcome, given the large potential benefits.

Providing high-quality extension services at scale can be challenging and is not as easy as subsidizing inputs. Scaling up depends on a combination of awareness building, providing technical information, social learning, and motivation, underlining the importance of implementation partners. Stakeholders who benefit from current input subsidy schemes are also resistant to reform, challenging a shift from a model of production support via input subsidies to one based on extension.

Facilitating, Enabling, and Triggering Sectoral Transitions: Egypt

Case Study 12. Motorization Management: Fleet Renewal and Recycling Program in Egypt

Contributors: Georges Darido and W. Nick Bowden

Context

Motorization management is a menu of measures to manage motor vehicle flows and stocks at all phases of their life cycle to support access and economic growth while reducing GHG emissions, improving air quality, and enhancing traffic safety (World Bank 2021h). Measures include fleet renewal mechanisms with replacement, recycling, and certification systems; and policies and financial incentives to modernize the most polluting, unsafe, and intensively used vehicles. In Egypt around 2010, the average age of the motor vehicle fleet was high, and many intensively used vehicles were poorly maintained, contributing to excessive emissions, breakdowns, and road traffic accidents. The bustling capital, Cairo, produces 40 percent of the country's transport-related GHG emissions, exposing residents to as much as 20 times the acceptable air pollution levels every day (Carbon Partnership Facility 2023; see also UNFCCC 2020). A significant share of these emissions come from older or poorly maintained vehicles, including up to 40-year-old taxis (Hereher et al. 2021).

Policy

In 2008, the government of Egypt adopted a new law mandating that fee-based transport vehicles (taxis, buses, trucks, and so on) over 20 years old would no longer be eligible for new operating licenses or license renewals. Because the law did not specify how eligible vehicles should be disposed of, owners could sell these vehicles, convert them for private use, or dismantle them and sell the engines for use in other vehicles. Without a national scrapping and recycling program, the law was not having its intended effect. In 2010, the World Bank, as trustee of the Danish and Spanish Carbon Funds, entered into an agreement with the Danish Carbon Fund of Egypt to purchase from the CDM certified emissions reductions (CERs) generated by vehicles participating in the scrapping and recycling program. This carbon finance transaction facilitated the sale and transfer of CERs from the Ministry of Finance's (MoF) program to Danish and Spanish Carbon Funds participants through a commercial contract referred to as an emissions reduction purchase agreement. The sale of these CERs would offset the costs incurred by MoF to set up a one-stop shop for scrapping and replacing taxis.

The Egypt Vehicle Scrapping and Recycling Program supported a fleet renewal mechanism through which taxi, microbus, trailer truck, and bus owners voluntarily surrendered their vehicles for managed scrapping and recycling, in exchange for financial incentives to purchase new vehicles from participating pre-registered vehicle dealers at a discounted price and with financing facilities (World Bank 2021c). Certified recycling and scrapping ensured that old vehicles were permanently taken off the roads and components such as tires, oils, and batteries disposed of and recycled in an environmentally safe manner. The program objective was to reduce emissions associated with the country's aging fleet of taxis, microbuses, minibuses, and buses through the purchase of CERs and included third-party auditing.

Results and Impacts

Between 2013 and 2017, more than 40,000 vehicles were turned in, scrapped, and recycled through the program in Cairo. The new vehicles, which represented over 90 percent of the city's taxi fleet, have reduced GHG emissions by over 300 $ktCO_2e$ as of 2017 and counting. MoF's project implementation success was based on strong internal technical capacity and in-house program and administrative design, including a one-stop shop for owners of eligible taxis. The one-stop shop meant that taxi drivers did not lose their source of income while waiting for their new taxi to arrive, which would have discouraged them from joining the program. The entire process—from application to surrendering the old vehicle and receiving the new one—took, on average, five to seven working days. The efficiency of the one-stop shop and the MoF incentives were so successful that the scrapping site was overwhelmed. The government then had to create a reservation system for a maximum of 120 vehicles per day for timely processing at the scrapping facility. As part of the project design, MoF was authorized to disburse a subsidy of up to LE 5,000 (about $270) per eligible surrendered vehicle and covered the taxes due from the sale of the new taxis. It also waived customs fees for importing vehicles parts, and MoF negotiated lower-interest rates for car loans (Ali 2016).

The new replacement vehicles used up-to-date technology that reduces pollution through lower fuel consumption and cost less to run, improving drivers' livelihoods. More than half of the new vehicles run on compressed natural gas (CNG), a more environment-friendly fuel producing fewer GHG emissions than gasoline or diesel. The government outsourced a recycling facility to ensure that the old vehicles were taken off the road permanently and that scrapped vehicle components such as tires, oils, and batteries were disposed of and recycled in an environmentally safe manner. As well as decreasing pollution, the upgraded vehicles have improved working conditions for taxi drivers (World Bank 2018a).

Key Takeaways

The program had a significant positive environmental impact, providing new and more energy-efficient vehicles and reducing CO_2, methane, nitric oxide, and nitrogen dioxide emissions in greater Cairo. The program is an example of how the sale of CERs can help accelerate the success of government programs, successfully reducing GHG emissions from transport, improving air quality, and creating safer road conditions. As of December 2018, it was the only World Bank transport sector operation in the Middle East to issue CERs and had sold more than 340,000 CERs. After its success in Cairo, the government is considering replicating the model in other locations. Other African countries—such as Burkina Faso and Côte d'Ivoire—have been inspired to develop similar initiatives, which the World Bank is supporting. The model could also be used to accelerate the penetration of zero-emission vehicles, such as electric vehicles (EVs), which may have higher capital investment requirements in vehicle and charging infrastructure but lower operating costs and other benefits over the long term.

Facilitating, Enabling, and Triggering Sectoral Transitions: Peru

Case Study 13. Nonmotorized Transport: Cycling Strategy and Infrastructure Plan for Lima, Peru

Contributors: Nicolas Peltier and Felipe Targa

Context

Lima faces challenges in providing proper transport services to its more than 11 million inhabitants (World Justice Project 2022). According to the Ministry of Transport and Communications of Peru, Lima has an excessive number of mass transport units (over 25,000 vehicles) and an oversupply of taxis (250,000 units when it should have half). Although 60 percent of trips in Lima take place on public transport, private vehicle use has increased rapidly in recent years, causing severe road congestion, air pollution, and road traffic accidents. Lima is ranked among the world's worst cities for traffic congestion, and the annual social cost of congestion in the city is $7 billion (GIZ 2014), around 1.8 percent of Peru's GDP. This has adverse effects on the working class, with 38 percent wasting 90 minutes a day commuting due to congestion (Federación Colombiana de Municipios and Dirección Nacional Simit 2020).

The city design is based on a motorized system, leaving few options for more sustainable means of transport. The lack of adequate infrastructure, legislation, and general cycling culture leaves bicyclists as a vulnerable group of users without tools to defend their rights. World Bank technical and financial support in recent years has aimed to produce several initiatives and policy suggestions that will make a positive impact on Lima's traffic and pollution challenges, and in so doing, empower others to choose more environmentally friendly means of transportation. Existing problems will be aggravated if the trend toward car-dominated cities and metropolitan areas continues (Lefevre 2014).

Cycling is a low-carbon activity, and its only emissions are related to bicycle manufacture. It produces only 21 grams of CO_2 per kilometer traveled, while private cars emit 270 grams, and a public transport bus, 101 grams (Blondel, Mispelon, and Ferguson 2011). The World Bank's recent proposals for a cycling strategy and infrastructure plan for Lima include development objectives to give Lima residents a healthy, low-carbon, efficient, and resilient transport option by making cycling safer, more convenient, and more accessible to the general population. In 2019, only 0.9 percent of all trips made in Lima were made by bicycle. By introducing new policies, the cycling strategy aims to increase this to 15 percent by 2050.

This analytical work conducted by the World Bank in 2020 and commissioned by the Metropolitan Municipality of Lima cites a lack of sound policy, infrastructure investment, and promotion for developing smarter and greener mobility systems, such as cycling and walking (World Bank 2021g). It outlines several transport problems, including a high rate of car accidents, an inefficient public transport system, an old fleet causing air pollution above the maximum permissible limits, an increase in new car numbers, and poor respect for the rule of law. The road network does not provide safe, comfortable, direct, and integrated transport options due to the lack of dedicated cycle lanes on arterial roads and safe traffic management (motor vehicle speeds and traffic volumes) on local roads. Developing and implementing a cycling system is crucial to develop a sustainable city. Local governments are underfunded, limiting the financial and technical resources needed to implement citywide climate-smart urban transport infrastructure. National, regional, and local regulations often promote car-centric urban development and infrastructure. Although there is a growing demand for using bicycles in the city, policies and infrastructure investments aimed at promoting their use are very limited. This is due to the incipient development of national and local policies and investment incentives on sustainable transport, ineffective strategies for informing the population about benefits of using of nonmotorized transport, and outdated laws and regulations with limited capacity to guarantee the road safety and security of cyclists, along with inadequate infrastructure.

Policy

A 2004–10 GEF project helped Peru establish a foundation for better, cleaner, more efficient, and safer urban transport in Lima and reduce GHG emissions. Fully blended with a World Bank loan, which financed the implementation of Lima's first bus rapid transit (BRT) corridor, the project financed bicycle infrastructure, promotion activities to complement the loan's nonmotorized transport activities, capacity building for sustainable urban transport, and the first bicycle infrastructure master plan for Lima (World Bank 2013).

In 2010, the Peruvian government issued the first countrywide policy (Law 29593) to improve biking conditions and promote cycling as a means of sustainable transportation. Although innovative, this law did not trigger concrete actions in terms of sound policy and infrastructure investments at local municipalities. Almost a decade later, and with concern about COVID-19 and crowded public transport risks, Lima is strengthening its cycling infrastructure with almost 50 kilometers of emergency cycle lanes and additional bicycle parking facilities. Lima's mayor during the pandemic, Jorge Muñoz, described this initiative as one that is "needed not only as a preventive measure for COVID-19, but also to help our citizens choose a healthier and more eco-friendly alternative." It also went hand in hand with the *Yo Respeto* (I Respect) campaign, which promoted road safety in the city. Road safety has become a top priority in Lima, which has upgraded and protected new bike lanes with vertical bollards, rubber humps, and painted markings to separate them from the roadway and installed dedicated bicycle traffic lights. The city is already making moves toward long-term change beyond the COVID-19 emergency. In June 2020, the Ministry of Transport and Communications of Peru accelerated the approval of the regulation under a new law that promotes and regulates bicycle use as a sustainable mode of transport (Law 30936 of 2019). Lima's city authorities have evaluated the success of their measures and are now planning to make their emergency cycle infrastructure permanent. Their experience shows that, with political will and the right policy landscape, it is possible to shift urban planning and citizen mobility habits to deliver long-term benefits in both population and environmental health (WHO 2020).

Law 30936 establishes measures to promote and regulate bicycle use as a sustainable and efficient means of transport in terms of road capacity and preservation of the environment. This law also assigned specific roles and mandates for public institutions at different government levels. The Ministry of Transport and Communications of Peru prepares and implements public policies for road infrastructure design and promotes urban and rural planning that favors bicycle use, in coordination with public entities at all three levels of government. The National Institute of Statistics and Informatics coordinates and produces basic statistics regarding bicycle use as a sustainable and efficient means of transport through censuses, sample surveys, and administrative public sector records. Under the Lima Metropolitan Municipal Government's Urban Mobility Management Office, the deputy manager of non-motorized transport oversees the development of policies to promote active mobility within the metropolitan area.

Bicycle use in Lima has increased since the start of the COVID-19 pandemic, though around 300 kilometers of cycle lanes remain unconnected, with poor-quality infrastructure design and unsafe intersections. The use of bicycles in Lima rose from 3.7 percent of total trips before the pandemic to 6.2 percent in 2021 (based on data from perception surveys, the actual mode share might be 50 percent lower). The existing 300 kilometers of cycle lanes are not yet fully connected, and few serve as last-mile connections to mass transit stations. Just a handful of BRT stations have integrated bike parking facilities. Despite recent achievements (in 2019 there were 200 kilometers of cycle lanes), there is still a long way to go to improve Lima's cycling infrastructure to consolidate a connected, low-stress network and make it more gender-inclusive (women account for just 18 percent of cyclists). Addressing road safety at key intersections along arterial avenues and collector streets is important to consolidate the growth in cycling demand for people of all genders, ages, and abilities. Another key step is to provide safe last-mile bicycle infrastructure connectivity to mass transit stations, schools, markets, and key public space destinations.

To reduce traffic congestion, decarbonize transport, and increase physical activity, in 2020, the World Bank provided analytical and advisory support to Lima's metropolitan government to increase cycling in the city. This included updating its Bicycle Infrastructure Plan (World Bank 2020c), developing a connected cycle network of 1,383 kilometers by 2040, and developing a proposal to adopt a bicycle strategy with policy recommendations to promote cycling, particularly among women (World Bank 2020d).[9] The plan supported the city's COVID-19 response approach for pop-up bike lanes during the pandemic, adding almost 100 kilometers of new cycle lanes during these two years. There are plans to add another 114 kilometers of cycle lanes with grant resources from the German government's development bank, KfW. The World Bank is also preparing an investment operation expected to be approved in 2023 under a programmatic approach to improve traffic management and support sustainable transport that includes building another 200 kilometers of cycle lanes and implementing bike-share systems and bike parking facilities at mass transit stations.

Results and Expected Impacts

For the update of Lima's Bicycle Infrastructure Plan, the World Bank supported an analysis of the ex ante social impacts of this plan. Using a standard social cost and benefit analysis to assess the relationship between the cost of a bicycle infrastructure investment and its benefits for communities, The total costs were projected to be S/1,210 million ($297,000) and the benefits, S/22,978 million ($6.1 million), with the social benefits outweighing the direct and indirect costs of infrastructure construction by a factor of 19. The analysis finds economic savings related with improved travel time reliability, reduced travel times, reduced risk of death or severe disease, cleaner air, less pollution and congestion, and healthier lifestyles. The plan also expects for the modal share for bikes to grow from 0.9 percent in 2019 to 11.6 percent by 2050 and estimates that the project could reduce emissions in Lima by 0.64 tCO_2e by 2030 and 1.03 tCO_2e by 2050.

Other initiatives across Lima have complemented the government's cycling policies, including the initiative "Promoting Access to Sustainable Transport in Lima through the Use of Bicycles as Means of Transport," a partnership between the World Justice Project, the Metropolitan Municipality of Lima, the Ministry of Environment, and the social movement for cycling, Actibisimo.

Key Takeaways

Cycling projects have a high return in terms of social benefits, which translate into significant economic savings. Presumably, similar initiatives in other cities and countries could also have net positive social effects. Over the past decades, several cities around the world have made substantial progress in promoting cycling. Bogotá, for example, has built more than 600 kilometers of cycling infrastructure, integrated cycle parking facilities into its BRT system, and continues to support its 48-year-old Ciclovía program, where over 1 million people enjoy more than 120 kilometers of car-free streets every week.

Despite the proven economic viability of cycling mobility projects, there are considerable obstacles to infrastructure programs. The following strategies can help countries and cities overcome these challenges, improving the possibility of implementation (World Bank 2021g):

- Prioritizing active mobility in national and local policies by aligning with broader goals on climate, road safety, health, equity, and build-back-better strategies
- Integrating cycling and pedestrian infrastructure into the following: long-term transport plans as a key component of integrated transport systems; standards for design in local practices for urban infrastructure; and national, regional, and metropolitan levels financing schemes
- Gearing international climate funding and investment toward active mobility and agreeing on corporate commitments for including active mobility projects in infrastructure loans from multilateral development banks
- Setting a minimum of 20 percent of the transport or infrastructure budget for active mobility as the most straightforward way to fulfill and sustain active mobility goals
- Screening transport and road infrastructure projects to ensure adequate and appropriate inclusion of walking and cycling components
- Training staff on best practices for active mobility, with the ultimate goal of creating a dedicated team or unit
- Encouraging tax incentives for private investors, developers, and suppliers
- Ensuring plans reflect the local or national political economy
- Realizing opportunities to finance active mobility in the developing world and make a shift that would meet transport needs, address the economic constraints, and relieve climate change impacts

The main challenges around building nonmotorized transport infrastructure projects are funding, technical capacity, and political economy considerations. To address these challenges, the World Bank's Lima Traffic Management to Support Sustainable Transport Expansion project will finance selected road safety interventions to improve conditions for cyclists (World Bank 2022c). Lima's government officials are also participating in the Latinoamérica Pedalea (Latin America Cycles, or LAP) knowledge exchange program. Under LAP, a program funded by the South-South Knowledge Exchange Facility, Lima's government staff received training directly from their counterparts in Mexico City and Bogotá, regional leaders in terms of planning and designing cycling projects. Representatives from civil society, media outlets, and business chambers also participated in the program, directly learning from the experiences of their peers in the Mexican and Colombian capitals. Such efforts are aimed at increasing the support base for cycling projects by disseminating the many social benefits that increased cycling rings to the city and forming cross-sectoral and multidisciplinary alliances in the LAP participating cities.

Facilitating, Enabling, and Triggering Sectoral Transitions: South Africa

Case Study 14. Public Transport in South Africa

Contributors: Georges Darido, Edward Beukes, and Gershwin Fortune

Context

The development objectives for public transport projects include improving efficient mobility and inclusive access to jobs, services, and socioeconomic opportunities, while also minimizing negative externalities such as local and global emissions, traffic injuries, and fatalities. To this end, many cities are implementing mass transit solutions, including BRT, which integrates dedicated road infrastructure, specialized vehicles and stations, advanced payment and management systems, and other features to maximize the efficiency, attractiveness, and sustainability of bus services. The main challenges include traffic congestion, a lack of priority for public and nonmotorized transport, maintaining affordable fares while minimizing public subsidies, and market failures leading to poor operating and maintenance practices, underinvestment, and poor performance in the sector.

Residents of South Africa's large cities, particularly the poor, suffer from long commutes and large spatial mismatches between jobs and housing as a legacy of apartheid. About two-thirds of public transport trips in South African cities are by paratransit by minibuses, the predominant transport mode for the working classes due to their affordability and ubiquity. Paratransit is usually a demand-responsive, self-organized service by an association of vehicle owners that contract drivers on a daily revenue target system and respond quickly to urban growth. Paratransit business models and relatively weak regulation enforcement contribute to cut-throat competition, reckless driving behaviors, and poor-quality vehicles, which in turn lead to excessive emissions and other negative impacts.

Policy

In 2007, the South African government approved a BRT strategy for its major cities in preparation for the 2010 World Cup. By 2014, the national government was spending R5.5 billion (around $500 million) annually on planning, building, and operating BRTs, and subnational governments were responsible for operating costs (Department of Transport 2022). Over 100 kilometers of dedicated bus lanes were operating in cities including Johannesburg, Cape Town, and Tshwane, and dozens of bus routes transported tens of thousands of persons per day. But the financial sustainability of these systems was a concern, as fare revenues relative to operating costs were lower than expected. Poor access and a lack of integration meant that many potential BRT users were unable to conveniently reach access points or their final destinations, and they walked or continued to use paratransit. Travel patterns with large tidal movements in peak hours, and low ridership in off-peak and the counter-peak direction also hampered the efficiency and sustainability of BRT systems, affecting ridership and increasing the need for public subsidy.

By 2014, the government recognized the need to improve BRT systems, including by extending their reach and access by connecting them to bus and paratransit services. The Department of Transport launched its Integrated Public Transport Network (IPTN) strategy in 13 cities. As part of this strategy, the city of Cape Town wanted to test the levers available to create a better service for users and a more sustainable business model for operators, while reducing externalities for society by incorporating paratransit to its IPTN. With these goals in mind, in 2017, the city launched a minibus taxi transformation pilot project in Mitchell's Plain, a densely populated township situated 27 kilometers from Cape Town's central business district. The pilot included five operating routes providing a scheduled paratransit feeder service connecting Tafelsig, a local suburb of Mitchell's Plain, and the Mitchell's Plain transport hub. The pilot focused on measures to improve business and operational efficiency, including pooling vehicles with centralized dispatch, centralized revenue and cost management, vehicle tracking and fleet management systems, introducing service headways, replacing drivers' daily revenue targets with monthly salaries, and an accounting system. The pilot did not include any public investment in vehicles or companies; rather, it was supported by business and consulting services facilitated by the city.

Results and Impacts

South Africa's transport sector contributes 12 to 15 percent of the country's total GHG emissions and is one of the fastest-growing sectors due to growing private motorization. The National Green Transport Strategy for South Africa (Department of Transport 2018) established several goals for 2030, including a 20 percent relative shift from private motorized transport to public transport; converting at least 10 percent of buses and minibuses to CNG, petrol, or EVs; and significantly expanding BRT systems in large cities while ensuring the security, reliability, and frequency of services. BRT systems operating in cities around the world have demonstrated the ability to reduce emissions by moving massive numbers of people more efficiently, attracting passengers from more polluting private motorized transport modes, and supporting compact urban development. The Johannesburg Rea Vaya BRT system was estimated to reduce public transport emissions by 69 percent (around 400 $ktCO_2e$ for 2011–21 for Phases 1A and 1B) through mode switching and improved efficiency of new and larger Euro IV buses. The Durban BRT system shows similar GHG emission potential reductions of 60 percent by inducing a shift to cleaner vehicles (principally Euro V BRT buses and minibuses) and more efficient operations (Gopaul, Friedrich, and Stretch 2019).

The Cape Town pilot shows that it is possible to achieve better services and reduce fuel consumption and emissions through improved business practices, operations, and labor and vehicle efficiency at negligible cost and without losing jobs. This is a triple win: for users, operators, and society. This small-scale pilot showed impressive results in terms of service quality, reliability, and emissions. First, it rationalized the fleet size from 78 mini-buses to 40 well-maintained vehicles (including three spares) while expanding service coverage from three to five licensed routes. Second, it improved employment conditions for drivers, moving from an average work pattern of 12-hour days in a 7-day week to 7.5-hour days with scheduled breaks and one day off in a 7-day cycle. Third, it reduced fuel consumption and associated emissions by 45 percent by transporting the same volume of passengers with fewer vehicle kilometers. A before-and-after passenger survey showed improvements in overall passenger satisfaction, waiting times, pick-up/drop-off locations, fares, crew conduct, vehicle comfort, road safety, and personal security.

The benefits of paratransit transformation projects and related sector reforms can be replicated in other cities and greatly expanded by including fleet renewal mechanisms and EVs. This will require greater public investment, as well as enabling private finance and fiscal incentives to support a green transition. Scalability also requires attention to the paratransit market structure, route lengths, travel behaviors, and competition with other operators. The World Bank is currently helping the South African government to analyze the technical, financial, and institutional feasibility of scaling up such policies and the possibility of creating a national program or financial facility to support fleet renewal, including EVs and other emerging vehicle technologies. The World Bank's South Africa Country Climate and Development Report estimates that electrifying 5 percent of South Africa's 412,000 public transport vehicles by 2030 would cost $2.8 billion and create some 58,000 new jobs (World Bank 2022l).

Key Takeaways

Improving public transport infrastructure and services is important, not only for equitable access to economic opportunities, but also as a pathway to decarbonize urban mobility. This is consistent with an avoid-shift-improve strategy (World Bank 2021e) that supports compact urban development patterns by reducing the need for private vehicles, shifting passengers away from more polluting motorized modes, and improving operations and technologies (World Bank 2021a). As the South Africa case shows, a comprehensive strategy should include mass transit investments supported by sector reforms and efficient regulations to create IPTNs and continuous improvement of existing operators with better business practices and technologies. Studies show that optimizing public transport planning and operations with the user in mind is as important as vehicle propulsion technology to achieving reduced emissions and other development objectives.

More than 3 million public transport and paratransit vehicles operate in Sub-Saharan Africa alone, from full-size buses to minivans and moto-taxis. If countries can modernize a share of these vehicles and improve their business practices, as shown by the Cape Town pilot, there is great potential for positive climate and development impacts. Investing in cleaner public transport fleets, improving paratransit operations, and supporting other sustainable urban mobility policies can help contain or reduce emissions while providing better services to users.

Facilitating, Enabling, and Triggering Sectoral Transitions: Türkiye

Case Study 15. Energy Efficiency in Türkiye's Public Buildings

Contributor: Jas Singh

Context

The building sector consumes about 30 percent of global final energy consumption and is responsible for about 27 percent of CO_2 emissions (IEA 2022a). Almost all the growth in energy demand in buildings will come from the developing world. As these countries develop, construction and energy demand from buildings will continue to rise. The rising middle classes demand larger housing units, more energy-using appliances, and, in tropical countries, air conditioning. This all requires more energy infrastructure and, is not sustainable. Within the building sector, there are publicly owned and operated buildings and private commercial and residential buildings. Among the former, government facilities—which can include central and municipal administrative buildings, universities and schools, hospitals and clinics, orphanages, museums, and other publicly owned facilities—are, collectively, the largest energy users in most countries. Available data suggest that the public sector typically accounts for 2 to 5 percent of a country's total energy consumption, although this figure is much higher (up to 30 percent) in countries with large heating loads (such as China, the EU, and the Europe and Central Asia region) or low energy access (as in many Sub-Saharan African countries).

The public sector represents a strategically important market segment for energy efficiency (EE). Public buildings, which are collectively large and visible consumers, can set examples for EE improvements in other sectors and demonstrate good energy management practices and high-performance technologies. The inclusion of energy-efficient criteria for products purchased for public offices, for example, can stimulate manufacturers to seek the necessary certifications for their products to compete in public tenders. The public sector can also use its purchasing power to stimulate EE markets; by purchasing in large volumes, it can bring down costs for all energy users. Businesses and institutions can also develop practices that promote public sector EE—such as standard contracts, tools, and protocols—while public campaigns can showcase the benefits of, and build confidence in, EE among citizens. Reducing government energy costs can open up fiscal space to invest in other socioeconomic priorities, such as improving the quality of and access to basic services, such as health care, education, and infrastructure.

Finally, public sector EE makes for a more resilient energy supply and lowers local and global emissions.

Barriers

Unfortunately, despite high potential and often attractive payback periods, the public sector, particularly in LMICs, often lags the rest of the economy on efficient energy use due to several barriers. Although the market barriers to EE in general are relevant here—low energy prices, high up-front and transaction costs, and limited access to data and information—other barriers are specific to the public sector. These include the following:

- Restrictive government policies and procedures, from budgeting to public procurement
- Limited financial resources for capital upgrades
- A lack of incentives, since government agencies are often unable to retain cost savings at all, or from one budget year to the next
- Behavioral inertia, as public employees have incentives to do things the same way and avoid taking risks.

Government Response

Governments have developed a range of policies, institutional setups, programs, and approaches to help overcome these barriers. Although they tend to rely on regulations, incentives, or market-based mechanisms, there are some universally applicable approaches. It is important to tailor solutions to each country's (or local government's) context and circumstances. Differences might stem from policy and regulatory frameworks, institutional setups, available resources, income levels, cultural norms, or other factors. A summary of tested approaches can be found in table 3.3.

In terms of legal frameworks, policies, and regulations, most countries have enacted overarching energy efficiency legislation, including building codes for new buildings and energy performance certificates for existing buildings, which are critically important to set performance standards and norms. Many countries also mandate annual reporting on energy use for larger facilities, periodic energy audits (typically every three to five years) to identify EE measures, appointment of energy managers, and other requirements.

Building codes and renovation programs also require strong institutional support structures to set standards, enforce regulations, share information, and train the market. Many governments have so-called nodal agencies, such as EE agencies or departments, to provide an overall framework for government programs, advise on policies and norms, provide technical information and training, develop tools such as EE calculators and model tender documents, implement awareness campaigns, and other actions to help public agencies reduce their energy use.

TABLE 3.3 Improving Public Sector Energy Efficiency: Dismantling Barriers

Barrier	Indicative action
Lack of information/awareness, including opportunities, costs, benefits, and risks	Initiate awareness campaigns and demonstrations; publish and disseminate information such as case studies, procurement guidelines, product catalogues, and specifications
Lack of technical capacity for audits, project design, procurement, implementation, monitoring; trust in EE potential	Create nodal agency to provide technical assistance for EE projects; appoint energy managers; develop training programs for facility operators and energy managers; encourage the formation and prequalification of ESCOs; develop EE analytical tools, audit and procurement guidelines, and measurement and verification protocols
Limited incentives to implement EE (potential loss of budget), try new approaches, and take risks	Revise budgeting to allow retention of energy savings; issue awards for agencies/staff; include EE in management performance reviews; develop risk sharing/financing programs; set EE targets
Lack of agency accountability for energy savings	Create public sector/agency targets with monitoring; set penalties for nonperformance; establish program to label energy performance of buildings, benchmark energy performance, and publish results
Restrictive procurement, contracting, and financing rules	Revise public policies on purchase of EE products (for example, to mandate the purchase of products with energy efficient labels or to make purchasing decisions based on life-cycle costing) and services; develop local ESCO models; create public EE funds
Lack of funding for up-front energy audits and project funding	Earmark public EE budgets; create dedicated grant/subsidy programs, public revolving funds; levy a demand-side management surcharge or "electricity surcharge" to mobilize funds for free energy audits
Small size and high transaction costs	Bundle public EE projects; generate model documents/templates to streamline projects; develop ESCO umbrella contracts; practice bulk procurement of EE products through cooperative purchasing agreements

Source: Singh 2018.

Note: EE = energy efficiency; ESCO = energy service company.

Financing

Financing is one of the most difficult challenges for public building EE. The financing ladder (figure 3.13) identifies options that policy makers can adapt to provide products suited to their country's needs. Over time, as local markets evolve, countries can move up the ladder to more commercial financing mechanisms. Once a country selects a mechanism, its design should include elements to facilitate transition to schemes that are higher up the ladder. Selecting and designing appropriate, locally relevant mechanisms depends on several factors, including the following:

- Legislative and regulatory conditions
- Maturity of financial and public credit markets
- State of local EE service markets, including energy service companies (ESCOs) and energy auditors
- Technical and financial capabilities of public entities for EE
- Local market and context

FIGURE 3.13 **Financing Energy Efficiency in Public Buildings: A Ladder of Options**

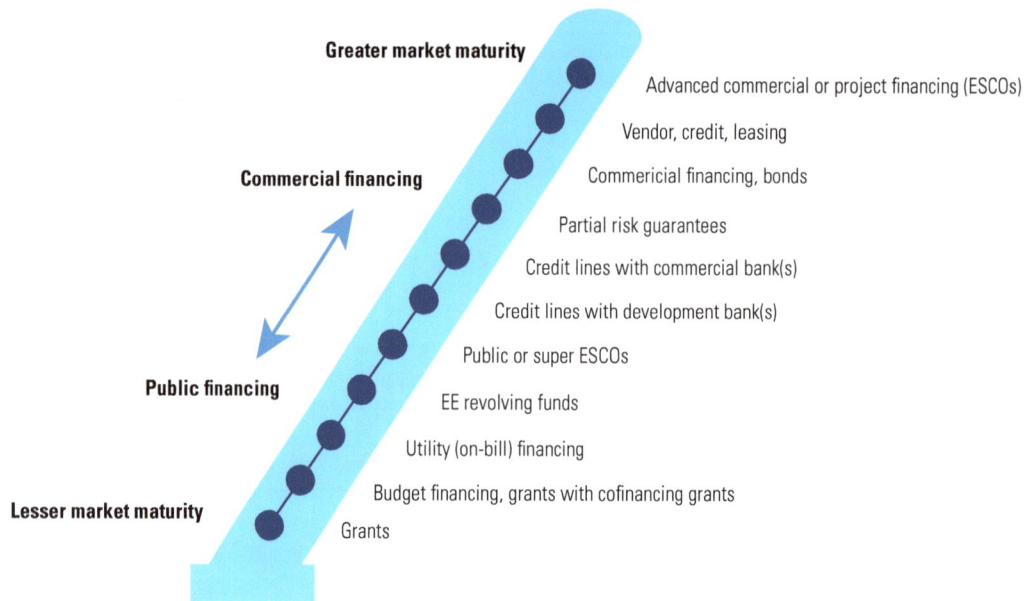

Greater market maturity

Advanced commercial or project financing (ESCOs)

Vendor, credit, leasing

Commercial financing

Commericial financing, bonds

Partial risk guarantees

Credit lines with commercial bank(s)

Credit lines with development bank(s)

Public or super ESCOs

Public financing

EE revolving funds

Utility (on-bill) financing

Budget financing, grants with cofinancing grants

Lesser market maturity

Grants

Source: World Bank 2014b.
Note: EE = energy efficiency; ESCOs = energy service companies.

The Türkiye Energy Efficiency in Public Buildings Project

A 2016 study estimated that there are over 175,000 public buildings (including central, regional, and municipal facilities) in Türkiye, with an annual technical EE potential of over 10,000 GWh, requiring about $18 billion in investments (Econoler International 2016). The government recognized that a strong public building renovation program could help develop and spur the market for the estimated 10 million public and private buildings across the country. In 2019, the World Bank, together with the Ministry of Energy and Natural Resources and Ministry of Environment and Urbanization (now the Ministry of Environment, Urbanization and Climate Change) developed an Energy Efficiency in Public Buildings Project designed to renovate 400 to 500 central government buildings and develop the market for a broader national public building renovation program. The project includes a $150 million International Bank for Reconstruction and Development (IBRD) loan, a $46.2 million concessional loan from the Clean Technology Fund (CTF), and a $3.8 million CTF grant (World Bank 2019a).

While the project includes many conventional aspects for public building renovation programs—such as selection of buildings with high energy savings potential, energy audits, technical designs, renovation works, and measurement and verification—it also has the following innovative features:

- *Deep renovations:* While the project has used the IBRD loan to support conventional renovations—that is, those that save a minimum of 20 percent energy and have simple payback periods of less than 12 years—the CTF loan has allowed support for deeper renovations that save at least 30 percent energy with longer payback periods, encouraging larger investments with thicker insulation, triple-pane windows, and newer technologies such as air-source heat pumps.
- *Energy service companies:* For a subset of eligible buildings, renovations can be done under energy performance contracts. Unlike traditional audit-design/works contracts, these involve an initial audit followed by a design-build contract, with some payments tied to verified energy savings. To defray the higher risks and uncertainties associated with ESCO contracts, the initial $10 million worth of ESCO contracts are financed by the CTF loan, subsequently replicated with $20 million in ESCO contracts financed and scaled up using the IBRD loan.
- *Near-zero energy buildings (NZEBs):* The project also uses the CTF loan to renovate 5 to 10 buildings with high demonstration value to showcase the concept of NZEB integrated design and renovation techniques, such as cool/green roofs, ventilated facades, daylighting/shading, water recycling/harvesting, advanced controls, and newer technologies, such as building-integrated solar photovoltaic (PV) and geothermal heat pumps. These renovations will also inform the introduction of a national NZEB standard and models for the broader buildings market.

To date, the project has completed renovations of 30 buildings, with average energy savings of 30 percent, with a range from 22 to 80 percent. It also successfully completed Türkiye's first publicly tendered ESCO contract—the Bursa Anatolian Girls' High School—with about 80 percent savings and 23 percent electricity generation from rooftop solar, making it essentially a net-negative energy building, as annual electricity consumption is being fully offset by rooftop solar PV generation, with some excess PV power being sold to the grid. Another 120 buildings started renovations in 2023, including additional ESCO contracts and NZEB pilots.

The project also includes critical technical assistance to capture experiences and lessons from the project to provide training for energy auditors, design companies, and construction firms, to learn from early experiences, share good practices, and build market capabilities. It will share case studies, model audit terms of references and reports, bidding documents, measurement and verification protocols, and so on with market actors to allow replication in the private building market.

Key Takeaways

Although the project is ongoing, the following important lessons have emerged:

- *Developing a clear and transparent screening methodology* is crucial to identify and prioritize eligible buildings that offer the greatest potential for energy savings.
- *Careful review and supervision of early subprojects—for example, energy audits, technical designs, and construction*—are important to ensure sound methodologies, consistent technical quality, and adherence to approved technical designs and material and equipment specifications.
- *Developing digestible case studies and targeting outreach* helps build project credibility and increases demand to join the project in later years.
- *Deeper renovations are possible under World Bank-financed building renovation programs.* Although they have longer payback periods, they can save substantially more energy (often 50 to 70 percent savings) compared with conventional renovations.
- *Developing alternative financing and business models is necessary to ensure sustainability, scale, and leverage.* Developing a renovation program as a way to inform a broader national program with sustainable financing mechanisms and different business models (that is, ESCOs) helps ensure sustainability beyond the project period.
- *Energy efficiency combined with rooftop solar systems allow buildings to reach net zero energy and emissions.* Demonstrating and then mainstreaming deep renovations alongside on-site RE generation can help make buildings carbon neutral while bringing their energy bills close to zero.

Looking to the Future

Despite these successes, the work is far from over. The project also provides funding to develop a national program for EE in public buildings, including schemes to introduce revolving financing to capture the energy cost savings from renovated buildings and use this to renovate additional buildings. This will be vital to demonstrate that building renovations can pay for themselves, allow for scale-up, and help bring commercial financing into the building renovations market. A national-scale program will also introduce greater consistency and predictability to the market, allowing new service providers and building materials and equipment suppliers to enter the market, which will ultimately drive down costs for everyone.

Facilitating, Enabling, and Triggering Sectoral Transitions: India

Demand Support Policies

Case Study 16. Solar Power in India

Contributors: Thomas Kerr, Emeka Nwangele, and Mehul Jain

Context

India's energy system is on the cusp of a paradigm shift toward renewables, driven by a concerted policy effort to spur wide-scale solar adoption. Growing from 4 to 13 percent of total electricity generation between 2014 and 2022 and projected to account for 30 percent of generation capacity by 2040, India's solar energy sector is rapidly growing (figure 3.14; IEA 2021b, 2022e; Ministry of Power 2022). Since 2004, $130 billion has been invested in India's RE sector. Of this, solar energy accounts for $71 billion, and its share of the country's renewable investment portfolio has risen from insignificant levels to 83 percent (figure 3.15; BloombergNEF 2022).

India's fast-growing economy and population have led to increased demand for energy services. Catalyzed by improved living standards, 40 percent population growth, increasing electrification, and advancing vehicle ownership, India's primary energy demand has doubled from 5,000 to 10,000 terawatt hours (TWh) in the past two decades. It is the third-largest energy consumer globally and projected to account for one-quarter of global energy demand growth between 2019 and 2040 (IEA 2020b).

To meet this demand, the government has prioritized utility-scale solar systems, home solar systems, and mini-grids for last-mile electricity connectivity in rural communities through an enabling political and economic framework. India has vast solar energy resources, with nearly 750 gigawatts (GW) of potential (Bandyopadhyay 2017). Since 2010, the government has prioritized solar energy as part of its economic transformation agenda, using favorable policies such as RE targets, fiscal incentives, FiTs, and reverse auction mechanisms (figure 3.16; *Economist* 2022).

Policy

India identified energy and climate challenges and set RE targets, backed by government programs and planning, as leverage points to solve its problems. As a first step, the government set out the National Action Plan for Climate Change in 2008 (Raina and Sinha 2019), creating initiatives with measurable objectives to advance the solar energy goal under the action plan. It introduced the National Solar Mission (NSM) in

FIGURE 3.14 **New Annual Energy Capacity Additions, in Gigawatts, 2015–21**

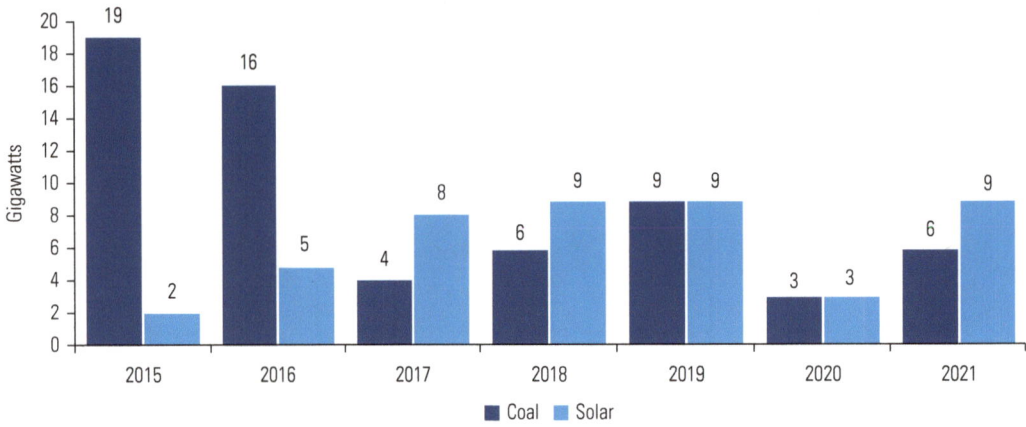

Source: Jaiswal and Gadre 2022.

FIGURE 3.15 **Renewable Energy Investment in India, 2004–22**

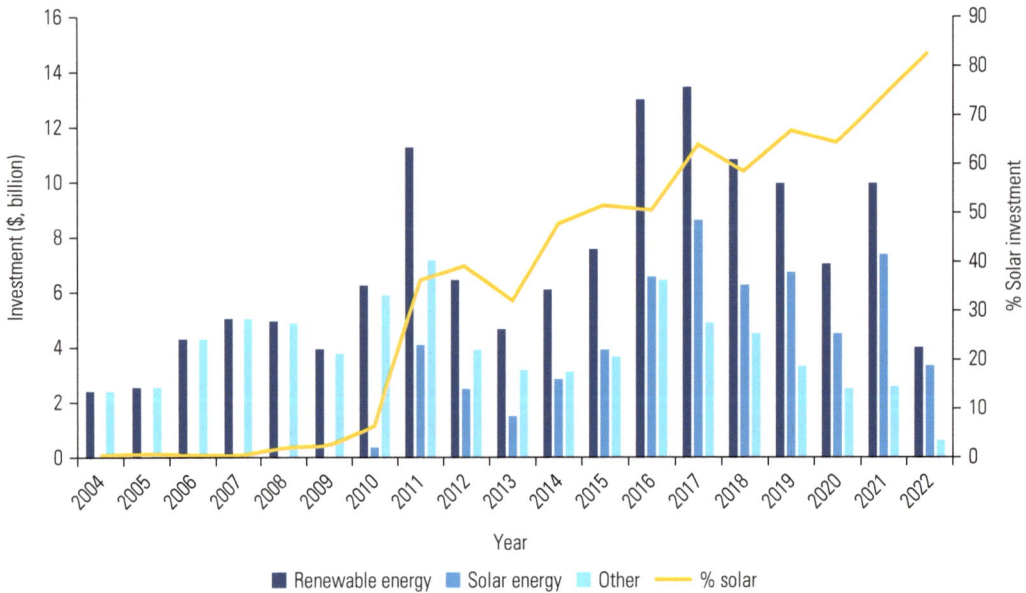

Source: BloombergNEF 2022.

2010 to develop other supporting systems for solar energy advancement, tasking the Ministry of New and Renewable Energy with implementing it. It has targeted achieving 500 GW of nonfossil energy capacity by 2030 in its NDC and 30 percent solar energy contribution to the electricity mix by 2040 in the 2070 Net-Zero plan announced by Prime Minister Narendra Modi at the 26th United Nations Climate Change Conference of the Parties (COP26) in Glasgow (Government of India 2014; IEA 2020b).

FIGURE 3.16 India's Solar Energy Expansion—Key Milestones

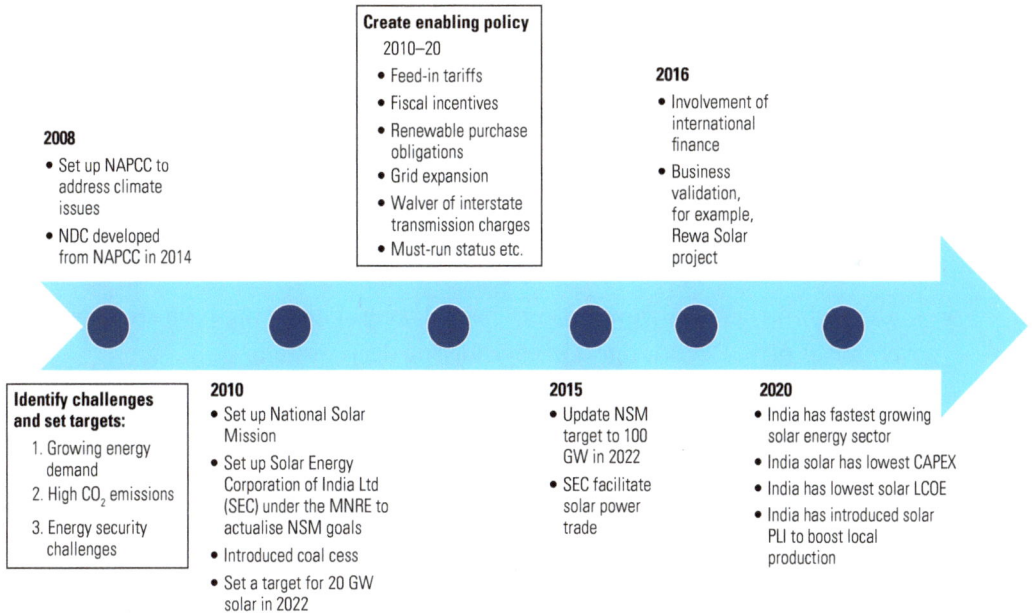

2008
- Set up NAPCC to address climate issues
- NDC developed from NAPCC in 2014

Create enabling policy
2010–20
- Feed-in tariffs
- Fiscal incentives
- Renewable purchase obligations
- Grid expansion
- Walver of interstate transmission charges
- Must-run status etc.

2016
- Involvement of international finance
- Business validation, for example, Rewa Solar project

Identify challenges and set targets:
1. Growing energy demand
2. High CO_2 emissions
3. Energy security challenges

2010
- Set up National Solar Mission
- Set up Solar Energy Corporation of India Ltd (SEC) under the MNRE to actualise NSM goals
- Introduced coal cess
- Set a target for 20 GW solar in 2022

2015
- Update NSM target to 100 GW in 2022
- SEC facilitate solar power trade

2020
- India has fastest growing solar energy sector
- India solar has lowest CAPEX
- India has lowest solar LCOE
- India has introduced solar PLI to boost local production

Source: BloombergNEF 2022.

Note: CAPEX = capital expenditures; GW = gigawatts; LCOE = levelized cost of energy; MNRE = Ministry for New and Renewable Energy; NAPCC = National Action Plan for Climate Change; NDC = nationally determined contribution; NSM = National Solar Mission; PLI = Production-Linked Incentive Scheme.

Fiscal policies and financial incentives have helped enhance RE investment. In 2010, the government created the National Clean Energy Fund through a *cess* (fee) on coal (originally $0.75/metric ton, revised to $5.7/ton in 2016) to support the nascent solar energy sector by creating initial capital for RE (IISD 2018). The federal and state governments alike have also provided other fiscal incentives, including solar project subsidies and tax incentives. For example, in the 2019 Pradhan Mantri Kisan Urja Suraksha evam Utthan Mahabhiyan scheme, many state governments agreed to provide 30 percent subsidies to deploy 10 GW solar energy plants. Accelerated depreciation tax benefits for developers also featured prominently in India's solar energy strategy, allowing them to depreciate RE assets at much higher rates than general fixed assets and claim tax benefits on each year's depreciated value. Between 2014 and 2017, the rate was set at 80 percent; this was revised to 40 percent in 2017.

In addition, the Government of India's NSM provided demand and technology support and policies for tariff and capacity building. These include the following:

- Interstate Transmission System charge waivers
- Dedicated solar parks for new projects, to address delays and difficulties in land acquisition caused by complex land permits, a lack of clarity over land titles, outdated records, and fragmented landholdings (Behuria 2020; IEA 2020b, 2021d; Raina and Sinha 2019)

- Reverse auctions to encourage competitive bidding and reduce solar energy tariffs
- State-dependent FiTs of $0.16–0.36 per kilowatt hour (kWh), and net metering, which credits solar energy owners based on surplus energy exported to the grid
- Renewable purchase obligations for utilities to buy 10.5 percent of their electricity from solar sources by 2022
- Must-run status policy, prioritizing the purchase of RE over fossil energy by grid operators
- Working with the International Solar Alliance to offer financial analysis of solar energy proposal training for financial institutions.

Although the national government retained control over long-term strategy, state governments played a critical role in engendering the transition:

- Signing solar power purchase agreements to encourage investment and facilitating the purchase of renewable electricity
- Facilitating land selection and approval and providing infrastructure for solar parks for projects
- Supporting interstate transmission through right-of-way access and environmental clearances
- Providing youth skills training to build technical competency for solar jobs (NRDC 2016).

Supported by these policies, the private sector and international financial agencies provided business models for bankable solar investment. Solar assets have historically been considered risky due to their high up-front costs, long payback periods, and project uncertainties (Sarangi 2022). As a result, banks offered high-interest rates for solar projects, making it difficult to access private capital. To address this, international financial institutions provided scalable PPP models, as in the case of the 750 MW World Bank–financed Rewa Solar Park in Madhya Pradesh, a flagship solar project that powers a metrorail line serving more than 2.6 million commuters a day. The World Bank provided technical and financial support in the form of concessional credits that improved investor confidence, while the state provided institutional support, including land and payment security. Overall, the project achieved tariffs that were 24 percent lower than the previous lowest national subsidy-free tariff (IFC 2020).

Results and Impacts

Thanks to this conducive policy environment and the global decline in solar energy costs, India's solar energy transition is underway. The up-front capital expenditure for utility-scale solar in India has decreased significantly, making India one of the cheapest places to deploy grid-scale solar power in the world. The attractiveness of India's solar sector has led to a $71 billion capital inflow over the past two decades, increasing solar installations from 65 MW in 2010 to more than 57 GW capacity in 2022 (table 3.4; IEA 2020b, 2022e; Ministry of Power 2022).

TABLE 3.4   Key Results of India's Solar Energy Expansion Drive

Objective	Results
Reduced up-front capital expenditure solar	$5,000/kW (2010)[a] $596/kW (2020)[a]
Reduced levelized cost of solar energy	$0.17/kWh (2010)[a] $0.038/kWh (2020)[a] 34% less than the global average[a]
Increased renewable investment	$71 billion since 2000[b]
Higher deployment and increased solar capacity targets	100 GW solar target for 2022[c]

Sources: BloombergNEF 2022; IEA 2022e; IRENA 2021.
Note: GW = gigawatts; kW = kilowatts; kWh = kilowatt hours.
a. Data from IRENA 2021.
b. Data from BloombergNEF 2022.
c. Data from IEA 2022e.

The increased deployment of solar has resulted in avoided CO_2 and air pollutant emissions, improved electricity access, and created jobs. With a carbon footprint of 4 to 6 grams of CO_2 per kWh, compared with the power grid's 718 grams of CO_2 per kWh (Ritchie and Roser 2022), solar power can reduce India's emissions by 1 $GtCO_2e$ by 2030, in line with its climate targets. Solar systems also improve electricity access: government-backed programs have provided 3.4 million solar lamps, more than 350,000 solar home systems, and mini-grids for last-mile electricity connectivity in many rural communities (Zaman, van Vliet, and Posch 2021). The sector has also created green jobs, with solar PV-related jobs in India reaching 163,500 in 2020 (IRENA 2021).

Key Takeaways

India shows how countries can achieve rapid scale-up of climate-smart solutions by leveraging the strengths of different stakeholders. The government prioritized the sector by setting a bold national target and provided both a stable policy ecosystem and a timely and adequate set of incentives. Development finance institutions provided concessional financing to kick-start the market and backed private investments by appropriating the necessary risk mitigation instruments. Finally, the private sector invested in India's solar energy scale-up and embraced technological advancements.

India aims to grow domestic solar manufacturing. In 2017, the largest bilateral solar export flow was from China to India, valued at $2.72 billion (Wang et al. 2021). Understanding the supply chain issues that emerge from India's dependence on China for solar cells, including transportation and shipping, which increase solar power costs and the increased geopolitical risks of energy security caused by import dependence (Shiradkar 2022), and in line with its plan to create green jobs, the government of India has earmarked funding for PV manufacturing as part of its $26 billion Production-Linked

Incentive (PLI) scheme (ET Bureau 2021). Of this, $2.6 billion will be made available to catalyze the development of domestic solar manufacturing for plants with more than 1 GW capacity (Rai-Roche 2022).

To address RE intermittency and storage requirements, the national government has set out initiatives to improve grid robustness. In 2013, the country achieved full regional power system connectivity. In 2015, it designed the Green Energy Corridor Policy to synchronize RE generation with conventional power stations in the grid. Under these policies, there was significant investment in grid capacity expansion, with a revised target of 9,700 circuit kilometers to export 20 GW of RE generation by 2022 (MNRE 2022). This national government, state equity, and loan-funded scheme has surpassed its target, adding 9,767 circuit kilometers. Other targets include increasing capacity from 75 GW in 2017 to 118 GW in 2022. The government is also harnessing battery and hydropower storage for ancillary market services and sponsoring research into new and more viable battery storage technologies. In 2021, it announced plans to float 4,000-megawatt hour (MWh) grid-scale battery storage tenders. These efforts have positively affected energy trade volumes and renewable power distribution and decreased blackouts due to low grid capacity, setting the stage for future expansion.

Rapid power sector transition will cause more grid operational constraints. To address these challenges, demand and supply-side flexibility, grid flexibility, storage, and power market frameworks will be needed. The government should therefore build a pricing mechanism and accelerate the rollout of advanced metering infrastructure to incentivize active participation in energy consumption and match peak production and consumption. It is possible to remove regulatory barriers to battery and hydro storage deployment by providing the proper remuneration framework for distributed storage projects to incentivize further investment. The government can also introduce measures to enhance interstate energy trade. In the long term, it can research innovative systems, such as EVs for storage using the vehicle-to-grid framework. Finally, with the reduced cost of solar power in India, the government can prioritize research into integrating solar-powered electrolyzers to produce green hydrogen for reliable short- and long-term storage that can improve India's grid robustness.

Facilitating, Enabling, and Triggering Sectoral Transitions: Colombia

Case Study 17. Gas Flaring in Colombia

Contributors: Zubin Bamji and Adam Pollard

Eliminating routine gas flaring must be central to decarbonization efforts. This burning of natural gas associated with oil extraction contributes to climate change and impacts the environment through CO_2, methane, and other emissions (World Bank 2021f). Each year, gas flaring contributes around 400 $MtCO_2e$ to global emissions; according to a World Bank study, it could cost as much as $100 billion to end all routine flaring (World Bank 2018c).

Reducing gas flaring provides energy conservation cobenefits, allowing the gas to be either conserved or used for productive purposes, such as generating power and expanding energy access. In 2021, the Global Gas Flaring Reduction Partnership estimated that more than 144 billion cubic meters of gas were flared at oil and gas production sites around the world (World Bank 2022g). This is enough to generate some 1,800 TWh of energy, almost two-thirds of the EU's net domestic electricity generation or equivalent to Sub-Saharan Africa's entire electricity generation capacity.

Colombia has made significant advancements in reducing gas flaring. Through a combination of government and business action, the volume of gas flared in Colombia has declined by almost 70 percent.

Context

Colombia is an emerging market economy with domestic oil reserves. Crude petroleum is Colombia's largest export (by value) and contributes almost $7.5 billion to the economy each year (OEC 2023). Its oil reserves are largely managed by the national oil company, Ecopetrol (EIA 2022). The majority of Colombia's gas is found in the form of associated gas, meaning the gas is produced as a by-product during crude oil extraction. Both oil and gas operations in Colombia have been troubled by strikes and protests.

Policy

Proactive company-led action helped kick-start progress on flare reduction. In 2010, Ecopetrol launched its current climate change strategy, which includes monitoring and reporting GHG emissions, reducing emissions from the company's operations and supply chain, engaging in research and development, and contributing to the national climate policy. The company developed a work plan to reduce flaring by 8 $MtCO_2e$ by 2021 and carried out some projects to reduce methane leaks from its equipment. Since 2010,

Ecopetrol has also committed to reducing its scope 1 and 2 emissions by 25 percent by 2030 compared with 2019 levels, and to achieving net zero emissions by 2050 (Ecopetrol 2020).

Ecopetrol has linked its targets to Colombia's NDC. At the end of 2020, Colombia submitted an updated NDC, increasing its commitment to reducing GHG emissions by 2030 from 20 percent to 51 percent, albeit from a slightly higher BAU scenario emission level. The new 2030 target for GHG emissions is 169 $MtCO_2e$, down from 265 $MtCO_2e$ in the original NDC submitted in 2018 (UNFCCC 2022b). The NDC notes gas utilization as an opportunity for emission reduction.

Government laws, regulations, and initiatives have supported gas utilization and flare reduction. The Colombian government has enabled progress by establishing a domestic gas market and implementing strong regulations that strictly prohibit and monetarily penalize unauthorized gas flaring. This has been led by the Ministry of Mines and Energy (MME), which is the principal governing body responsible for upstream oil and gas operations. The National Hydrocarbon Agency, Agencia National de Hidrocarburos, operates autonomously under the MME and is in charge of administering and regulating hydrocarbons, including granting flaring authorizations, setting measuring standards, and monitoring compliance. Key legislation related to gas flaring includes the following:

- *Law 10/1961*, which explicitly prohibited gas flaring in production fields for the first time. Article 14 requires all operators to avoid wasting any gas produced. If the operator does not stop wasting gas within three years, the government has the right to take ownership of gas free of charge to improve utilization.
- *MME Resolution 181495/2009*, which constitutes the main regulatory framework for exploring and producing hydrocarbons. Articles 52 and 53 prohibit gas flaring and wasting. Article 64 imposes a fine of up to $5,000 for violations.
- *MME Resolution 41251/2016*, which covers measurement and reporting requirements, including monthly reporting of flare volumes.
- *MME Resolution 40687/2017*, which establishes technical standards for offshore hydrocarbon exploration projects and regulates gas flaring and venting for these activities.
- *MME Resolution 40066/2022*, which updates provisions for flaring, venting, and fugitive methane emissions, with more detail on when flaring exemptions may be granted and greater financial penalties for infringements (fines of 2,000 to 100,000 times the legal monthly minimum wage for each breach).

Colombia has joined a global movement for tackling unnecessary flaring and methane emissions. In 2020, Ecopetrol endorsed the World Bank's Zero Routine Flaring by 2030 initiative. The following year during COP26, the government signed the Global Methane Pledge, demonstrating a commitment to voluntarily act toward reducing global methane emissions by at least 30 percent from 2020 levels by 2030. Adopting Resolution 40066/2022 has made Colombia one of the first countries to regulate flaring, venting, and fugitive methane emissions.

Results and Impacts

A combination of strong legal and regulatory action with proactive business leadership means that Colombia has made significant progress in reducing gas flaring over the past decade. The volume of gas flared has declined by almost 70 percent, from 1 billion cubic meters in 2012 to 0.3 billion cubic meters in 2021 (figure 3.17). Flaring intensity also declined steadily during this period, decreasing from 2.86 cubic meters of gas per barrel of oil produced in 2012 to 1.22 in 2021.

Gas flaring reductions have provided environmental, health, and economic cobenefits. Through the reductions made between 2012 and 2021, Colombia reduced its GHG emissions by 1.76 $MtCO_2e$, equivalent to 2 percent of its total emissions. These reductions have also decreased the volume of black carbon particulate matter released through flaring, which has been associated with adverse health effects. At a sales value of $2.5 per metric billion British thermal unit, the country avoided approximately $75 million of lost value in 2021, compared with 2012.

A focus on gas utilization has benefited Colombia's domestic energy supply. Unlike many other oil-producing nations, Colombia does not have an abundant supply of domestic natural gas. Its proven gas reserves have been in continuous decline since 2012, almost halving in volume between 2012 and 2020. In 2016, Colombia imported natural gas for the first time to meet the shortfall between domestic production and

FIGURE 3.17 Flare Volume and Intensity in Colombia, 2012–21

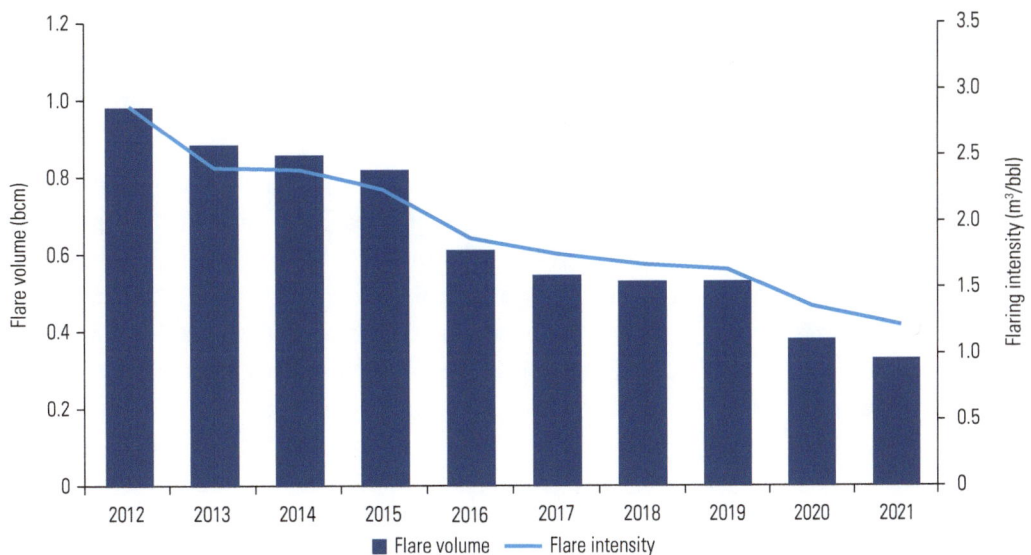

Source: World Bank 2021f. Taken from the National Oceanic and Atmospheric Administration, Payne Institute and Colorado School of Mines, Global Gas Flaring Reduction Partnership, and Energy Information Administration.

Note: bcm = billion cubic meters ; m³/bbl = cubic meters of gas per barrel of oil produced.

demand (IEA 2020a). The focus on improving gas utilization through flare reduction has been an important measure for the country's energy self-sufficiency. Access to natural gas has also played a role in the nation's sustainable development goals. Over the past two decades, Colombia has made meaningful progress in improving access to clean cooking fuels and technologies, increasing population access rates from 78 percent in 2000 to 93 percent in 2020 (IEA 2022g). Clean-burning gas stovetops have contributed to some of these improvements.

Key Takeaways

The Colombian government has implemented widespread regulations around measuring, reporting, monitoring, and complying with regulations related to gas flaring. An autonomous government body, the National Hydrocarbon Agency, has monitored and enforced compliance with these regulations, making them more effective.

Establishing a domestic gas market has provided financial incentives for local operators to comply with regulations and reduce unnecessary flaring. Simultaneously, the presence of financial penalties for noncompliance provides further incentives for operators to conform.

Ecopetrol's proactive climate change strategies and commitments demonstrate how aligning business and government objectives on flare reduction can accelerate progress.

Looking to the Future

Reducing unnecessary flaring could help alleviate current gas shortages. Russia's invasion of Ukraine has sparked a global energy crisis and a large reduction in gas supplies flowing to the EU (IEA 2022d). Building new projects and infrastructure to address these shortages will take time, but the Colombian case study demonstrates that proactive action on flaring can return relatively fast results and deliver gas-saving benefits.

Further work is needed to achieve zero routine flaring. In 2015, the World Bank launched the Zero Routine Flaring by 2030 (ZRF) initiative to support cooperation between all relevant stakeholders to find solutions to gas flaring through appropriate regulation, application of technologies, and financial arrangements. To date, the ZRF initiative has garnered endorsements from 87 governments and companies, representing over 60 percent of global flaring (World Bank 2022o). Further work is needed to continue progress and eliminate routine flaring by 2030.

Facilitating, Enabling, and Triggering Sectoral Transitions: India

Case Study 18. Public Transport Systems in India

Contributor: Gerald Paul Ollivier

Context

India's updated NDC targets a 45 percent reduction in GHG emissions intensity by 2030, compared with 2005 levels (Government of India 2022). The transport sector contributes approximately 10 percent of India's GHG emissions and has the world's fastest energy usage growth rate, averaging 6.8 percent per year since 2000 (LBNL 2022). Oil products, mostly diesel and gasoline, supplied 95 percent of total energy in the sector, and road transport energy demand accounted for 90 percent of the total oil demand in 2017 (IEA 2020b). Heavy-duty vehicles, such as buses and trucks, consumed 55 percent of total energy within India's road transport sector in 2010; this share is expected to reach 67 percent by 2030 (Sharma et al. 2017). As a result, the government of India has identified the electrification of heavy-duty vehicles—particularly buses—as a priority policy intervention.

Policy

The government of India is taking up several fiscal and regulatory measures to accelerate EV manufacturing and adoption across vehicle segments (World Bank 2022d). A total of $7.1 billion has been earmarked across incentives, including $5.8 billion for production-linked incentives for EV manufacturers, component manufacturers, and advanced chemistry cells, and $1.3 billion for end-user incentives under the Faster Adoption and Manufacturing of Electric (and Hybrid) Vehicles in India (FAME-II) scheme. Electrification of public transportation is a key priority under FAME-II, with about 35 percent of the total subsidy outlay earmarked for buses. Electrifying buses provides the twin benefits of mitigating emissions and improving mobility access for the masses, as buses are the mainstay of mobility in India.

The first phase of FAME-II for buses witnessed procurement of close to 3,500 buses across 36 tenders floated between April 2019 and March 2021 (World Bank 2022i). Prices under Phase 1 of FAME II varied widely between cities, despite procuring similar types of bus. This was driven by variations in contractual parameters, the volume of buses procured (from 25 buses in some cities to 300 in others), different procurement specifications with cities requiring different technical and financial commitments from the bidders, and cities' creditworthiness, which posed varying levels of credit risk to the bidders.

Building on the learnings from Phase 1, the government of India adopted an aggregated procurement approach, with concentrated large-scale deployment and standardized procurement specifications to achieve economies of scale. Convergence Energy Services Limited (CESL), a government enterprise, was entrusted with the job of aggregating demand across nine Indian metropolitan cities with a population of more than 4 million. CESL invited cities to subscribe to the numbers and types of electric bus they needed against harmonized procurement specifications to be adopted across all cities. The available subsidy was allocated to cities in proportion to their subscribed demand. Five out of the nine eligible cities participated in the process, subscribing for a total of 5,450 buses, of which 3,472 buses were eligible for subsidy. The rest were tendered without subsidy. This initiative adopted a gross-cost, contract-based business model wherein private service providers invest in the purchase of bus and charging infrastructure and undertake operations and maintenance throughout the contract tenure. The government bus authority defines service levels, monitors implementation, pays the operator, and collects revenue.

CESL floated a request for proposals (RfP) from cities to discover the prices in Indian rupees (Rs) per kilometer for the 5,450 buses split across different lots, according to technical specifications such as length, floor height, and air-conditioning. The eligible bidders with the least-cost quote would be the selected service provider for each lot. The RfP covers a wide range of technical and financial specifications, covering items such as eligibility criteria, vehicle and charger requirements, operational requirements such as depots and routes, contract tenure, grounds for early termination, payment terms such as assured kilometers of payment, periodicity of payment, payment guarantee mechanisms, penalties for underperformance against service-level agreements, and arbitration mechanisms. CESL adopted a collaborative and technically sound approach toward harmonizing procurement specifications across cities and ensuring their robustness. This reduced the number of lots and maximized lot sizes wherever technically, commercially, and practically feasible, enabling economies of scale. The World Bank provided technical support to NITI Aayog and CESL in harmonizing the specifications, and enhancing and calibrating contract terms to balance risks to all parties, thereby reducing costs.

Results and Impacts

The RfP attracted four eligible bidders, post-technical evaluation. Financial evaluation of eligible bidders found that the lower quote for a 12-meter air-conditioned, low-floor bus was Rs 47.99 (~$0.64) per kilometer, and for a 9-meter air-conditioned bus, Rs 44.99 (~$0.60) per kilometer. Prices were about 37 percent lower than procurement under Phase 1 of FAME II with the same subsidy, equivalent to saving more than Rs 10,800 crore (CR) ($1.45 billion) over the 12 years of the corresponding contracts. This was made possible due to the economies of scale offered by the large contract volume, improved procurement specifications that made the contract more bankable, and the five selected cities being among the more mature bus systems in India, with depot infrastructure in place.

As well as being lower than previous electric bus procurements, the prices were also better than the cost of operating on-road diesel and CNG buses in these cities. The quoted costs for electric buses, excluding subsidy, was 27 and 23 percent lower than the cost of the diesel and CNG buses operating in these cities, respectively. Including the available subsidy, they were 35 and 31 percent lower, respectively. However, factors such as the recent rise in fuel prices and lower bus kilometers per day due to passenger demand not yet reaching pre-COVID levels are leading to higher-than-usual costs per kilometer for diesel and CNG buses, so it is likely that the cost difference may narrow as fuel prices and operations stabilize. That said, services run with electric buses are expected to remain cheaper. Together, these 5,450 buses are anticipated to deliver GHG emissions savings of over 1 $MtCO_2e$ across their 12-year life cycle, indicating significant mitigation potential without accounting for the mode shift they enable.

Key Takeaways

The results of the aggregated procurement policy mark a clear inflection point in India's electric bus adoption story. For the first time, the prices quoted for electric buses are cheaper than their diesel and CNG counterparts. Such low prices have encouraged more cities to adopt electric buses as their primary choice in the future. Following this national-level aggregated procurement, the city of Mumbai has procured another 2,100 buses at similar costs. The national government is now looking to scale up the aggregated procurement model across India to secure about 50,000 electric buses over the next two to three years. Such large-scale procurement will ensure the adoption of electric buses even in rural and intercity bus markets, which represent 90 percent of the country's fleet and bus kilometers. The GHG emission mitigation estimates also point to significant decarbonization of India's bus services through large-scale electrification. Bus agencies are now likely to consider electric buses as their primary choice, only opting for diesel and CNG buses if electric ones are not feasible.

Facilitating, Enabling, and Triggering Sectoral Transitions: Colombia

Case Study 19. Green Building Market Transformation in Colombia

Contributors: Corinne Figueredo, Sarah Megan Santucci, and Cecilia Lozada Andrade

When it comes to green buildings, no market has seen a more remarkable transformation than Colombia. Between 2021 and 2022, 27 percent of new buildings in Colombia were certified green with EDGE, a building certification tool that enables investors and developers to calculate the cost of going green (Lozada Andrade 2021). As of December 2022, a cumulative 11.5 million square meters (roughly equivalent to $11.5 billion worth of floor space) of EDGE-certified green spaces had either been built or were under construction. Colombia owes the transformation of its construction sector in large part to strong government support and a strong local partner, the Colombian Chamber of Construction (CAMACOL).

Context

Colombia has a supportive policy framework and active commitment to climate mitigation and adaptation. In 2015 with International Finance Corporation (IFC) support and as part of its National Green Growth Strategy, the Colombian government enacted Latin America's first mandatory green building code. Soon after, it also introduced tax incentives for technical solutions such as insulation and energy-efficient air conditioning systems. By setting targets for energy and water savings through the code and offering incentives to support the financial viability of these new practices, Colombia achieved a progressive application of sustainable construction practices.

Opening Finance for Green Buildings

In 2016, IFC invested in Colombia's first private green bond, issued by Bancolombia for a total of $115 million. Using its own resources alongside the proceeds of the green bond, the bank offered a reduced interest rate as an incentive to strengthen its green building portfolio. This gave rise to an aggressive green mortgages program in 2017.

IFC's investment also encouraged other banking institutions to follow suit. In 2017, Davivienda's $149 million green bond, purchased by IFC, became the largest green-bond issuance by a private financial institution in Latin America. By 2021, five commercial banks in Colombia were offering green mortgages and green construction finance: Bancolombia, Davivienda, Banco Bilbao Vizcaya Argentaria (BBVA), Banco Bogotá, and Caja Social. Colombia has the most financial institutions offering this type of financial product targeting the construction sector across Latin America.

In 2017, IFC started working with CAMACOL to promote EDGE. An IFC innovation, EDGE provides a platform for designing and certifying green and zero carbon buildings. CAMACOL delivered dozens of EDGE training and capacity-building sessions to its members. Encouraged by access to green finance and with support from CAMACOL, Colombia's largest social housing developer, Constructora Bolivar, has certified over $2 billion worth of floor space across the country.

In August 2022, IFC provided a loan of up to $200 million to BBVA Colombia to support the bank's lending program for climate-smart projects, with a focus on green buildings and an emphasis on projects that achieve EDGE's advanced certification (IFC 2019). This is the first loan supported by the Market Accelerator for Green Construction Program in Colombia. Sponsored by the UK Department for Business, Energy and Industrial Strategy, this program aims to expand the green building market by encouraging financial intermediaries to develop new financing products for green construction.

IFC has also provided a $40 million loan to Visum Rentas Inmobiliarias Real Estate Collective Investment Fund (Visum), the fifth-largest real estate investment fund in Colombia. Visum will use the loan to support its 2022–24 investment plan in green construction, which includes developing a world-class 80,000 square meter custom-built distribution center for leading regional retailer Falabella for its retail operations and electronic commerce.

Results and Impacts

IFC estimates that EDGE-certified floor space now exceeds 20 percent of new construction and represents a cumulative private sector investment of more than $11.5 billion. There are now more than 157,000 EDGE-certified housing units across the country, and two-thirds of these are low-income and affordable housing. Taking into consideration that a low-income family can spend up to 15 percent of their monthly income on utility costs, reducing these through more efficient housing is a significant achievement. The key results of Colombia's green building expansion are summarized in table 3.5.

TABLE 3.5 Key Results of Colombia's Green Building Expansion

Result	Details
Increased EDGE certification	By June 2021, over 20% of all new builds in Colombia were EDGE-certified
Reduced energy and water consumption	Some of Colombia's EDGE-certified green buildings are are using 45% less energy and 42% less water, respectively
Technical assistance to local governments	Building on its experiences in Peru, IFC is helping cities across Colombia to encourage the construction of green buildings through municipal incentives

Note: For more information on EDGE, see https://edgebuildings.com/project-studies/foresta-etapa-1/. IFC = International Finance Corporation.

Key Takeaways

There are four key elements to Colombia's successful green building market transformation:

- *Government support:* Creating the Green Building Code and appropriate tax incentives to bolster the interest of the private sector to build green provided the foundations for this transformation.
- *Financial institutions offering green products:* Colombia has the most financial institutions offering green mortgages, or a green product for the construction sector, in Latin America. The availability of these products has proven a game changer not only for developers, who receive attractive rates to finance their projects, but also for the end clients, giving Colombian families better interest rates for financing their green homes.
- *A committed local partner:* CAMACOL's commitment to forging a green real estate sector, its solid institutional position in Colombia's construction industry, and its interest in promoting EDGE as an effective tool to design green buildings was vital to effectively reach a large number of developers. CAMACOL estimates that 230 construction companies are certifying their projects as green.
- *Training of developers and professionals:* To date, Colombia has 136 EDGE experts, 42 percent of whom are women (IFC 2023). CAMACOL and its regional offices have offered dozens of trainings to guide developers and construction companies to design and build green projects in Colombia's major cities.

Looking to the Future

To achieve compliance with the Paris Agreement, new buildings must be net zero carbon in their operations by 2030, and existing buildings by 2050. Despite the green growth of the construction sector in recent years, sustainable buildings have yet to be consolidated as a general practice in all territories. For this reason, IFC and CAMACOL, with the support of the Colombia Green Building Council, are undertaking a capacity-building program to help municipal governments create municipal bylaws that offer incentives for green building. This program gathers the experience IFC has accumulated in fostering green building incentive ordinances in Peru. In January 2023, IFC's technical support resulted in the approval of Colombia's first-ever local bylaw to offer incentives for green buildings, in the city of Envigado.

Facilitating, Enabling, and Triggering Sectoral Transitions: China

Case Study 20. Climate-Smart Agriculture in Guangdong, China

Contributors: William R. Sutton and Bethany Linton

Context

While China has achieved tremendous success over recent decades in increasing agricultural production and feeding its population, this success has come at the cost of significant environmental degradation (World Bank 2022h). Agriculture in China is a major source of air, land, and water pollution. China's agri-food system also generates more GHG emissions than any other country in the world and accounts for more than 14 percent of its total GHG emissions.[10] The sector releases substantial amounts of CO_2, methane, and nitrous oxide, which trap up to 25 and 300 times the heat of CO_2, respectively. When it comes to agricultural production, the largest sources of GHG emissions are synthetic fertilizers, livestock manure, and enteric fermentation from ruminant livestock, at 18, 18, and 24 percent, respectively (figure 3.18). Poor agriculture practices—such as excessive fertilizer and pesticide use, and mismanaged livestock waste—are also the leading cause of water pollution (World Bank, forthcoming b), affecting sources for drinking, recreation, crops, and fisheries. Improved manure management, dietary changes, more efficient fertilizer use, and reducing waste in the food system could contribute to important emissions reductions from the sector.

FIGURE 3.18 China's Farm Gate Emissions, 2020

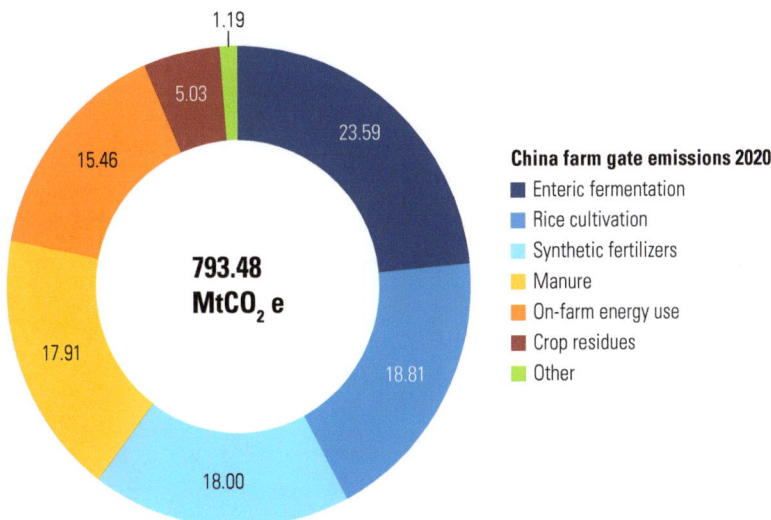

Source: World Bank staff calculations, based on 2020 data from FAOSTAT (FAO 2020).

China's 12th Five-Year Plan called for pollution control from crop production through soil management and efficient use of pesticides. The plan also defined improved agricultural targets for each level of local government as part of their performance evaluations.

In Guangdong Province, heavy pesticide and fertilizer use—60 to 70 percent of which ended up as residue on crops or was released into the environment (World Bank 2022b)—and waste from a standing pig population of more than 20 million has led to significant water contamination. Following public demand for improved water quality, the government asked for World Bank assistance in developing policy reform and greener practices on farms.

Policies

As part of this policy reform, the Guangdong Department of Agriculture, alongside the World Bank and GEF, funded the Guangdong Agricultural Pollution Control Project in 2013, which aimed to reduce nutrient pollution in local water supplies from crop and livestock production in the province. This would improve water quality in the province's estuary systems and the coastal ecosystems of the South China Sea, generating global environmental benefits in the form of reduced GHG emissions.

The project strengthened institutional capacity to implement agricultural pollution control activities, including monitoring and evaluation methodologies and verification procedures. It generated policy studies on various technical packages related to the excessive application of chemical fertilizer and pesticide, low fertilizer use efficiency, high rice production costs, and the increase in pig manure and waste pollution in Guangdong and across China. The project activities targeted agricultural officers, farmers, cooperatives, and enterprises, training them in livestock waste management, fertilizer and pesticide application, and how to develop standards and regulations for certification of safe and green agricultural products. Although external financial support for project activities concluded in 2021, the policies for greener agricultural production are ongoing.

Results and Impacts

The interventions supported by the project resulted in multiple benefits, including demonstrating a rural circular economy by replacing chemical fertilizers with treated livestock waste. This reduced both water pollution and GHG emissions. To source this natural fertilizer and reduce pollution, the project subsidized the piloting of several new, greener pig production technologies that either used livestock waste to generate biogas for energy on the farms, using the solids for organic fertilizer, or innovative zero discharge piggery designs that incorporate complete capture and rapid composting of livestock waste for use as organic fertilizer. The project also promoted more modern, compound, slow-release, and organic fertilizers for farmers to use on their crops instead of overapplying single-nutrient ammonia fertilizer. Together with training on how and when to effectively apply fertilizers for maximized crop bioavailability, and promoting modern fertilizers among suppliers, the policies resulted in improved practices that decreased costs to farmers, increased crop yields, reduced water pollution, and lowered GHG emissions.

Reducing nutrient pollutants in waterways also generated tremendous local financial and environmental benefits. These included provincial economic savings, avoided expenditures in downstream water quality improvement, avoided health care costs, reduced deforestation, and reducing annual average GHG emissions by almost 84,000 $mtCO_2e$. Much of this was by reducing methane and nitrous oxide. Policies addressing pollutant reduction practices and livestock waste management activities developed under the project are being upscaled throughout Guangdong Province and across China. For example, Guangdong Province has recently written upscaling good pollutant reduction practices developed under the project to the whole province into its 14th Five-Year Plan for Agriculture and Rural Development.

Key Takeaways

- Agriculture is not only a source of GHG emissions; it can also serve as a source of practical decarbonization actions, even when it involves many smallholder farmers.
- Improved agricultural policies can provide multiple wins at once, mitigating GHG emissions while also reducing water pollution, increasing crop yields, and reducing costs to farmers.
- Promoting local environmental benefits can generate global public goods. Although the project's main objective was to reduce water pollution in response to local public demand, it also generated important reductions of global climate pollutants.
- Positive results can be achieved without a heavy-handed approach. Rather than banning polluting practices such as chemical fertilizer use or pig production, the project secured the collaboration of farmers and the private sector by working to green existing practices.

Getting the Finance Flowing: Chile

Case Study 21. E-buses in Santiago de Chile

Contributors: Nicolas Peltier, Cecilia Briceno-Garmendia, and Wenxin Qiao

Context

The integration of e-buses in Santiago's public transport system is driven by Chile's broader commitment to achieve carbon neutrality by 2050, its National Electromobility Strategy (established in 2017, updated in 2021), and other programs.[11] This is in addition to nationwide initiatives such as the National Climate Change Plan 2017–22, the Energy Route 2018–22, and more recently the approval of a Decarbonization Plan in the context of COP25. The transport sector was responsible for 25 percent of Chile's CO_2 equivalent emissions in 2018, with roads accounting for 86 percent, 65 percent of which is traceable to trucks and buses (Ministerio del Medio Ambiente 2019). While oil dominates the energy mix, power generation is quickly shifting to renewables, tapping into the country's vast resources of solar energy and abundant unexploited potential for wind, hydro, and geothermal (IEA 2018).

Santiago, with a population of 6.8 million in 2018, has almost 40 percent of the country's population and is the most densely populated city. Its public transport system, the Red Metropolitana de Movilidad—known simply as Red, and formerly Transantiago—records an average of 5.5 million daily transactions. Known for recent decades of economic and political stability, Chile's inequality remains a salient problem. In this context, providing sustainable and affordable mobility is a high priority.

The National Electromobility Strategy seeks to contribute to the mitigation of GHG emissions by improving the mobility and quality of life for Chileans. It outlines the actions that Chile must take in the short and medium term to ensure that 100 percent of all urban public transport buses and light and medium vehicles sold are electric by 2035 (Government of Chile 2021).

Chile faces operational, infrastructure, and financial challenges to adopting e-buses. First, the e-buses have lower passenger capacity per vehicle than regular buses (with internal combustion engines), so to achieve the same level of supply, more buses and frequency are necessary. This requires new operating plans, more drivers and maintenance staff, and additional infrastructure and finance. Training enough workers to operate and support the new systems and technology is also a challenge. Second, e-buses require custom modifications and charging infrastructure for urban operations. This includes designing, building, and installing charging depots, electric infrastructure, power management systems, and possibly energy storage. Implementing regulatory systems and streamlined approval processes to manage infrastructure installations and maintenance presents another challenge. Third, at $450,000 per bus, the cost of Chile's first e-buses was more than double the diesel Euro VI vehicles. As the e-bus fleet grew and manufacturers expanded into the Latin American market, prices went down to $300,000 per e-bus by 2020 and are expected to decline further as technology advances. A key challenge is harnessing the full potential of e-buses' lower operating expenditures to offset this higher capital cost.

The Experience of E-buses in Santiago

Santiago's public transport system is based on six bus companies: Metbus, Buses Vule, Servicio de Transporte de Personas (STP) Santiago, RedBus, Subus, and Express. Each company is assigned a group of bus services, integrated through a seamless electronic payment system that uses a smart card called Bip!. The regulator collects and manages revenues. Concession contracts were originally 10 years, and the life cycle of a bus fleet is defined as at least 1 million kilometers and/or 12 years of operation, after which there is an imminent need to renew the fleet.

The business model used to implement e-buses in Santiago consists of a PPP between the Ministry of Transport and Telecommunications and private energy companies Enel and Engie, who serve as bus operators and investors. Fleet provision and depot ownership are separated from the operation of buses in the street, introducing two types of contract: one for operations, and the other for enabling infrastructure and assets. The transition involved a proactive government role in supporting fleet renewal with better and cleaner technologies through the adoption of vehicle and fuel standards and vehicle certification. Chile's Center for Vehicle Control and Certification has a technical laboratory to certify the characteristics of different types of vehicles, including assessing the emissions and energy efficiency of buses in the public transport system. The transition also involved bold government actions to facilitate the process, reduce approval and authorization times, and support e-bus planning and regulation.

As an innovation, financing for the charging infrastructure and e-buses was developed as part of a scheme in the core business of Enel and Engie. They developed leasing contracts with the private bus operator companies with monthly payments to cover fleet provision, charging infrastructure, and energy supply, allowing operators' quotes for fleet provision to be paid directly to the bus provider (and investor). A financial entity in charge of collecting revenue and managing operators' payments deducts from each operator's payment the amount corresponding to the leasing contract it has with the energy company, reducing the risk for investors. The providers and operators sign provision contracts, approved by the state, that specify that no matter what company operates the e-buses, the state guarantees that the buses will remain in the system until the debt is paid. Managing and monitoring the e-buses' operation is mainly the responsibility of the bus operator but depends on contractual agreements between the different actors, especially regarding fleet and electric infrastructure maintenance, but also charging management issues.

Metbus was the first operator to include e-buses in its fleet (285 vehicles), operating the first e-corridor in Latin America, and was followed by Buses Vule (76 vehicles), STP (25 vehicles), and RedBus (25 e-buses in 2020). These buses represent approximately 6 percent of the Santiago fleet (411 e-buses in a total fleet of 6,849 in 2019), making Chile's the world's second-biggest e-bus fleet, after China. Under the existing plan, the bus fleet will be evenly split between Euro VI diesel and e-buses by 2030; consequently, emissions and particulate matter (PM) are expected to drop significantly: nitric oxide, nitrogen dioxide, and hydrocarbons (by 90 percent); CO_2 (by 15 percent); and PM2.5 and PM10 (by 70 and 56 percent, respectively). This will have a direct impact on air pollution and thus health outcomes in the city. Meanwhile, the overall quality of the public transport system has increased, with passengers preferring e-buses for their smooth ride, lower noise levels, and good air conditioning. The shift would also create energy cost savings of 70 percent.

Key Takeaways

Building a cooperative partnership between private companies (bus operators, bus manufacturers, and financiers) and the public sector is vital. Although financing can come from traditional sources, creating adequate policies to incentivize private companies, such as utilities, to invest can help minimize the fiscal burden. The government's role in minimizing nonpayment risks cannot be overemphasized, either as facilitator or as policy maker. The planning stage should include construction time for the electric infrastructure as well as technical operational adjustments to adapt to the capacity of the new buses. Planners should also consider the selection of bus routes suitable for e-buses, in terms of slope and length, and possible adjustments to buses for operating on certain routes.

Pilot projects are an essential element to consider when implementing e-bus fleets, to test the battery range and e-bus capabilities for specific city conditions. A salient priority is training e-bus drivers, maintenance technicians, and other personnel in charge of electrical infrastructure. At the same time, universities and technical institutions should adapt their degrees and other courses to the future challenges of e-mobility.

Having viable and enforceable contractual arrangements for fleet and charging infrastructure maintenance is also essential. Maintenance is an important issue to guarantee e-fleet availability and the proper operation of e-buses. Similarly, the bus performance should be guaranteed from the first moment of operation.

Getting the Finance Flowing: Colombia

Case Study 22. Greening Colombia's Financial System

Contributors: Martijn Gert Jan Regelink and Fiona Stewart

Context

Colombia's financial sector is exposed to climate risks, while also playing an increasingly important role in mobilizing finance for climate action. Climate change can affect the Colombian economy and destabilize its financial sector through the materialization of both *physical risks*, which emanate from natural disasters and global warming and can lead to economic costs and financial losses, and *transition risks*, which are associated with economic adjustment costs during the transition toward a greener, carbon-neutral economy. For example, the large-scale riverine floods of 2010 and 2011 led to combined damages of $7 billion (2 percent of GDP), which induced a significant increase in bank loan loss provisions (Reinders et al. 2021). The decarbonization plan in Colombia considers a 51 percent reduction of GHG emissions in 2030 compared with 2010; during that transition, banks may face write-offs on loans to polluting companies that face additional costs or cannot comply with regulations. At the same time, climate change represents an opportunity to mobilize new and greater resources for climate-resilient and low-carbon iinvestment (DNP 2022). In October 2021, Colombia became the first Latin American country to issue local currency green bonds on the domestic market, raising Col$750 billion (World Bank 2022k). Banks have also issued green bonds, and pension funds have invested in them.

Policy

Against this background, Colombia's financial supervisor, the Superintendencia Financiera de Colombia (SFC), with support from the World Bank, has initiated several high-impact activities to further green the Colombian financial sector. Following its membership of the Central Bank and Regulators Network for Greening the Financial System and the introduction of a climate action plan, SFC—with support from the World Bank and IFC—has initiated several key actions to green its financial sector, including a climate risk stress test, regulatory reforms for banks and investors, and a green taxonomy. These actions aim to stimulate private-sector investments for Colombia's ambitious climate targets, while also building resilience in the financial sector against the impacts of climate change and climate policy.

To build understanding in the financial sector of climate risks, SFC and the World Bank conducted a stress test to examine the impact of different climate scenarios on the banking sector. This first-of-its-kind exploration for an emerging market focused on the most relevant climate physical and transition risk scenarios for Colombia, such as large-scale flooding and introducing a carbon tax to decarbonize the economy. In the most severe forward-looking flooding scenarios, some banks would be affected by significant losses, with the results underlining the need for adaptation and resilience measures. The transition risk stress test assessed the impacts of decarbonization targets, including a scenario envisioning the late and abrupt introduction of a high carbon tax to support the 51 percent reduction in GHG emissions by 2030. While Colombia's credit exposure to highly CO_2-intensive sectors is moderate for the region, assessed impacts from transition scenarios are not trivial, with significant heterogeneity of impacts among banks and losses up to almost 3 percent of total assets. And while we should interpret results with caution, they point to the importance of Colombia's financial sector regulators incorporating these risks in their supervisory approach. Results also show that timely and coordinated mitigation policy can help smooth impacts on the banking sector.

Informed by the risk assessment, SFC has also introduced climate risk management guidelines for the banking sector and climate disclosure regulations for institutional investors. In alignment with global principles (Basel Committee 2022) and sound practices, SFC has presented guidelines for banks on how to further integrate climate risks in risk management, governance, and disclosure practices. It has also undertaken a set of activities to support the development of environmental, social, and governance (ESG) and climate risk disclosure regulations for institutional investors. This included developing ESG and climate risk reporting requirements for institutional investors, launched in 2021 (Centro de Estudios Regulatorios 2021a, 2021b). These guidelines and regulations will help banks and investors better integrate climate considerations into their operational frameworks, building a financial sector that is more resilient against climate shocks and that better aligns its investments with sustainable development.

In 2021, Colombia introduced a Green Taxonomy, which provides a classification of green economic activities and assets (Azizuddin 2022). By helping investors determine whether a project is green and aligned with Colombia's NDC to the Paris Agreement, the taxonomy can support growth of green-labeled products in the country's capital markets and banking sector, while also providing a framework to start measuring green finance flows. Its creation was supported by a large group of stakeholders, including various ministries, the National Planning Authority, SFC, and international initiatives such as the Green Bond Initiative and the Sustainable Banking and Finance Network. The World Bank also supported the development of Colombia's sustainable bond market, facilitating a second-party opinion on the Sovereign Green Bond Framework's alignment with the issuer's sustainable strategic priorities and climate-change commitments and goals.

Results and Impacts

These actions provide important building blocks for a more sustainable and greener financial system in Colombia. The strengthening of climate and environmental risk management practices not only supports the resilience of the financial sector against transition impacts but could also incentivize the reduction of carbon-intensive investments while increasing greener investments. A taxonomy—and subsequent green products that are issued using the taxonomy—is foundational in creating an enabling environment of public and private sector climate finance. Although the initiatives were first launched in 2020 and the impact on mobilizing funding for climate action remains to be assessed, the steps taken closely align with best practice from advanced markets, including examples from the EU (World Bank 2021i). SFC has clearly put some of the enabling pillars in place that will allow for further alignment of financial sector flows with decarbonization objectives and strengthen climate risk management and disclosure practices.

Following the establishment of the Sovereign Green Bond Framework, the inaugural sovereign green bonds issued on the local market in September 2021 raised Col$750 million, with a maturity of 10 years. The green bond secured a coupon of 7.56 percent, compared with 7.63 percent for a conventional bond with the same financial characteristics. Following support to develop a green bond issuance framework, the national development bank, Financiera de Desarrollo Nacional, issued the first tranche ($40 million) of a nine-year $116 million securitized bond in local currency to finance the renovation of the Transmilenio BRT buses. An official second-party opinion provider certified it as a green and social bond, and it was listed in the exchange and purchased mostly by local insurance companies, pension funds, and mutual funds.

Key Takeaways

This example, and the actions of SFC in particular, provide key learnings for other emerging markets and developing economies. First, while part of a broader picture, this case study underlines the central and systemic role that a financial sector regulator can play in greening the financial sector and the economy, not only through its direct microprudential (risk-based) mandate, but also by playing a catalyzing role in the development of key enablers for green finance markets and direct change by households and firms. Second, it underlines the importance of a clear strategy and vision to guide the work. And third, greening the financial system involves working with a large group of stakeholders. Ministries, financial sector regulators, financial sector institutions, firms, and academics all need to work together to assess climate impacts, design relevant tools, create climate regulations, socialize findings, and drive action across agencies and the financial sector.

Getting the Finance Flowing: Kenya

Case Study 23. Power Sector Reform in Kenya

Contributors: Vivien Foster and Mumba Ngulube

Context

After independence, Kenya relied primarily on hydropower to meet its demand for electricity. But this left it heavily exposed to hydrological risks. As drought periods intensified during the 1990s, the country was pushed into a situation of acute supply insecurity, forcing it to ramp up fossil fuel–based generation by the end of the decade, which increased both the cost and carbon intensity of the power supply (figure 3.19). High fossil fuel generation costs combined with low electricity tariffs, heavy government involvement in state-owned enterprise operations and management, and inadequate coverage of aging transmission and distribution networks resulted in a poorly performing and financially constrained energy sector.

Policy

It was under these conditions of acute supply insecurity and poor financial performance that the country's first wave of power sector reforms took place in the early 2000s. Given the pressing need to release the aid embargo in place at that time and

FIGURE 3.19 **CO_2 Intensity of Power in Kenya, 1990–2020**

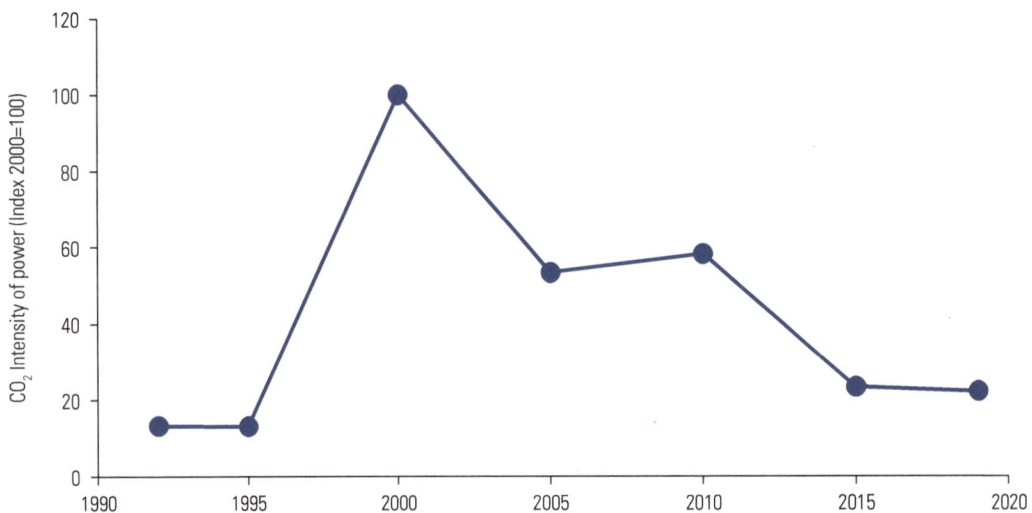

Source: World Bank calculations based on data from IEA 2019.
Note: CO_2 = carbon dioxide.

attract private investment into the sector, Kenya overhauled its approach to planning and funding power generation, unbundling it from transmission and distribution and putting the national generation company KenGen in charge of all state-owned generation capacity. The first phase reforms also separated policy and regulatory functions from commercial activities, introduced cost-reflective tariffs, and attracted private capital by liberalizing generation activities.

The Energy Act 2006 initiated a second wave of reform, including the establishment of the Energy Regulatory Commission (ERC) as the regulatory body responsible for overseeing and regulating the energy sector in Kenya. The ERC was given powers to set tariffs, issue licenses, and monitor the performance of market participants, including KenGen. Retaining its long-standing capacity for comprehensive and technically sound planning of the power sector, Kenya moved away from the more traditional industry model to the complex hybrid sector created by the reform, and third-party access was established to the grid. Significantly, the Energy Act vested responsibility for power development planning in the ERC, which works through multistakeholder steering and technical committees to produce a rolling Least Cost Power Development Plan for the power sector.

Results and Impacts

Kenya has been one of East Africa's most successful countries at attracting private-sector financing for developing power generation assets. This has happened in two distinct ways. First, KenGen raised private finance from the capital market by issuing corporate bonds and rights, listing 30 percent of its shares on the securities exchange to bolster its ability to secure commercial lending, which accounted for 15 percent of its debt as of 2021 (KenGen 2021). Second, by modernizing the legal framework and establishing a regulatory framework for the power sector, Kenya became an investment destination for independent power producers (IPPs). By the end of 2020, 28 IPPs were operating in Kenya, supplying 26 percent of its total electricity supply (figure 3.20; Kenya National Bureau of Statistics 2021). As of 2022, generation capacity financed and installed by IPPs had reached a cumulative total of 1,172 MW (Energy and Petroleum Regulatory Authority 2021). Although Kenya's early IPPs used diesel-fired generation, over time, this has shifted markedly toward clean power generation sources. Today, as much as 70 percent of IPP-installed capacity has an RE source, including geothermal, wind, and solar.

Notwithstanding the growth in IPPs, the public sector has retained a significant role in power generation. The major expansion of geothermal energy in Kenya would not have been possible without publicly funded exploration between 2007 and 2015, and subsequent investment by KenGen to develop generation capacity, as the private exploration of steam fields would otherwise have proved too risky. In the process, KenGen has become Africa's largest developer of geothermal power and ranks in the world's top 10.

FIGURE 3.20 Electricity Suppliers in Kenya, 2020

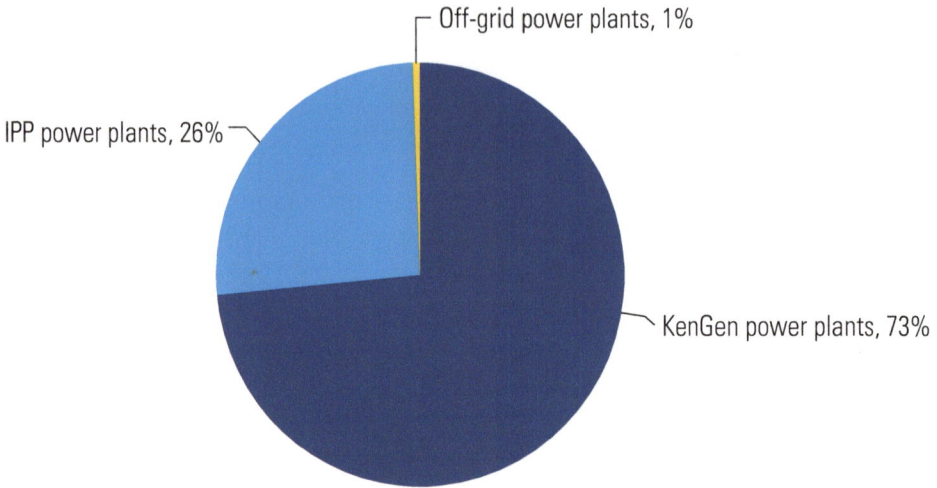

Off-grid power plants, 1%

IPP power plants, 26%

KenGen power plants, 73%

Source: World Bank calculations based on data from Kenya National Bureau of Statistics 2021b.
Note: IPP = independent power producer.

The combined result is that Kenya's generation capacity tripled between 1990 and 2022, from 829 MW to 3,076 MW. Considering a peak demand of 2,036 MW in November 2021, the country's reserve margin is more than 30 percent. Expanding its generation capacity has made electricity supply more reliable in many parts of the country. The marked diversification of the energy mix has also improved security of supply. Kenya now has 949 MW of geothermal capacity and is less exposed to hydrological risk. The increased share of geothermal generation has also displaced energy from thermal plants, which fell from 53 percent in 2000 to just 11 percent in 2019, reducing Kenya's carbon intensity of power index by 62 percent between 2010 and 2019 (figure 3.21). Further, the country is on its way to achieving 100 percent RE supply by 2030, in line with its COP26 commitment, through a combination of developing indigenous geothermal resources, competitive auctions for solar and wind resources, and energy trading through regional interconnections.

Expanding the country's generation capacity has increased people's access to electricity, setting Kenya on a path to achieve universal access before 2030. Kenya's electrification experience has been exceptionally rapid, owing to a combination of grid densification, by targeting more connections in neighborhoods where infrastructure is already present, and off-grid programs. The population with access to electricity increased from 15 percent in 2000 to 75 percent (54 percent on-grid and 22 percent off-grid; Dubey et al. 2020) by 2018 (figure 3.22). This sharp increase, induced by power sector reforms, has positive implications for the economy due to the strong link between electrification and development. Several case studies in Sub-Saharan Africa reveal that increase in electrification is positively associated with increased economic

FIGURE 3.21 **Electricity Generation in Kenya, by Source, 1990–2020**

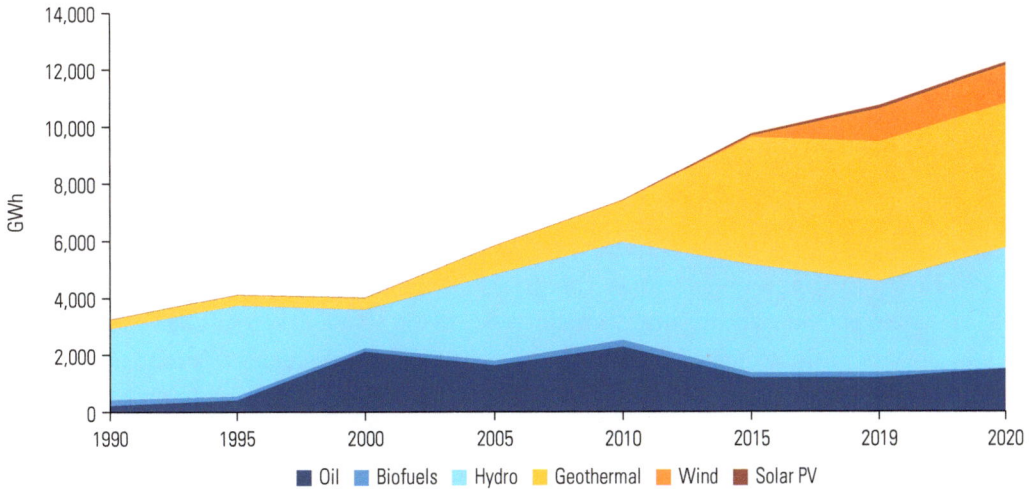

Source: World Bank calculations based on data from IEA 2019 and Kenya National Bureau of Statistics 2021a.
Note: GWh = gigawatt hours; PV = photovoltaic.

FIGURE 3.22 **Access to Electricity, Kenya, 1993–2018**

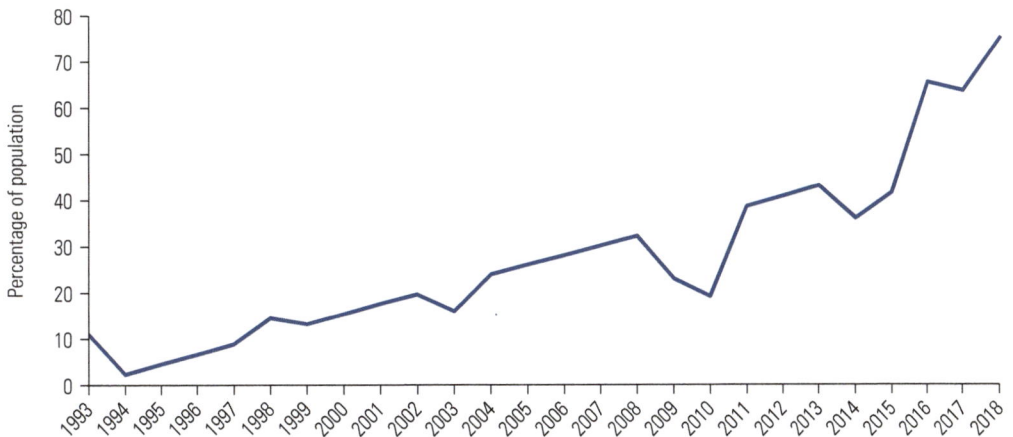

Source: World Bank calculations based on data from the World Bank Global Infrastructure Dashboard.

growth, jobs, productivity, incomes, health outcomes, and human capital development (Dinkelman 2011; Jimenez 2017; Foster et al. 2023; Fried and Lagakos 2021; Salmon and Tanguy 2016; World Bank 2015). One review of 50 studies on electrification reports that, on average, electrification leads to increases of around 7 percent in school enrollment, 25 percent in employment, and 30 percent in incomes (Jimenez 2017). Another finds that rural electrification in KwaZulu-Natal positively impacts female employment, increasing it by about 10 percentage points (Dinkelman 2011). Newly electrified communities also experience substantial shifts away from using wood at home toward electric cooking and lighting, which improves air home quality and health. The rapid electrification, however, has resulted in a deteriorating financial position of Kenya Power and Lighting Company, which is being addressed through a new set of policy and institutional reform measures.

Key Takeaways

Kenya's power sector reform has been successful from a variety of standpoints, including the decarbonization of electricity. Several important lessons emerge from this experience. First, it is important for countries to develop the technical capacity for power system planning and ensure strict adherence to the plan that supports least-cost development of the sector and guides the choice of clean technologies. Second, creating a modern regulatory framework provides the necessary enabling environment to support privately financed IPPs, notably for RE. And third, while the private sector is often willing to invest in RE, state actors retain an important role for addressing early development risks of new technologies, such as geothermal. Partially listing state-owned enterprises, such as KenGen and Kenya Power and Lighting Company, allows them to access significant volumes of private sector finance.

Ensuring a Just Transition: South Africa

Case Study 24. Toward a Just Transition and Greener Future for South Africa's Coal Sector

Contributors: Katie Polkinghorne and Bandita Sijapati

Context

South Africa is increasingly adopting measures to address climate change, demonstrating the government's commitments toward a low-carbon economy and resilient society. The country is facing a severe energy crisis. The breakdown of several coal-fired power plants in late 2021 and early 2022 caused widespread blackouts and load shedding, which had a significant impact on the country's economy and disrupted the lives of millions of people.

To address the energy crisis, the South African government announced plans to invest in RE sources such as wind and solar power while also making commitments to decommission coal mines. In accordance with the Integrated Resource Plan (IRP) created in 2019, Eskom, the country's primary electricity supplier, has revealed plans to shut down 8 to 12 GW (30 percent) of coal-fired power generation in the next 10 years. South Africa's updated NDC in September 2021 raises the country's mitigation ambition further by committing to reduce annual GHG emissions to 398 to 510 $MtCO_2e$ by 2025 and 350 to 420 $MtCO_2e$ by 2030 (UNFCCC 2021). However, 12 of South Africa's 15 coal-fired power stations are more than 30 years old, and this inefficient and outdated infrastructure makes the country increasingly susceptible to carbon lock-in and other hazards (World Bank 2019b). The government is aware of such risks and is pushing to transition away from a predominantly coal-based economy and energy grid as it seeks to increase RE.

South Africa has the most carbonized electrical grid of all G20 countries, and its power system is the biggest in Sub-Saharan Africa, representing about half of the region's installed capacity. The energy mix (figure 3.23) is dominated by fossil fuels (89 percent), of which coal makes up over 75 percent and gas and diesel over 10 percent. Nuclear contributes around 5.6 percent, followed by RE at 5.5 percent, but this number has been increasing. There are three main groups of electricity generators: the public utility Eskom, which operates 89 percent of South Africa's total generation capacity; municipal generators, which operate about 1 percent; and IPPs and private generators, which operate about 10 percent, including cogeneration. In kilowatt-hour terms, IPPs contribute less than 5 percent of total electricity.

To uphold national commitments toward a low-carbon economy while focusing on improving the livelihoods of those most vulnerable to climate change, South

FIGURE 3.23 **Breakdown of South Africa's Energy Mix**

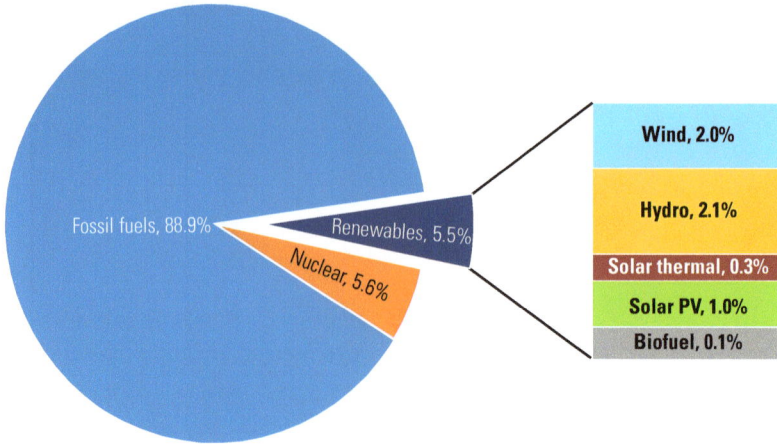

Source: Akinbami, Oke, and Bodunrin 2021, based on data in IEA 2023.
Note: PV = photovoltaic.

Africa has embraced the just transition principle. Already outlined in various national plans since 2009, the just transition principle was reinforced in June 2022 with the endorsement of the cabinet of the Just Energy Transition Framework (JETF), led by the Presidential Climate Commission (PCC), a multistakeholder body that aims to advise on the country's climate change response and support the just transition agenda at a political level (PwC South Africa 2022). However, the PCC lacks the mandate and resources to implement JETF at the local level. More inclusive movements are forming—such as local municipal climate change task forces and local government climate change support programs—but they require more support and funding from influential powers, including government and business (ICLEI Africa 2019).

South Africa has always relied heavily on its abundant coal reserves as a source of energy and jobs (Hodder and Richards 2022). In 2019, the coal industry employed over 92,000 people, representing about 19 percent of total employment in the mining sector (Makgetla 2021; Minerals Council South Africa 2022). The Social and Labour Plan, introduced in 2002 to support local economic development by addressing social conflicts associated with mining, describes how mining companies will share benefits with local communities; yet there has been a lack of accountability and enforcement (Strambo, Burton, and Atteridge 2019). Over 42,000 mining jobs have already been lost in Mpumalanga province between 2008 and 2015, and it is estimated that a further 120,000 will be lost to future planned coal mine closures (Gatticchi 2020; Steyn et al. 2021). Long overdue transition planning in the province has now taken place with, among others, the establishment of the Mpumalanga Green Cluster Agency to advance a sustainable and inclusive green economy and create shared values in the Mpumalanga province (Steyn et al. 2021). This is one of many examples, as South Africa has implemented several national policies that are helping translate policy commitments into concrete actions.

Policies

In 2012, the PCC proposed a framework for a national-level social dialogue, later launched as the Social Partner Dialogues on Pathways for a Just Transition. Aimed at building toward including the just transition in South Africa's National Development Plan (National Planning Commission 2022). These dialogues called together the four social partners—government, labor workers and unions, business, and civil society—to build a common vision for the just transition and create pathways to achieve this vision. Participants reached a consensus on the importance of just management of the energy–water–land use nexus for a sustainable socioeconomic future in South Africa supported with corruption-free governance, social dialogue, and participatory decision-making. However, several issues remain under discussion, including emissions reduction pathways, state versus private ownership of energy resources, conservation versus equitable access to natural resources, the timing of the coal phaseout, and the future of Eskom and a reformed electricity industry (National Planning Commission 2019).

The IRP sets out a long-term diversification of the power mix by 2030. The plan helps the country move toward reducing the energy sector's carbon footprint, replacing coal power with RE while meeting growing energy demand and ensuring a socioeconomically just transition. The IRP aims to retire 12 GW of aging coal-fired power plants by 2030 while installing 18 GW of RE (World Bank 2022n). The government is also accelerating its Coal Transition Investment Plan and the Department of Mineral Resources and Energy's JETF.

The Eskom Just Energy Transition (JET) Project was selected as a demonstration project by the government to establish a pathway for retiring future coal plants in a sustainable manner. For example, the project will decommission the Komati coal-fired power plant and repurpose the site with renewables (150 MW solar PV, 70 MW wind) and 150 MW battery storage. The project will also mitigate socioeconomic impacts on affected workers and communities while enhancing opportunities to support them during the transition process. Expediting the repurposing and repowering of its power stations and actively pursuing a larger share of RE generation are part of the JET Project. The strategy aligns with South Africa's IRP (Department of Mineral Resources and Energy 2019).

The development of South Africa's Just Energy Transition Investment Plan (JET IP) 2023–27 is key for longer-term success and planning. It includes priority investments over the next five years in the electricity, EV, and green hydrogen sectors, focused on supporting South Africa's goals of energy security, just transition, and economic growth. The JET IP was prepared through a joint engagement between the Presidential Climate Finance Task Team established in February 2022 and the International

Partners Group comprising France, Germany, the United Kingdom, the EU, and the United States. To support implementation of the JET IP, they agreed to channel $8.5 billion over five years as a catalytic contribution toward addressing the JET IP priorities (Presidency of the Republic of South Africa 2022).

Challenges and Opportunities

Eskom's coal-fired plants are concentrated in Mpumalanga province, which has no RE plants, making a just transition a complex challenge. Having identified the communities most at risk in the distributional analysis and identified how to engage with and build trust with them through inclusion and procedural justice, there is an acute need for restorative justice plans (Mahachi and Rix 2016). Restorative justice looks at repairing harm caused from the just transition against marginalized communities (Montmasson-Clair 2021). It is rooted in union movements demanding the restoration of lost jobs, with unions agreeing to support the shift to renewables and cleaner technology on the condition that job losses for coal communities could be (at least) restored to previous levels (Stevis and Felli 2015). One solution is Renewable Energy Development Zones (REDZs), such as the eMalahleni REDZ in Mpumalanga. The South African Wind Energy Association emphasizes that REDZs will play a key role in the just transition, as they create priority areas for investment in the electricity grid and increase South Africa's green energy map by enabling higher levels of renewable power penetration (Bungane 2021).

Recent bouts of load-shedding and subsequent outcries from civil society and public and private enterprise have also placed further pressure on Eskom to act. A missed opportunity to sign RE contracts in 2014 is causing high load-shedding and has recently sent the country into a declared state of disaster (Nyathi 2023). In response, Eskom has issued an RfP to lease land to IPPs in Mpumalanga to create RE projects. The process will involve auctioning suitable land near power stations to develop RE generation sites that can deliver rapid additional generation capacity to the grid. Eskom says it views this process as validation of its commitment to being part of the just transition (Smith 2022). The National Development Plan also includes a critical action that states the need for "New spatial norms and standards—densifying cities, improving transport, locating jobs where people live, upgrading informal settlements and fixing housing market gaps" (National Planning Commission 2022, 4). These all seem to be steps in the right direction, and a monitoring mechanism would help hold such actions accountable.

The transition process is expected to have a significant impact on people's well-being through its effects on the economic growth trajectory, composition of GDP, employment, relative prices, and health cobenefits. For example, an estimated 0.6 million jobs will be lost—mainly in sectors with large proportions of unskilled or low-skilled employees—with the impacts felt most acutely by vulnerable groups (Kilumelume et al. 2022). In 2021, over 90 percent of coal workers were low- or semi-skilled, which would make it more difficult for them to find other jobs (World Bank 2022j). Women will also be widely affected, as they generally work in indirect jobs, such as services provided by small firms to workers and firms in coal-related industries. The spatial dimension of transition is equally important—in the coal belt of Mpumalanga Province, which is home to over 80 percent of the country's coal-fired power plants and coal mines, an estimated 150,000 to 200,000 jobs are at risk (about 18 percent of the employed provincial labor force); this includes about 75,000 coal miners and 15,000 jobs in the transport sector (World Bank 2022l). However, the exact number of jobs lost in the coal sector will depend on the number of power plants decommissioned (IASS 2022). Municipality revenues and services will also be affected—for example, in eMalahleni, coal accounts for almost half of local revenues (TIPS 2020). Eskom and coal mining companies provide key public services, such as water and electricity, to communities close to their sites. However, a recent study from IASS (2022) shows that the transition from coal to RE could create an estimated 150,000 to 300,000 new jobs by 2030.

Key Takeaways

Accelerating the transition away from coal is crucial. Early planning with policy makers and all stakeholders, including affected coal communities, is key to achieving justice, with a specific focus on implementing restorative plans for vulnerable communities in coal-dependent regions. Immediate, deeper baseline mapping will enable early lending that provides comprehensive, on-the-ground support on pending closures, using learning to improve on future closures and new opportunities for people and communities.

Establishing an independent statutory body, the PCC, to lead, coordinate, and oversee the just transition provided the political weight required to steer the process across various government institutions and stakeholders. The broad representation of the PCC—which comprises commissioners represented by government ministers, business, labor, youth, academia and research institutions, advocacy groups, civil society, and traditional leadership—is equally important, providing legitimacy in terms of both representation and credibility. Likewise, extensive and robust stakeholder engagement led by the PCC while drafting and finalizing the JETF helped create a shared vision of how South Africa can build a zero-carbon economy by 2050 while upholding the three principles of procedural, distributional, and restorative justice.

Managing impacts will require a multisectoral approach, with collaboration and coordination between the national governments, local governments, the private sector, community groups, and so on. Taking such an approach has allowed South Africa to secure commitments from the private sector and others.

A just transition protects people and the environment. It helps workers and communities build and access new economic opportunities in the transition to clean energy.

It also ensures that those most impacted by the transition help create the plans, policies, and reforms that will strengthen the institutions and mobilize the investments needed to remediate the land, support people in their post-transition jobs and lives, and build a new economic future. Deeply vested international, national, and local political economy issues can hamper early planning discussions, and a poorly managed closure process will only build opposition, eroding public support for further closures. Proper planning and preparation are essential to demonstrate from the outset that there is a better way to transition away from coal. If planned and implemented effectively, the transition process can create significant opportunities. For example, while 0.6 million jobs are expected to be lost during the transition, 1.6 million jobs may be gained.

The current energy crisis has highlighted the need for a long-term strategy for energy production and distribution in South Africa. In the coming years, the country will need to invest in modernizing its energy infrastructure and diversifying its energy sources to ensure it can meet the growing demand for electricity and avoid future crises. The government of South Africa will need to make difficult decisions as it aims to diversify its energy sources and reduce its environmental impact. Its integrated policymaking, robust regulations, and effective incentives for low-carbon investments—including private investments—give it an advantage in accomplishing this task (IEA 2021e), while its emphasis on energy efficiency and regional integration strengthens its position.

Ensuring a Just Transition: United Kingdom, Germany, and the Netherlands

Case Study 25. Lessons from the United Kingdom, Germany, and the Netherlands

Contributor: Catrina Godinho

Evidence from previous structural transitions away from coal reveals several key issues and approaches that are decisive in determining the socioeconomic impacts of these transitions. Although insights are collected and organized in different ways across the literature, there is a good degree of convergence on high-level lessons and approaches. These are outlined here with reference to ongoing coal transitions in the United Kingdom (on track to phase out by 2024), the Netherlands (by 2030), and Germany (by 2038).

Lesson 1. Declining Employment in the Coal Sector Is Unavoidable, Driven as It Is by Multiple Factors and Not Just the Result of Environmental Policies

Historical and present-day coal transitions are not solely the result of policies targeting the coal sector. Rarely motivated primarily by environmental concerns, they are more often driven by other factors, including the following:

- The declining performance of domestic coal industries, especially where subsidies or other public support are rationalized or removed, or where global trade dynamics shift
- The declining competitiveness of coal compared with other energy technologies—historically, oil and gas; currently, renewables—especially where market rules, procurement, or other institutional factors select for least-cost options
- Economic transitions that lead to offshoring some industries, reducing energy or coal demand and employment shifts from primary to secondary and tertiary sectors
- Gains in efficiency, mechanization, and automation, which can change the structure of the coal sector, especially in terms of final energy demand and employment

These drivers lead to declining employment in the coal sector, even in cases where coal production and use increase. So, declining employment in the coal sector is not only driven by environmental or climate considerations. It is something to be expected, and planned for, in all possible scenarios.

Lesson 2. Well-Managed Coal Transitions Have Lesser Short-Term Impacts and Can Avoid Long-Term Effects

Even when accelerated, coal transitions typically take decades, with older, poor-performing, or economically unviable mines and power plants closing first. Without proper planning and policies to facilitate the transition, shocks can lead to volatile sociopolitical conditions, and coal regions ultimately suffer economic and social decline. The "unmanaged shock" of the British coal transition provides examples of both risks: first, with the dramatic mining strikes and industrial disputes in response to coal closure plans in the 1970s and 1980s; and second, in the long-term negative impacts in former coal communities, which continue to suffer lower job density, worse health outcomes, and higher unemployment, deprivation, and depopulation than the national average (Brauers, Oei, and Walk 2020). At the other extreme, the "managed delay" approach of Germany's ongoing 60+ year coal decline (figure 3.24)—with its protectionist policies and public subsidies to the sector—was much more expensive. The German parliament estimated that just the phaseout period from 2006 to 2018, during which hard coal but not lignite was phased out, cost an estimated €38 billion, but the socioeconomic impacts have been better (Oei, Brauers, and Herpich 2019). The Dutch 10-year coal phase-down, by contrast, shows that a well-planned transition does not have to have severe long-term adverse impacts or high costs, although the sector was relatively small and the transition was aided by significant natural gas availability. But the Dutch adjustment was also well planned, with substantial support for workers who lost their jobs. As such, it was supported by the trade unions and, for the most part, went smoothly.

FIGURE 3.24 Coal Production and Employment in the United Kingdom and Germany, 1958–2018

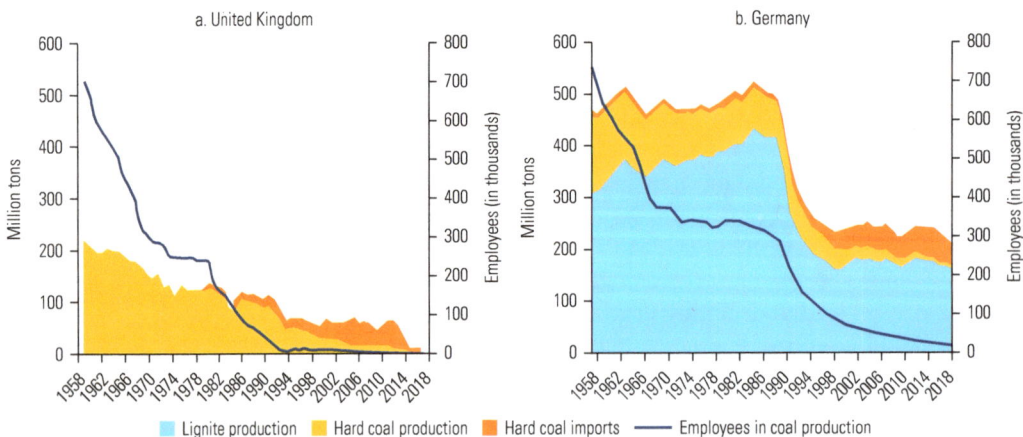

Source: Brauers, Oei, and Walk 2020.

Note: The United Kingdom phased out coal production in around 30+ years, while it took Germany 60+ years, despite similar economic conditions.

Lesson 3. Long-Term Policy Package Approaches, Developed with Key Stakeholders, Underpin Successes

There are large benefits to starting coal transition planning early, before significant negative impacts are visible. This can include early efforts to gradually reduce coal production and consumption to smooth the transition, prevent lock-in effects and reduce stranded asset risks, and favor diversification (thus avoiding industrial concentration). Successful strategies also tend to involve policy packages that combine structural reforms with more targeted support. For example, structural policies may be geared toward increasing resilience to shocks—such as improving access to financial instruments and borrowing; strengthening social safety nets, critical infrastructure and related services, and health care; facilitating greater labor market flexibility and mobility; and creating alternative employment by incentivizing economic innovation and diversification. Targeted policies aimed at affected workers, such as early retirement packages or financial and reemployment support, can exist alongside broader community or regional level initiatives, such as skills training, investments in human capital, local economic development programs, and environmental regeneration.

A key lesson is the importance of human and economic development interventions, as opposed to simple compensation mechanisms, for managing longer-term impacts. Using this approach ensures that coal transition planning can be part of or a catalyst for regional and national socioeconomic development plans, including attracting financing. Common elements include investing in and putting measures in place to improve infrastructure; developing policies and regulations to attract new businesses, education, and skills programs; supporting research and development; and expanding soft location factors in mining regions—such as tertiary education institutions and cultural, leisure, and natural infrastructure—to attract the inward and prevent the outward migration of people, business, and investment (Diluiso et al. 2021).

Local ownership of, participation in, and early mobilization for policy design and implementation are also important. Local economic development and diversification are key, and policy design needs to respond to local needs and wants. Economic structures in coal regions are often concentrated around coal and related industries, and coal tends to be important culturally. Inclusive processes; local leadership; and mobilizing public, private, nongovernmental, and other actors can help develop locally relevant and responsive transition plans. Building consensus around the need to transition and developing policies that are guided by community needs and visions of an attractive alternative contributes to political acceptability. In Germany's Ruhr coal region, for example, the transition was made tangible by transforming previous industrial sites into landmarks or cultural sites, marking a break with the past and unveiling a more forward-looking vision for the region while still maintaining a distinct local identity, in addition to extensive training and reskilling for renewable energy jobs.

Other initiatives included opening universities, expanding the education system, and improving transport infrastructure.

Activating local stakeholders can also help with implementation. For example, coal companies can provide skills training and jobs transition support; local government, unions, or community groups can coordinate dialogue processes; and local business initiatives can collaborate to create alternative or diversify employment opportunities—for example, by repurposing coal plants or pivoting production or services to an alternative industry. Institutional capacity support may also be needed to ensure local actors can, and are incentivized to, fulfill these functions. In the Ukraine coal adjustment, which is slightly different from a coal transition, employment was reduced by one-third in just four years (1998–2002) without any major sociopolitical backlash. In this case, strengthening coal industry management by introducing commercial and operational plans and management contracts helped improve governance capacity, accountability, and acceptability. Other success factors included stakeholder engagement and reemployment support.

Gender dimensions can be mainstreamed for more inclusive outcomes. When it comes to specific support for workers, it is worth noting that many indirect jobs are also affected. Policies that only target miners may contribute to excluding and disadvantaging the female workers who rely on the coal sector. There is also some evidence that job transitions might contribute to crowding out female workers when competition for limited jobs increases. For example, before Romania restructured its mining sector, women accounted for 16 percent of the workforce; seven years later, this had reduced to just 7 percent. Gender mainstreaming in policy development can help ensure gender-inclusive transitions and economic development pathways. Policies that include psychological health and support for households or family members are other gender-sensitive approaches.

Lesson 4. Environmental Rehabilitation and Regeneration Are Key Enablers of Alternative Economic Development

Coal mining, power generation, and related industries cause significant environmental degradation that can limit the potential for alternative economic activities, such as farming or tourism. Communities living in coal regions can experience long-term impacts of such environmental pollution—including negative health impacts, poor water quality, soil contamination, and safety issues—long after the industry has left. Historical experiences suggest that this element of coal (or other industrial) transitions is not always adequately planned for, hindering the longer-term economic renewal of former coal-dependent regions. As well as strengthening regulations and enforcement mechanisms (including clearly establishing "polluter pays" mechanisms in mining licenses to create appropriate incentives), earlier and more progressive rehabilitation efforts can ensure environmental legacies are addressed while coal mining companies are still present.

Lesson 5. Nationally Coordinated Fiscal Support Plays an Important Role

Bottom-up and locally led approaches are important, but a successful coal transition requires significant national-level support and coordination. Considerable resources are needed for sectoral adjustments or transitions, and in most historical cases (primarily from the EU), national governments have had to cover them, as local resources have been insufficient and local fiscal capacity was eroded by the economic impact of the coal transition. A full cost-benefit analysis needs to include the cost of direct and hidden coal sector subsidies, and the costs of environmental and public health externalities from coal mining and combustion, which are typically several magnitudes larger than the direct economic benefits of coal use (or the fiscal costs of the coal transition). Countries can use carbon pricing, levies, taxes, and other tools to compensate for these costs and raise revenues to pay for the coal transition. National coordination is especially important in this regard to ensure that raised funds are appropriately directed and fully utilized.

Notes

1. This case study draws heavily from World Bank (forthcoming a), *Operationalizing Long-Term Decarbonization Strategies: Lessons for Practitioners.*

2. Presidential Regulation No. 98/2021.The text of the regulation is available at https://jdih.setkab .go.id/PUUdoc/176561/Salinan_Perpres_Nomor_98_Tahun_2021.pdf.

3. For more information, see the website of the Forest Carbon Partnership Facility at https://www.forestcarbonpartnership.org/country/indonesia.

4. See "Measurement Monitoring and Reporting: Indonesia: East Kalimantan Province," available on the website of the government of East Kalimantan Province at https://mrv.kaltimprov.go.id /en.

5. Emissions data in this paragraph is for 2021 and is provided by the Ministry of Environment and Forestry.

6. The text of the act is available at https://www.legislation.gov.uk/ukpga/2008/27/contents.

7. For example, see the literature summary in Heine and Black (2019).

8. Data are from the Green Transition Navigator, which is available at https://green-transition -navigator.org/.

9. The proposal is still pending formal approval.

10. Based on 2020 data from FAOSTAT, Emissions Total, at https://www.fao.org/faostat/en/#data /GT.

11. This case study draws heavily from World Bank (2020a), "Clean Bus in LAC: Lessons from Chile's Experience with E-mobility: The Integration of E-buses in Santiago."

References

Acosta, P., and M. D. Curt. 2019. "Understanding the Expansion of Oil Palm Cultivation: A Case-Study in Papua." *Journal of Cleaner Production* 219: 199–216. https://doi.org/10.1016/j .jclepro.2019.02.029.

Ahmadi, Y., and A. Yamazaki. 2020. "The Effectiveness of Revenue-Neutral Carbon Taxes." GRIPS Discussion Paper 19-36, National Graduate Institute for Policy Studies.

Aker, J. C., and J. Kelsey. 2021. "Harvesting the Rain: The Adoption of Environmental Technologies in the Sahel." Working Paper 29518, National Bureau of Economic Research. https://doi.org/10.3386 /w29518.

Akinbami, O. M., R. O. Samuel, and M. O. Bodunrin. 2021. "The State of Renewable Energy Development in South Africa: An Overview." *Alexandria Engineering Journal* 60 (6): 5077–93.

Ali, S. 2016. "Egypt, Arab Republic of—Egypt Vehicle Scrapping and Recycling Program: P119483—Implementation Status Results Report: Sequence 03 (English)." World Bank, June 22. https:// documents.worldbank.org/en/publication/documents-reports/documentdetail /554341468023371923/egypt-arab-republic-of-egypt-vehicle-scrapping-and-recycling-program -p119483-implementation-status-results-report-sequence-03.

Arifanti, V. B. 2020. "Mangrove Management and Climate Change: A Review in Indonesia." *IOP Conference Series: Earth and Environmental Science* 487: 012022.

Assunçãoa, J., C. Gandoura, and R. Rochad. 2019. "DETERring Deforestation in the Amazon: Environmental Monitoring and Law Enforcement." https://www.climatepolicyinitiative.org /wp-content/uploads/2019/11/Assuncao-Gandour-Rocha-WP2019-DETERring-Deforestation -in-the-Amazon-1.pdf.

Azevedo, D., H. Wolff, and A. Yamazaki. Forthcoming. "Do Carbon Taxes Kill Jobs? Firm-Level Evidence from British Columbia." *Climate Change Economics.*

Azizuddin, K. 2022. "Colombia Launches First LatAm Green Taxonomy, Excludes Nuclear and Gas." *Responsible Investor*, April 13. https://www.responsible-investor.com/colombia-launches-first -latam-green-taxonomy-excludes-nuclear-and-gas/.

Bandyopadhyay, S. 2017. "Renewable Targets for India." *Clean Technologies and Environmental Policy* 19 (2): 293–94. https://doi.org/10.1007/s10098-017-1335-z.

Banerjee, O., M. Cicowiez, R. Vargas, E. Molina-Pérez, and Ž. Malek. 2022. "Decarbonization of Costa Rica's Agriculture, Forestry and Other Land Uses Sectors: An Application of the IEEM+ ESM Approach." IDB Working Paper 01200. https://publications.iadb.org/en/decarbonization-costa -ricas-agriculture-forestry-and-other-land-uses-sectors-application-ie em-esm.

Basel Committee. 2022. "Principles for the Effective Management and Supervision of Climate-Related Financial Risks." https://www.bis.org/bcbs/publ/d532.htm.

Bataille, C., H. Waisman, and A. Vogt-Schib. 2021. "Deep Decarbonization Pathways in Latin America and the Caribbean (DDP-LAC): An Assessment of Low-Emission Development Strategies in Six LAC Countries." *Energy Strategy Review*. https://www.sciencedirect.com/journal/energy -strategy-reviews/special-issue/105SPX6M5R6.

Beck, M., N. Rivers, R. Wigle, and H. Yonezawa. 2015. "Carbon Tax and Revenue Recycling: Impacts on Households in BC." *Resource and Energy Economics* 41: 40–69.

Behuria, P. 2020. "The Politics of Late Development in Renewable Energy Sectors: Dependency and Contradictory Tensions in India's National Solar Mission." *World Development* 126. https://doi .org/10.1016/j.worlddev.2019.104726.

Blondel, B., C. Mispelon, and J. Ferguson. 2011. "Cycle More Often 2 Cool Down the Planet: Quantifying CO_2 Savings of Cycling." European Cyclists' Federation. https://ecf.com/files /wp-content/uploads/ECF_BROCHURE_EN_planche.pdf.

BloombergNEF. 2022. "Energy Transition Investment. Investment and Valuation." https://www.bnef .com/interactive-datasets/2d5d59acd9000005?data-hub=3.

Bocca, R., and M. Ashraf. 2022. "Net-Zero Industry Tracker, 2022 Edition." World Economic Forum. https://www.weforum.org/reports/the-net-zero-industry-tracker/.

Braganca, A., and R. Dahis. 2021. "Cutting Special Interests by the Roots: Evidence from the Brazilian Amazon." Working Paper 004, Climate Policy Initiative, Rio de Janeiro.

Brauers, H., P.-Y. Oei, and P. Walk. 2020. "Comparing Coal Phase-Out Pathways: The United Kingdom's and Germany's Diverging Transitions." *Environmental Innovation and Societal Transitions* 37: 38–253.

Bungane, B. 2021. "SAWEA: Mpumalanga Is a Key Location to Drive Just Energy Transition." *ESI Africa*, January 19. https://www.esi-africa.com/renewable-energy/sawea-mpumalanga-is-a-key -location-to-drive-just-energy-transition/.

Calfucoy, P., M. T. Gunfaus, A. Fazekas, and A. Vogt-Schilb. 2022. *Long-Term Strategies for Decarbonization in Latin America: Learnings from Actor-Based Insights into the Drafting Process.* IDB Working Paper 1361. https://unfccc.int/sites/default/files/resource/202209061139---Long -Term-Strategies-for-Decarbonization-in-Latin-America-Learnings-.pdf.

Cao, J., M. S. Ho, R. Ma, and F. Teng. 2021. "When Carbon Emission Trading Meets Regulated Industry: Evidence from the Electricity Sector in China." *Journal of Public Economics* 200: 104470.

Carattini, S., M. Carvahlo, and S. Fankhauser. 2018. "Overcoming Public Resistance to Carbon Taxes." *Wiley Interdisciplinary Reviews: Climate Change* 9 (2): e531.

Carbon Partnership Facility. 2023. "Egypt: Vehicle Scrapping and Recycling Program." https://cpf .wbcarbonfinance.org/programs/egypt-vehicle-scrapping-and-recycling-program.

Castrejón-Godínez, M. L., L. Ortiz-Hernandez, E. Sanchez-Salinas, and A. Rodriguez. 2015. "Management of Municipal Solid Waste in Mexico." https://www.researchgate.net/publication /292326943_MANAGEMENT_OF_MUNICIPAL_SOLID_WASTE_IN_MEXICO.

CCAC (Climate and Clean Air Coalition) Secretariat. 2021. "Improved Waste Management Is Key to Delivering the Methane Cuts Needed to Prevent Catastrophic Warming." CCAC Secretariat, Paris. https://www.ccacoalition.org/en/news/improved-waste-management-key-delivering-methane-cuts-needed-prevent-catastrophic-warming.

CCC (Climate Change Committee). 2020. "The UK Climate Change Act." CCC Insights Briefing 1. https://www.theccc.org.uk/wp-content/uploads/2020/10/CCC-Insights-Briefing-1-The-UK-Climate-Change-Act.pdf.

CCC (Climate Change Committee). 2021. "International Action on Climate Change." https://www.theccc.org.uk/international-action-on-climate-change/#:~:text=TheUKClimateChangeCommittee,2008UKClimateChangeAct.

CCC (Climate Change Committee). 2022. *Progress in Reducing Emissions: 2022 Report to Parliament.* https://www.theccc.org.uk/publication/2022-progress-report-to-parliament/.

Centre for Public Impact. 2016. "Green Legislation: The Climate Change Act 2008." https://www.centreforpublicimpact.org/case-study/climate-change-act-uk.

Centro de Estudios Regulatorios. 2021a. "Superfinanciera Circular Externa 007 de 2021." https://www.cerlatam.com/normatividad/superfinanciera-circular-externa-007-de-2021/.

Centro de Estudios Regulatorios. 2021b. "Superfinanciera Circular Externa 008 de 2021." https://www.cerlatam.com/normatividad/superfinanciera-circul ar-externa-008-de-2021/.

Cheng, C., A. Blakers, M. Stocks, and B. Lu. 2022. "100% Renewable Energy in Japan." *Energy Conversion and Management* 255: 115299. https://doi.org/10.1016/j.enconman.2022.115299.

Chiavari, J., and C. Leme Lopes. 2015. "Brazil's New Forest Code. Part I: How to Navigate the Complexity." Policy Brief, Climate Policy Initiative (CPI) and NAPC/PUC-Rio.

Chrysolite, H., A. F. Utami, D. Mahardika, A. Wijaya, J-C. Altamirano, and M. Ge. 2020. "Looking Past the Horizon: The Case for Indonesia's Long-Term Strategy for Climate Action." Working Paper, WRI Indonesia. https://files.wri.org/d8/s3fs-public/looking-past-horizon.pdf.

Client Earth. 2022. "We've Won Our Case against the UK Government's Inadequate Net Zero Strategy." *ClientEarth Communications.* https://www.clientearth.org/latest/latest-updates/news/clientearth-are-suing-the-uk-government-over-its-net-zero-strategy/.

ClimateWatch. 2022. "Global Historical Emissions." https://www.climatewatchdata.org/ghg-emissions?end_year=2019&start_year=1990.

ClimateWatch. (n.d.). "Historical GHG Emissions." https://www.climatewatchdata.org/ghg-emissions?break By=countries&end_year=2019&regions=GBR&sectors=total-including-lucf&start_year=1990 (retrieved July 21, 2022).

Cui, J., C. Wang, J. Zhang, and Y. Zheng. 2020. "The Effectiveness of China's Regional Carbon Market Pilots in Reducing Emissions." *Proceedings of the National Academy of Sciences* 118 (52): e109912118.

De Janvry, A., E. Sadoulet, and T. Suri. 2017. "Field Experiments in Developing Country Agriculture." In *Handbook of Economic Field Experiments,* vol. 2, edited by Abhijit Vinayak Banerjee and Esther Duflo, 427–66. Amsterdam: North-Holland.

Department of Mineral Resources and Energy. 2019. "Integrated Resource Plan 2019." Pretoria. http://www.energy.gov.za/IRP/2019/IRP-2019.pdf.

Department of Transport. 2018. "Green Transport Strategy for South Africa: (2018–2050)." Pretoria. https://www.transport.gov.za/documents/11623/89294/Green_Transport_Strategy_2018_2050_onlineversion.pdf/71e19f1d-259e-4c55-9b27-30db418f105a.

Department of Transport. 2022. "Bus Rapid Transit System (BRT)." Pretoria. https://www.transport.gov.za/bus-rapid-transport.

Dercon, S., and L. Christiaensen. 2011. "Consumption Risk, Technology Adoption and Poverty Traps: Evidence from Ethiopia." *Journal of Development Economics* 96 (2): 159–73.

Diluiso, F., P. Walk, N. Manych, N. Cerutti, V. Chipiga, A. Workman, C. Ayas, et al. 2021. "Coal Transitions—Part 1: A Systematic Map and Review of Case Study Learnings from Regional, National, and Local Coal Phase-Out Experiences." *Environmental Research Letters* 16: 113003. https://iopscience.iop.org/article/10.1088/1748-9326/ac1b58/pdf.

Dinkelman, T. 2011. "The Effects of Rural Electrification on Employment: New Evidence from South Africa." *American Economic Review* 101 (7): 3078–108.

DNP (Departmento Nacional de Planeación). 2022. "Financiamiento Climático General en Cifra." https://mrv.dnp.gov.co/Financiamiento_en_cifras/Paginas/general_cifras.aspx.

Dubey, S., E. Adovor, D. Rysankova, and B. Koo. 2020. *Kenya: Beyond Connections*. Washington, DC: World Bank. https://elibrary.worldbank.org/doi/abs/10.1596/35268.

Econoler International. 2016. "Market Assessment Report for Energy Efficiency in Public Buildings." Prepared by Econoler International on behalf of the Turkish Ministry of Energy and Natural Resources under the World Bank–GEF Small and Medium Enterprise Energy Efficiency Project.

Economist. 2022. "India Is Likely to Be the World's Fastest-Growing Big Economy This Year." May 14. https://www.economist.com/briefing/2022/05/14/india-is-likely-to-be-the-worlds-fastest -growing-big-economy-this-year.

Ecopetrol. 2020. "Mitigation." https://www.ecopetrol.com.co/wps/portal/Home/en/Corporate responsibility/Environment/Climate%20action.

EIA (Energy Information Administration). 2022. "Colombia." https://www.eia.gov/international /analysis/country/COL.

ELLA (Evidence and Lessons from Latin America). 2011. "Turning Waste into Resources: Latin America's Waste-to-Energy Landfills. Evidence and Lessons from Latin America."

Energy and Petroleum Regulatory Authority. 2021. "Electricity and Petroleum Report: Quarter Two (April–June 2021)." Nairobi.

ESMAP (Energy Sector Management Assistance Program). 2017. "Energy Subsidy Reform Facility Country Brief: Egypt." Report 120075, ESMAP. https://documents.worldbank.org/en /publication/documents-reports/documentdetail/873871506492500301/energy-subsidy-reform -facility-country-brief-egypt.

ET Bureau. 2021. "Govt to Float 4,000 MWh Battery Storage Tenders: R K Singh." *Economic Times,* July 15. https://economictimes.indiatimes.com/industry/renewables/govt-to-float-4000-mwh -battery-storage-tenders-r-k-singh/articleshow/84434524.cms?from=mdr.

European Parliamentary Research Service. 2023. "EU Carbon Border Adjustment Mechanism. Implications for Climate and Competitiveness." https://www.europarl.europa.eu/thinktank/en /document/EPRS_BRI(2022)698889#:~:text=The%20CBAM%20aims%20to%20contribute, supported%20in%20their%20climate%20transitions.

Evans, S. 2019. "In-Depth Q&A: The UK Becomes First Major Economy to Set Net-Zero Climate Goal." *Carbon Brief.* https://www.carbonbrief.org/in-depth-qa-the-uk-becomes-first-major -economy-to-set-net-zero-climate-goal/.

Ezawa, M. 2021. "Energy Efficiency Benchmark System of Japan." Agency for Natural Resources and Energy. https://iea.blob.core.windows.net/assets/2867cfa4-5184-4d4e-801b-c545de7e8900/2 .Mr.MasanaEZAWA%2CMETI17-03BenchmarkingWorkshop.pdf.

Fankhauser, S., A. Averchenkova, and J. Finnegan. 2018. "10 Years of the UK Climate Change Act." Policy Report, London School of Economics. https://www.lse.ac.uk/granthaminstitute/publication /10-years-climate-change-act/.

FAO (Food and Agriculture Organization of the United Nations). 2018. "Emissions Due to Agriculture: Global, Regional and Country Trends 2000–2018." FAOSTAT Analytical Brief 18, Rome.

FAO (Food and Agriculture Organization of the United Nations). 2020. "FAOSTAT: Emissions Total, 2020 Data." https://www.fao.org/faostat/en/#data/GT.

Faye, B., H. Webber, J. B. Naab, D. S. MacCarthy, M. Adam, F. Ewert, J. P. A. Lamers, et al. 2018. "Impacts of 1.5 Versus 2.0°C on Cereal Yields in the West African Sudan Savanna." *Environmental Research Letters* 13 (3): 034014.

Fearnside, P. 2017. "Deforestation of the Brazilian Amazon." In *Oxford Research Encyclopedia of Environmental Science.* Oxford University Press. https://doi.org/10.1093/acrefore/9780199389414 .013.102.

Federación Colombiana de Municipios and Dirección Nacional Simit. 2020. "Transitemos 2019." https://www.fcm.org.co/wp-content/uploads/2021/04/Transitemos_v4-comprimido.pdf.

Fischer, C., and A. Fox. 2012. "Comparing Policies to Combat Emissions Leakage: Border Carbon Adjustments Versus Rebates." *Journal of Environmental Economics and Management* 64 (2): 199–216.

Foster, V., N. Gorgulu, S. Straub, and M. Vagliasindi. 2023. "The Impact of Infrastructure on Development Outcomes: A Qualitative Review of Four Decades of Literature." Policy Research Working Paper 10343, World Bank, Washington, DC. http://hdl.handle.net/10986/39515 License: CC BY-NC 3.0 IGO.

Fried, S., and D. Lagakos. 2021. "Rural Electrification, Migration and Structural Transformation: Evidence from Ethiopia." *Regional Science and Urban Economics* 91: 103625.

Gatticchi, G. 2020. "Energy Transition Threatens 120,000 South African Coal Jobs." *Bloomberg,* November 5.

GEF (Global Environment Facility). 2001. "Methane Capture and Use (Landfill Demonstration Project)." https://www.thegef.org/projects-operations/projects/784.

GIZ (Deutsche Gesellschaft für Internationale Zusammenarbeit). 2014. "TRANSPeru: Peru's Sustainable Urban Transport NAMA: An Overview." http://www.transferproject.org/wp-content /uploads/2014/04/Overview_PERU_TRANSPeru.pdf.

Gopaul, A., E. Friedrich, and D. Stretch. 2019. "Public Transportation and Greenhouse Gas Emissions: A Case Study of the eThekwini Municipality, South Africa." *Current Trends in Civil and Structural Engineering* 3 (1). https://doi.org/10.33552/CTCSE.MS.ID.000553.

Government of Chile. 2021. "National Electromobility Strategy Launch: Government Announces that Only Electric Vehicles Will Be Sold in Chile by 2035." Press release, October 18. https://www.gob .cl/en/news/national-electromobility-strategy-launch-government-announces-only-electric-vehicles -will-be-sold-chile-2035/.

Government of Costa Rica. 2000. *Primera Comunicación Nacional ante la Convención Marco de Cambio Climático.* https://unfccc.int/resource/docs/natc/cornc1.pdf.

Government of Costa Rica. 2019. *Cuarta Comunicación Nacional: Convención Marco de las Naciones Unidas sobre Cambio Cllimático.* https://unfccc.int/sites/default/files/resource/Cuarta ComunicacionCC202_Costa%20Rica.pdf.

Government of Costa Rica. 2020. *Contribución Nacionalmente Determinada 2020.* https://unfccc.int /sites/default/files/NDC/2022-06/Contribucio%CC%81n%20Nacionalmente%20 Determinada%20de%20Costa%20Rica%202020%20-%20Versio%CC%81n%20Completa.pdf.

Government of India. 2014. "India INDC to UNFCCC." https://www4.unfccc.int/sites/ndcstaging /PublishedDocuments/India%20First/INDIA%20INDC%20TO%20UNFCCC.pdf.

Government of India. 2022. "India's Updated First Nationally Determined Contribution under Paris Agreement (2021–2030)." Submission to UNFCCC. https://unfccc.int/sites/default/files/NDC /2022-08/India%20Updated%20First%20Nationally%20Determined%20Contrib.pdf.

Government of Indonesia. 2016. "Indonesia's Nationally Determined Contribution (NDC)." Jakarta.

Government of the United Kingdom. 2019. "The Climate Change Act 2008 (2050 Target Amendment) Order 2019." https://www.legislation.gov.uk/ukdsi/2019/9780111187654.

Government of the United Kingdom. 2021. "UK Enshrines New Target in Law to Slash Emissions by 78% by 2035." Press release, April 20. https://www.gov.uk/government/news/uk-enshrines-new -target-in-law-to-slash-emissions-by-78-by-2035#:~:text=change%20and%20energy-,UK%20 enshrines%20new%20target%20in%20law,emissions%20by%2078%25%20by%20 2035andtext=The%20UK's%20sixth%20Carbon%20Budget,to%20net%20zero%20by%202050.

Groves, D. G., and R. J. Lempert. 2007. "A New Analytic Method for Finding Policy-Relevant Scenarios." *Global Environmental Change* 17 (1): 73–85.

Groves, D. G., E. Molina-Perez, J. Syme, G. Alvarado, F. De León Denegri, J. D. Acuña Román, and A. Jenkins Rojas. 2022. *A Green Costa Rican COVID-19 Recovery: Aligning Costa Rica's Decarbonization Investments with Economic Recovery.* Santa Monica, CA: RAND. https://www .rand.org/pubs/research_reports/RRA1381-1.html.

Groves, D. G., J. Syme, E. Molina-Perez, C. Calvo Hernandez, L. F. Víctor-Gallardo, G. Godinez-Zamora, J. Quirós-Tortós, F. De León Denegri, M. Meza Murillo, V. Saavedra Gómez, and A. Vogt-Schilb. 2020. *The Benefits and Costs of Decarbonizing Costa Rica's Economy: Informing the Implementation of Costa Rica's National Decarbonization Plan under Uncertainty.* Santa Monica, CA: RAND. https://www.rand.org/pubs/research_reports/RRA633-1.html.

Hallegatte, S., J. Rentschler, and J. Rozenberg. 2020. *Adaptation Principles: A Guide for Designing Strategies for Climate Change Adaptation and Resilience.* Washington, DC: World Bank. https:// openknowledge.worldbank.org/handle/10986/34780.

Heine, D., and S. Black. 2019. "Benefits beyond Climate: Environmental Tax Reform." In *Fiscal Policies for Development and Climate Action*, edited by M. A. Pigato, 1–63. Washington, DC: World Bank.

Hereher, M., R. Eissa, A. Alqasemi, and A. M. El Kenaw. 2021. "Assessment of Air Pollution at Greater Cairo in Relation to the Spatial Variability of Surface Urban Heat Island." *Environmental Science and Pollution Research* 29: 21412–25.

Hill, R., N. M. Chaherli, N. Nguyen, A. Ouedraogo, E. Ouedraogo, N. Traore, J. Tougma, B. Nyamba, and F. Bayala. 2019. *Burkina Faso Rural Income Diagnostic.* Washington, DC: World Bank.

Hodder, G., and M. Richards. 2022. "Transitioning from Coal to Renewables in Africa." White & Case, May 31. https://www.jdsupra.com/legalnews/transitioning-from-coal-to-renewables-6194777/.

IASS (Institute for Advanced Sustainability Studies), IET (International Energy Transition), and CSIR (Council for Scientific and Industrial Research). 2022. "From Coal to Renewables in Mpumalanga: Employment Effects, Opportunities for Local Value Creation, Skills Requirements, and Gender-Inclusiveness—Assessing the Co-benefits of Decarbonising South Africa's Power Sector." COBENEFITS Executive Report, Potsdam and Pretoria. https://publications.rifs-potsdam.de /rest/items/item_6001449_5/component/file_6001450/content.

ICAP (International Carbon Action Partnership). 2021. "China Releases Instructions for the First Compliance Cycle of the National ETS and Procedures for Offset Use." *ETS-News*, November 23. https://icapcarbonaction.com/en/news/chin a-releases-instructions-first-compliance-cycle-national -ets-and-procedures-offset-use.

ICAP (International Carbon Action Partnership). 2023. "China Releases Allocation Plan and Compliance Arrangements for 2021 and 2022." *ETS-News*, March 27.

ICCN (International Climate Councils Network). 2021. "ICCN Work." https://climatecouncilsnetwork .org/iccn-work/.

ICLEI Africa. 2019. *Local Government Climate Change Support Programme: A Practical Systematic Guide Towards Unlocking Municipal Climate Finance.* Pretoria: Department of Environment Forestry and Fisheries

IEA (International Energy Agency). 2017. "Act on the Rational Use of Energy (Energy Efficiency Act)." https://www.iea.org/policies/573-act-on-the-rational-use-of-energy-energy-efficiency-act.

IEA (International Energy Agency). 2018. *Energy Policies Beyond IEA Countries: Chile 2018 Review.* https://www.iea.org/reports/energy-policies-beyond-iea-countries-chile-2018-review.

IEA (International Energy Agency). 2019. "Kenya Key Energy Statistics 2019." https://www.iea.org/countries/kenya.

IEA (International Energy Agency). 2020a. "Colombia Key Energy Statistics, 2019." https://www.iea.org/countries/colombia.

IEA (International Energy Agency). 2020b. "India 2020." *Energy Policy Review.* https://iea.blob.core.windows.net/assets/2571ae38-c895-430e-8b62-bc19019c6807/India_2020_Energy_Policy_Review.pdf.

IEA (International Energy Agency). 2020c. "Japan Key Energy Statistics." https://www.iea.org/countries/japan.

IEA (International Energy Agency). 2021a. *Energy and Climate Change.* Paris: IEA. https://www.iea.org/reports/energy-and-climate-change.

IEA (International Energy Agency). 2021b. "India Energy Outlook 2021." https://www.iea.org/reports/india-energy-outlook-2021.

IEA (International Energy Agency). 2021c. "Japan 2021." *Energy Policy Review.* https://iea.blob.core.windows.net/assets/3470b395-cfdd-44a9-9184-0537cf069c3d/Japan2021_EnergyPolicyReview.pdf.

IEA (International Energy Agency). 2021d. "Jawaharlal Nehru National Solar Mission (Phase I, II and III)." https://www.iea.org/policies/4916-jawaharlal-nehru-national-solar-mission-phase-i-ii-and-iii.

IEA (International Energy Agency). 2021e. "South Africa." https://www.iea.org/countries/south-africa.

IEA (International Energy Agency). 2022a. "Buildings: Sectorial Overview." https://www.iea.org/reports/buildings.

IEA (International Energy Agency). 2022b. "Egypt: Key Energy Statistics." https://www.iea.org/countries/egypt

IEA (International Energy Agency). 2022c. "Global CO_2 Emissions Rebounded to Their Highest Level in History in 2021." Press release, March 8. https://www.iea.org/news/global-co2-emissions-rebounded-to-their-highest-level-in-history-in-2021.

IEA (International Energy Agency). 2022d. "IEA Key Statements and Communications on the Natural Gas Crisis in EU." https://www.iea.org/news/iea-key-statements-and-communications-on-the-natural-gas-crisis-in-europe.

IEA (International Energy Agency). 2022e. "India: IEA Country Energy Profile." https://www.iea.org/countries/india#analysis.

IEA (International Energy Agency). 2022f. "Russia's War on Ukraine." https://www.iea.org/topics/russia-s-war-on-ukraine.

IEA (International Energy Agency). 2022g. "Ten Milestones in 2021: Increasing Natural Gas Users." https://www.iea.org/policies/13176-ten-milestones-in-2021-increasing-natural-gas-users.

IEA (International Energy Agency). 2022h. "United Kingdom." https://www.iea.org/countries/united-kingdom.

IEA (International Energy Agency). 2023. "Data and Statistics. South Africa." https://www.iea.org/data-and-statistics (accessed March 8, 2023).

IFC (International Finance Corporation). 2019. "IFC Invests $200 Million in a New Fund to Boost Small Business Lending in Emerging Markets." Press release, July 28. https://pressroom.ifc.org /All/Pages/PressDetail.aspx?ID=27116

IFC (International Finance Corporation). 2020. "Scaling Infrastructure: Rewa Solar (India)— Removing Barriers to Scale." https://www.ifc.org/en/types/insights-reports/2010/scaling-infra -rewa-solar-india.

IFC (International Finance Corporation). 2023. "EDGE: Find an Expert." https://app.edgebuildings .com/edge-experts.

IISD (International Institute for Sustainable Development). 2018. "Story 8: The Evolution of the Clean Energy Cess on Coal Production in India." https://www.iisd.org/system/files/publications /stories-g20-india-en.pdf.

INPE (National Institute for Space Research). 2021. Portal TerraBrasilis. http://terrabrasilis.dpi.inpe .br/en/home-page.

IPAC (International Programme for Action on Climate). 2021. "The UK's Pioneering Climate Change Act." https://www.oecd.org/climate-action/ipac/webbooks-practices/dynamic/ipac-case-studies /c08c3d7a/pdf/the-united-kingdom-s-pioneering-climate-change-act.pdf.

IPCC (Intergovernmental Panel on Climate Change). 2007. Climate Change 2007: Synthesis Report. Geneva: IPCC. https://www.ipcc.ch/report/ar4/syr/.

IPCC (Intergovernmental Panel on Climate Change). 2019. 2019 Refinement to the 2006 IPCC Guidelines for National Greenhouse Gas Inventories. Geneva: IPCC. https://www.ipcc.ch/report /2019-refinement-to-the-2006-ipcc-guidelines-for-national-greenhouse-gas-inventories/.

IPCC (Intergovernmental Panel on Climate Climate). 2022. "Africa." In Climate Change 2022: Impacts, Adaptation and Vulnerability—Working Group II Contribution to the Sixth Assessment Report of the Intergovernmental Panel on Climate Change, edited by H.-O. Pörtner, D. C. Roberts, et al., 907–1040. Cambridge, UK: Cambridge University Press.

IRENA (International Renewable Energy Association). 2021. Renewable Energy and Jobs: Annual Review 2021. Masdar City, United Arab Emirates: IRENA. https://www.irena.org/-/media/Files /IRENA/Agency/Publication/2021/Oct/IRENA_RE_Jobs_2021.pdf.

Jaiswal, S., and R. Gadre. 2022. "Financing India's 2030 Renewables Ambition." White paper, BloombergNEF. https://about.bnef.com/blog/financing-indias-2030-renewables-ambition/.

Jaramillo, M., J. Quirós-Tortós, A. Vogt-Schilb, A. Money, and M. Howells. 2023. Data-to-Deal (D2D): Open Data and Modeling of Long-Term Strategies to Financial Resource Mobilization—The Case of Costa Rica. Cambridge Open Engage. https://www.doi.org/10.33774/coe-2023-sqbfm-v3.

Jimenez, R. 2017. "Development Effects of Rural Electrification." Policy Brief, InterAmerican Development Bank, Washington, DC.

Johnson, C. 2013. "Indonesia: Forest Rights of Indigenous Peoples Affirmed." https://www.loc.gov/item /global-legal-monitor/2013-06-03/indonesia-forest-rights-of-indigenous-peoples-affirmed/.

Jones, M., F. Kondylis, J. Loeser, and J. Magruder. 2022. "Factor Market Failures and the Adoption of Irrigation in Rwanda." American Economic Review 112 (7): 2316–52.

Jong, H. N. 2022. "Mapping of Indigenous Lands Ramps Up in Indonesia—Without Official Recognition." Mongabay, September 7. https://news.mongabay.com/2022/09/mapping-of -indigenous-lands-ramps-up-in-indonesia-without-official-recognition/.

Kaza, S., S. Shrikanth, and S. Chaudhary. 2021. "More Growth, Less Garbage." World Bank, Washington, DC. https://openknowledge.worldbank.org/handle/10986/35998.

KenGen. 2021. Honouring Our Promise: Integrated Annual Report Financial Statements for the Year Ended 30 June 2021. https://www.kengen.co.ke/images/2021/15-KenGen-IR.pdf.

Kenya National Bureau of Statistics. 2021a. *Kenya National Bureau of Statistics Economic Survey.* Nairobi: Kenya National Bureau of Statistics. https://www.knbs.or.ke/wp-content/uploads/2021/09/Economic-Survey-2021.pdf.

Kenya National Bureau of Statistics. 2021b. "Kenya Data Portal." https://kenya.opendataforafrica.org/.

Kiely, L., D. V. Spracklen, S. R. Arnold, E. Papargyropoulou, L. Conibear, C. Wiedinmyer, C. Knote, and H. A. Adrianto. 2021. "Assessing Costs of Indonesian Fires and the Benefits of Restoring Peatland." *Nature Communications* 12 (1): 7044.

Kilumelume, M., B. Morando, C. Newman, and J. Rand. 2022. "Spillovers from Extractive Industries." WIDER Working Paper 2022/10, United Nations University World Institute for Development Economics Research, Helsinki.

Lal, R. 2004. "Soil Carbon Sequestration to Mitigate Climate Change." *Geoderma* 123 (1): 1–22.

LBNL (Lawrence Berkeley National Laboratory). 2022. "Pathways for Electrification of South Asia's Transportation Sector." Policy Brief. https://international.lbl.gov/publications/pathways-electrification-south-asia-s.

Lefevre, B. 2014. "Peru's Climate Leaders Awarded over $11 Million for Low-Carbon Urban Transport." *Insights,* December 12. https://www.wri.org/insights/perus-climate-leaders-awarded-over-11-million-low-carbon-urban-transport.

Lozada Andrade, C. 2021. "The Transformation of Colombia's Green Buildings Market: From Zero to 20% in Four Years." EDGE. https://edgebuildings.com/the-transformation-of-colombias-green-building-market-from-zero-to-20-percent/.

LSE (London School of Economics and Political Science). 2022. "Climate Change Laws of the World: Japan." https://climate-laws.org/geographies/japan/laws/law-concerning-the-rational-use-of-energy-energy-conservation-act-law-no-49-of-1979.

Mahachi, T., and A. Rix. 2016. "Energy Yield Analysis and Evaluation of Solar Irradiance Models for a Utility Scale Solar PV Plant in South Africa." Doctoral dissertation, Stellenbosch University. https://core.ac.uk/download/pdf/188220231.pdf.

Makgetla, N. 2021. "The Just Transition in Coal." TIPS Working Paper for the Presidential Climate Commission, Trade and Industrial Policy Strategies, Pretoria. https://www.tips.org.za/images/Working_Paper_PCC_The_Just_Transition_in_coal_2021.pdf.

Manning, D. A. C. 2008. "Biological Enhancement of Soil Carbonate Precipitation: Passive Removal of Atmospheric CO_2." *Mineralogical Magazine* 72 (2): 639–49.

Matlon, P. J. 1985. *Annual Report of ICRISAT/Burkina Economics Program.* Ouagadougou, Burkina Faso: International Crops Research Institute for the Semi-arid Tropics.

Metcalf, G. E. 2019. "On the Economics of a Carbon Tax for the United States." Conference Draft, Brookings Papers on Economic Activity. Brookings Institution, Washington, DC.

Minerals Council South Africa. 2022. "Coal: Facts and Figures." https://www.mineralscouncil.org.za/sa-mining/coal.

Ministerio del Medio Ambiente. 2019. "Tercera Comunicación Nacional de Cambio Climático: Chile."

Ministry of Ecology and Environment. 2020. "2019–2020 National Carbon Emissions Trading Quota Total Setting and Allocation Implementation Plan (Power Generation Industry)" [in Chinese]. https://www.mee.gov.cn/xxgk2018/xxgk/xxgk03/202012/t20201230_815546.html.

Ministry of Ecology and Environment. 2022. "The First Compliance Cycle of the National Carbon Market Ended Successfully" [in Chinese]. Press release, January 1. https://www.mee.gov.cn/ywgz/ydqhbh/wsqtkz/202112/t20211231_965906.shtml.

Ministry of Environment and Forestry. 2021. *State of Indonesia's Forests, 2020.* Jakarta.

Ministry of Environment and Forestry. 2022a. *Operational Plan for Indonesia's FOLU Net Sink 2030.* Minister of Environment and Forestry Decree 168/Menlhk/PKTL/PLA.1/2/2022. https://www .menlhk.go.id/uploads/site/post/1647334063.pdf.

Ministry of Environment and Forestry. 2022b. "State of Indonesia's Forests: Towards FOLU Net Sink 2030." Ministry of Environment and Forestry, Jakarta.

Ministry of Power. 2022. "Power Sector at a Glance: All India." https://powermin.gov.in/en/content /power-sector-glance-all-india.

MNRE (Ministry of New and Renewable Energy). 2022. "Green Energy Corridors." https://mnre.gov .in/green-energy-corridor.

Montmasson-Clair, G. 2021. "A Policy Toolbox for Just Transitions." TIPS Working Paper, Trade and Industrial Policy Strategies. https://justtransitionforall.com/wp-content/uploads/2022/10/TIPS _Working_Paper_Policy_toolbox_for_a_just_transition.pdf.

Moutinho, P., and C. Azevedo-Ramos. 2023. "Untitled Public Forestlands Threaten Amazon Conservation." *Nature Communications* 14: 1152. https://www.nature.com/articles/s414 67-023 -36427-x.

Mullan, K., T. Biggs, J. Cavaglia-Harris, J. Rodrigues Ribeiro, T. O. Santiao, E. Sills, and T. A. P. West. 2022. "Estimating the Value of Near-Real-Time Satellite Information for Monitoring Deforestation in the Brazilian Amazon." Working Paper 22-22, Resources for the Future, Washington, DC.

Murray, B., and N. J. Rivers. 2015. "BC's Revenue-Neutral Carbon Tax: A Review of the Latest 'Grand Experiment' in Environmental Policy." *Energy Policy* 86: 674–683.

National Planning Commission. 2019. "Social Partner Dialogue for a Just Transition May 2018–June 2019: Revised Proposal Following the Outcomes of the Concluding Conference Held on 29 May 2019." Department of Planning Monitoring and Evaluation, Pretoria.

National Planning Commission. 2022. "National Development Plan 2030: Our Future—Make It Work." https://www.gov.za/documents/national-development-plan-2030-our-future-make-it-work.

NRDC (Natural Resources Defense Council). 2016. "Filling the Skill Gap in India's Clean Energy Market: Solar Energy Focus." https://www.nrdc.org/sites/default/files/renewable-energy-solar -skill-gap.pdf.

Nyathi, M. 2023. "Eskom Needs Big Money to Fix Kusile's Chimney to Cut Load-Shedding." *Mail and Guardian,* January 24. https://mg.co.za/environment/2023-01-24-eskom-needs-big-money-to -fix-kusiles-chimney-to-cut-load-shedding/.

OEC (Observatory of Economic Complexity). 2023. "Colombia." https://oec.world/en/profile /country/col#:~:text=Exports%20The%20top%20exports%20of,and%20Brazil%20(%241.28B).

OECD (Organisation for Economic Co-operation and Development). 2021. "Taxing Energy Use for Sustainable Development: Country Notes—Egypt." https://www.oecd.org/tax/tax-policy/taxing -energy-use-egypt.pdf.

Oei, P.-Y., H. Brauers, and P. Herpich. 2019. "Lessons from Germany's Hard Coal Mining Phase-Out: Policies and Transition from 1950 to 2018." *Climate Policy* 20 (8): 963–79. https://www .tandfonline.com/doi/full/10.1080/14693062.2019.1688636?cookieSet=1.

PMR (Partnership for Market Readiness). 2015. "INDC Costa Rica: A Summary of the Process." Presented at the Partnership Assembly Meeting (PA 12), Barcelona, Spain, May 29–30. https:// www.thepmr.org/system/files/documents/Presentaci%C3%B3n%20Barcelona%202015%20 PMR%20%28Guion%29.pdf.

Presidency of the Republic of South Africa. 2022. *Just Energy Transition Investment Plan (JET IP) 2023–2027.* Pretoria. https://www.thepresidency.gov.za/content/south-africa%27s-just-energy -transition-investment-plan-jet-ip-2023-2027.

Pretis, F. 2022. "Does a Carbon Tax Reduce CO_2 Emissions? Evidence from British Columbia." *Environmental and Resource Economics* 83 (1): 115–44.

Pryor, J., P. Agnolucci, C. Fischer, D. Heine, and M. M. de Oca Leon. 2023. "Carbon Pricing around the World." In *Data for a Greener World: A Guide for Practitioners and Policymakers*, edited by S. Arslanalp, K. Kostial, and G. Quirós-Romero, 79–94. Washington, DC: International Monetary Fund.

PwC South Africa. 2022. "Just Energy Transition Framework Endorsed." Press release.

Raina, G., and S. Sinha. 2019. "Outlook on the Indian Scenario of Solar Energy Strategies: Policies and Challenges." *Energy Strategy Reviews* 24: 331–41. https://doi.org/10.1016/j.esr.2019.04.005.

Rai-Roche, S. 2022. "India Unveils Four-Fold Increase of Solar PLI Scheme Funding to $2.6 Billion." *PVTech*, February 1. https://www.pv-tech.org/india-unveils-four-fold-increase-of-solar-pli-scheme-funding-to-us2-6-billion/.

Reij, C., G. Tappan, and M. Smale. 2009. "Re-greening the Sahel: Farmer-Led Innovation in Burkina Faso and Niger." In *Millions Fed: Proven Successes in Agricultural Development*, edited by David Spielman and Rajul Pamdya-Lorch, 53–58. Washington, DC: International Food Policy Research Institute.

Reinders, H. J., M. G. J. Regelink, P. Calice, and M. E. Uribe. 2021. "Not-So-Magical Realism: A Climate Stress Test of the Colombian Banking System." World Bank, Washington, DC. https://documents.worldbank.org/en/publication/documents-reports/documentdetail/957831635911537578/not-so-magical-realism-a-climate-stress-test-of-the-colombian-banking-system.

Ritchie, H., and M. Roser. 2020. "China: CO_2 Country Profile." Our World in Data. https://ourworldindata.org/co2/country/china.

Ritchie, H., and M. Roser. 2022. "India: CO_2 Country Profile." Our World in Data. https://ourworldindata.org/co2/country/india.

Ritchie, H., M. Roser, and P. Rosado. 2020. "CO_2 and Greenhouse Gas Emissions." Our World in Data. https://ourworldindata.org/co2-and-other-greenhouse-gas-emissions.

Roe, S., C. Streck, R. Beach, J. Busch, M. Chapman, V. Daioglou, A. Deppermann, et al. 2021. "Land-Based Measures to Mitigate Climate Change: Potential and Feasibility by Country." *Global Change Biology* 27: 6025–58. https://doi.org/10.1111/gcb.15873.

Sales, V. G., E. Strobl, and R. J. R. Elliott. 2022. "Cloud Cover and Its Impact on Brazil's Deforestation Satellite Monitoring Program: Evidence from the Cerrado Biome of the Brazilian Legal Amazon." *Applied Geography* 140: 102651. https://doi.org/10.1016/j.apgeog.2022.102651.

Salmon, C., and J. Tanguy. 2016. "Rural Electrification and Household Labor Supply: Evidence from Nigeria." *World Development* 82: 48–68.

Sarangi, G. K. 2022. "Green Energy Finance in India: Challenges and Solutions." ADBI Working Paper 863, Asian Development Bank Institute. https://www.adb.org/publications/green-energy-finance-india-challenges-and-solutions.

Sari, A. A., A. Mayastuti, A. Roanto, and Z. Lutfiya. 2018. "Indigenous People's Forest Management to Support REDD Program and Indonesia One Map Policy." *IOP Conference Series: Earth and Environmental Science* 200: 0120480.

Sharma, S., A. Dutta, C. Sitalakshami, and S. Sundar. 2017. "Developing Pathways for Fuel Efficiency Improvements in HDV Sector in India." Shakti Foundation. https://shaktifoundation.in/wp-content/uploads/2017/06/Pathways-for-fuel-efficiency-improvements-in-HDV-sector-in-India.pdf.

Shiradkar, N., R. Arya, A. Chaubal, K. Deshmukh, P. Ghosh, A. Kottantharayil, S. Kumar, and J. Vasi. 2022. "Recent Developments in Solar Manufacturing in India." *Solar Compass* 1: 100009. https://doi.org/10.1016/j.solcom.2022.100009.

SIMEPRODE (Sistema Integral para el Manejo Ecológico y Procesamiento de Desechos). 2020. "Manejo Integral de Residuos Sólidos en Monterrey y su Área Metropolitana." https://remoxenergy.com/wp-content/uploads/2021/07/3.JOSE-MANUEL-VAZQUEZ-JUAREZ-MANEJO-INTEGRAL

-DE-RESIDOS-SOLIDOS-URBANOS-EN-MONTERREY-Y-SU-AREA-METROPOLITANA6.500
-TONELADAS-POR-DIA.pdf.

Singh, J. 2018. "Energy Efficiency in the Public Sector." World Bank, Washington, DC. https://
openknowledge.worldbank.org/handle/10986/31023.

Singh, S., D. Stanway, and M. Xu. 2021. "Explainer: How Will China's New National Carbon Emissions
Trading Scheme (ETS) Work?" Reuters, July 14. https://www.reuters.com/business/chinas
-national-emissions-trading-scheme-ets-2021-07-14/#:~:text=Its%20nationwide%20
scheme%20had%20been,in%20the%20world%20by%20volume.

Smith, P., J. Nkem, K. Calvin, et al. 2019. "Interlinkages between Desertification, Land Degradation,
Food Security and Greenhouse Gas Fluxes: Synergies, Trade-offs and Integrated Response
Options." In *Climate Change and Land: An IPCC Special Report on Climate Change, Desertification,
Land Degradation, Sustainable Land Management, Food Security, and Greenhouse Gas Fluxes in
Terrestrial Ecosystems*, edited by P. R. Shukla et al., 551–672. Cambridge, UK: Cambridge
University Press. https://doi.org/10.1017/9781009157988.008.

Smith, T. 2022. "Eskom Issues RFP for Renewable Energy Projects in Mpumalanga." *ESI Africa*, April 13.
https://www.esi-africa.com/industry-sectors/business-andmarkets/eskom-issues-rfp-for
-renewable-energy-projects-in-mpumalanga/.

Srouji, J., C. Schumer, C. Fyson, A. Geiges, and M. Gidde. 2021. "Closing the Gap: The Impact of G20
Climate Commitments on Limiting Global Temperature Rise to 1.5°C." Working Paper, World
Resources Institute. https://www.wri.org/research/closing-the-gap-g20-climate-commitments
-limiting-global-temperature-rise?auHash=oZwy9HINuvJpev4nvILtOOvhZ53_HoQf7ad4bRxcgd
8andutm_medium=socialandutm_source=twitterandutm_campaign=socialmedia.

Stassart, J., R. Torsiano, F. Cardoso, and F. M. de A. Collaço. 2021. "Weak Land Governance, Fraud
and Corruption: Fertile Ground for Land Grabbing." Transparency International. https://
comunidade.transparenciainternacional.org.br/land-grabbing.

Stern, N. 2006. *The Economics of Climate Change: The Stern Review.* https://www.lse.ac.uk
/granthaminstitute/publication/the-economics-of-climate-change-the-stern-review/

Stevis, D., and R. Felli. 2015. "Global Labour Unions and Just Transition to a Green Economy."
International Environmental Agreements: Politics, Law and Economics 15: 29–43.

Steyn, S., E. Tyler, A. Roff, C. Renaud, and L. Mgoduso. 2021. *The Just Transition Transaction: A
Developing Country Coal Power Retirement Mechanism.* Cape Town: Meridian Economics.
https://meridianeconomics.co.za/wp-content/uploads/2021/09/2021-09-28_What-is-the-JTT
_Final-Report.pdf.

Strambo, C., J. Burton, and A. Atteridge. 2019. *The End of Coal? Planning a "Just Transition" in South
Africa.* Stockholm: Stockholm Environment Institute.

TIPS (Trade and Industrial Policy Strategies). 2020. "Sector Jobs Resilience Plan: Coal Value Chain."
https://www.tips.org.za/research-archive/sustainable-growth/green-economy-2/item/3986
-sector-jobs-resilience-plan-coal-value-chain.

Udry, C. 1996. "Efficiency and Market Structure: Testing for Profit Maximization in African
Agriculture." Working Paper, Department of Economics, Northwestern University.

UNDP (United Nations Development Programme). 2020. "Human Development Index." https://hdr
.undp.org/data-center/human-development-index#/indicies/HDI.

UNEP (United Nations Environment Programme). 2021. "The Heat Is On: A World of Climate
Promises Not Yet Delivered—Emissions Gap Report 2021." https://www.unep.org/resources
/emissions-gap-report-2021.

UNEP (United Nations Environment Programme). 2022. "Solid Waste Management." https://www
.unep.org/explore-topics/resource-efficiency/what-we-do/cities/solid-waste-management.

UNFCCC (United Nations Framework Convention on Climate Change). 2020. "Egypt Vehicle Scrapping
and Recycling Program." Clean Development Mechanism, PoA 2897. https://cdm.unfccc.int
/ProgrammeOfActivities/poa_db/JMC6IEOPXNUS TA2Q78DFZ4GW9LHKV1/view.

UNFCCC (United Nations Framework Convention on Climate Change). 2021. "South Africa: First Nationally Determined Contribution under the Paris Agreement." September 2021 update.

UNFCCC (United Nations Framework Convention on Climate Change). 2022a. "Indonesia's Enhanced NDC." https://unfccc.int/node/615082.

UNFCCC (United Nations Framework Convention on Climate Change). 2022b. "NDC Registry." https://unfccc.int/NDCREG.

Wang, M., X. Mao, Y. Xing, J. Lu, P. Song, Z. Liu, Z. Guo, K. Tu, and E. Zusman. 2021. "Breaking Down Barriers on PV Trade Will Facilitate Global Carbon Mitigation." *Nature Communications* 12 (1). https://doi.org/10.1038/s41467-021-26547-7.

Warren, M., K. Hergoualc'h, J. B. Kauffman, D. Murdiyarso, and R. Kolka. 2017. "An Appraisal of Indonesia's Immense Peat Carbon Stock Using National Peatland Maps: Uncertainties and Potential Losses from Conversion." *Carbon Balance Manage* 12: 12. https://doi.org/10.1186/s13021-017-0080-2.

Werneck, F., C. Angelo, and S. Araújo. 2022. *A conta chegou: O terceiro ano de destruição ambiental sob Jair Bolsonaro.* Brasília: Observatório do Clima. https://www.oc.eco.br/wp-content/uploads/2022/02/A-conta-chegou-HD.pdf.

West, T. A. P., and P. M. Fearnside. 2021. "Brazil's Conservation Reform and the Reduction of Deforestation in Amazonia." *Land Use Policy* 100: 105072. https://doi.org/10.1016/j.landusepol.2020.105072.

WHO (World Health Organization). 2020. "Lima Responds to the COVID-19 Pandemic on Wheels." News release, October 23. https://www.who.int/news-room/feature-stories/detail/lima-responds-to-the-covid-19-pandemic-on-wheels.

World Bank. 2001. "Project Appraisal Document for Mexico—Methane Gas Capture and Use at a Landfill—Demonstration Project." World Bank, Washington, DC. http://documents.world-bank.org/curated/en/996281468774581878/Mexico-Methane-Gas-Capture-and-Use-at-a-Landfill-Demonstration-Project.

World Bank. 2007. "Implementation Completion Report for Mexico—Methane Gas Capture and Use at a Landfill—Demonstration Project." World Bank, Washington, DC. https://documents1.worldbank.org/curated/en/242731468300678517/pdf/37925.pdf.

World Bank. 2012. *Carbon Sequestration in Agricultural Soils.* Washington, DC: World Bank.

World Bank. 2013. "Peru: Better Transport for Lima to Mitigate Climate Change." https://www.worldbank.org/en/results/2013/04/24/Peru-better-transport-for-Lima-to-mitigate-climate-change.

World Bank. 2014a. "Implementation Completion Report for Mexico Waste Management and Carbon Offset Project." World Bank, Washington, DC.

World Bank. 2014b. "Western Balkans: Scaling Up Energy Efficiency in Buildings." Working Paper 89321, Europe and Central Asia Region, World Bank, Washington DC.

World Bank. 2015. "Bringing Electricity to Kenya's Slums: Hard Lessons Leads to Great Gains." https://documents.worldbank.org/en/publication/documents-reports/documentdetail/572561638253471313/bringing-electricity-to-kenya-s-slums-hard-lessons-lead-to-great-gains.

World Bank. 2016a. "Costa Rica. (Intended) Nationally Determined Contribution (I)NDC." https://unfccc.int/documents/497422.

World Bank. 2016b. *The Cost of Fire: An Economic Analysis of Indonesia's 2015 Fire Crisis.* Washington, DC: World Bank.

World Bank. 2016c. "Program Document for Second Fiscal Consolidation, Sustainable Energy and Competitiveness Programmatic Development Policy Financing." Report 110036-EG, World Bank, Washington, DC.

World Bank. 2017. "Program Document for Third Fiscal Consolidation, Sustainable Energy and Competitiveness Programmatic Development Policy Financing." Report 100978-EG. World Bank, Washington, DC.

World Bank. 2018a. "Egypt: Scrapping and Recycling Old Vehicles to Lower Pollution and Improve Livelihoods." https://www.worldbank.org/en/news/feature/2018/10/25/egypt-scrapping-and-recycling-old-vehicles-to-lower-pollution-and-improve-livelihoods

World Bank. 2018b. "Urban Population (% of total population)—Brazil." https://data.worldbank.org/indicator/SP.URB.TOTL.IN.ZS?locations=BR.

World Bank. 2018c. "Zero Routine Flaring by 2030 (ZRF) Initiative." https://www.worldbank.org/en/programs/zero-routine-flaring-by-2030/qna.

World Bank. 2019a. "Project Appraisal Document for Turkey Energy Efficiency in Public Buildings." Report PAD3159, World Bank, Washington, DC.

World Bank. 2019b. "South Africa: Over-reliance on Coal Leading to Carbon Lock-In and Environmental Degradation." World Bank, Washington, DC.

World Bank. 2020a. "Clean Bus in LAC: Lessons from Chile's Experience with E-mobility: The Integration of E-buses in Santiago." Report AUS0001853. https://documents1.worldbank.org/curated/en/656661600060762104/pdf/Lessons-from-Chile-s-Experience-with-E-mobility-The-Integration-of-E-Buses-in-Santiago.pdf.

World Bank. 2020b. "Implementation Completion and Results Report of First, Second, and Third Fiscal Consolidation, Sustainable Energy and Competitiveness Programmatic Development Policy Financing." Report ICR00005121, World Bank, Washington, DC.

World Bank. 2020c. *Propuesta de Actualización del Plan de Infraestructura Cicloviaria para Lima y Callao.* Washington, DC: World Bank. https://documents1.worldbank.org/curated/en/294041589874919754/pdf/Propuesta-de-actualizacion-del-Plan-de-Infraestructura-Cicloviaria-para-Lima-y-Callao.pdf.

World Bank. 2020d. *Propuesta y Recomendaciones para la Formulación de una Estrategia para la Bicicleta en Lima Metropolitana.* Washington, DC: World Bank. https://documents1.worldbank.org/curated/en/804721589870386400/pdf/Propuesta-y-recomendaciones-para-la-formulacion-de-una-estrategia-para-la-Bicicleta-en-Lima-Metropolitana.pdf.

World Bank. 2020e. "World Bank Reference Guide to Climate Change Framework Legislation." https://openknowledge.worldbank.org/bitstream/handle/10986/34972/World-Bank-Reference-Guide-to-Climate-Change-Framework-Legislation.pdf?sequence=6.

World Bank. 2021a. "Decarbonizing Cities by Improving Public Transport and Managing Land Use and Traffic." https://openknowledge.worldbank.org/handle/10986/36517

World Bank. 2021b. "The Economics of Large-Scale Mangrove Conservation and Restoration in Indonesia." Technical Report, World Bank, Washington, DC.

World Bank. 2021c. "Egypt Vehicle Scrapping and Recycling Program." https://projects.worldbank.org/en/projects-operations/project-detail/P119483.

World Bank. 2021d. "GDP (current $)." World Bank. 2021. "GDP (current $)." https://data.worldbank.org/indicator/NY.GDP.MKTP.CD?locations=GBandmost_recent_value_desc=true.

World Bank. 2021e. "Global Facility to Decarbonize Transport." https://www.worldbank.org/en/topic/transport/brief/global-facility-to-decarbonize-transport.

World Bank. 2021f. "Global Gas Flaring Tracker Report." https://thedocs.worldbank.org/en/doc/1f7221545bf1b7c89b850dd85cb409b0-0400072021/original/WB-GGFR-Report-Design-05a.pdf.

World Bank. 2021g. "Investing for Momentum in Active Mobility. Transport Decarbonization Investment." Discussion Paper. https://thedocs.worldbank.org/en/doc/c6de7aa3e8b4b081029f639767c1486c-0190062021/original/TDI-paper-Investing-for-Momentum-in-Active-Mobility-October-2021.pdf.

World Bank. 2021h. "Motorization Management and the Trade of Used Vehicles: How Collective Action and Investment Can Help Decarbonize the Global Transport Sector." Discussion Paper, World Bank, Washington, DC. https://openknowledge.worldbank.org/handle/10986/36518.

World Bank. 2021i. "Toolkits for Policymakers to Green the Financial System." https://openknowledge.worldbank.org/handle/10986/35705.

World Bank. 2022a. "Carbon Pricing Dashboard." https://carbonpricingdashboard.worldbank.org/map_data.

World Bank. 2022b. "China–Guangdong Agricultural Pollution Control Project. Implementation Completion and Results Report, Guangdong Agricultural Pollution Control Project, Final," June 30. http://documents.worldbank.org/curated/en/099330007082259474/BOSIB0a594b0970a90a2df0fd9b2dc1114f.

World Bank. 2022c. "Concept Project Information Document (PID)—Lima Traffic Management and Sustainable Transport—P178842." https://documentos.bancomundial.org/es/publication/documents-reports/documentdetail/099830011112213273/p17884201e713c00095 b206f72ebc7a3da.

World Bank. 2022d. *Electric Mobility Market Assessment, Business Model and Action Plan in India.* Washington, DC: World Bank. http://hdl.handle.net/10986/37898.

World Bank. 2022e. "GDP (current $)." https://data.worldbank.org/indicator/NY.GDP.MKTP.CD?most_recent_value_desc=true.

World Bank. 2022f. *G5 Sahel Country Climate and Development Report.* Washington, DC: World Bank. https://openknowledge.worldbank.org/handle/10986/37620.

World Bank. 2022g. "Global Gas Flaring Reduction Partnership (GGFR)." https://www.worldbank.org/en/programs/gasflaringreduction/global-flaring-data. World Bank, Washington, DC.

World Bank. 2022h. "Greening of China's Agriculture: A Policy Brief." https://documents.worldbank.org/en/publication/documents-reports/documentdetail/099555512222217554/p17151805469f30f0b9040575969f41541.

World Bank. 2022i. "Improving Bankability of E-bus Procurement in India." Working Paper, World Bank, Washington, DC. https://documents1.worldbank.org/curated/en/099551506152217472/pdf/IDU0a1555f8407326 048dd09 f08069157b590e67.pdf.

World Bank. 2022j. "National Employment Vulnerability Assessment (2019) and Quarterly Labor Force Survey (2022, Q1)." In *South Africa Climate Change and Development Report.* Washington, DC: World Bank.

World Bank. 2022k. "Republic of Colombia Equitable and Green Recovery DPF." Report PGD326. https://documents1.worldbank.org/curated/en/302551648600963407/pdf/Colombia-Equitable-and-Green-Recovery-Development-Policy-Financing.pdf.

World Bank. 2022l. *South Africa Country Climate and Development Report.* Washington, DC: World Bank. http://hdl.handle.net/10986/38216.

World Bank. 2022m. *State and Trends of Carbon Pricing 2022.* Washington, DC: World Bank. https://openknowledge.worldbank.org/handle/10986/37455.

World Bank. 2022n. "World Bank Group President David Malpass' Visit to Komati Power Station Highlights the Plant's Repurposing from Coal to Clean Energy." Press release, November 7. https://www.worldbank.org/en/news/press-release/2022/11/07/world-bank-group-president-david-malpass-s-visit-to-komati-power-station-highlights-the-plant-s-repurposing-from-coal-to.

World Bank. 2022o. "Zero Routine Flaring by 2030." https://www.worldbank.org/en/programs/zero-routine-flaring-by-2030.

World Bank. Forthcoming a. *Operationalizing Long-Term Decarbonization Strategies: Lessons for Practitioners.* Washington, DC: World Bank.

World Bank. Forthcoming b. *Transforming Rural China: Greening of Agriculture Modernization.* Synthesis Report, World Bank, Washington, DC

World Justice Project. 2022. "Promoting Access to Sustainable Transport in Lima through the Use of Bicycles as Means of Transport." https://worldjusticeproject.org/our-work/programs/promoting-access-sustainable-transport-lima-through-use-bicycles-means-transport.

Xu, M., and D. Stanway. 2022. "China Slams Firms for Falsifying Carbon Data," *Reuters,* March 15.

Xue, Y. 2022. "Explainer: What Is the China Certified Emission Reduction Scheme and Why Is It Important for Beijing's Carbon Neutral Goal?" *South China Morning Post,* January 31. https://www.scmp.com/business/article/3165425/what-china-certified-emission-reduction-scheme-and-why-it-important.

Yamazaki, A. 2017. "Jobs and Climate Policy: Evidence from British Columbia's Revenue-Neutral Carbon Tax." *Journal of Environmental Economics and Management* 83: 197–216.

Yin, I. 2021. "China Wary of Socio-economic Impact of Unregulated Carbon Market." *S&P Global Commodity Insights* (blog). https://www.spglobal.com/commodityinsights/en/market-insights/blogs/energy-transition/070721-china-carbon-market-emissions-socio-economic-impact-power-industry.

Yin, I. 2023a. "China Relaxes Compliance Carbon Market Rules for Coal-Fired Power Plants." *S&P Global Commodity Insights* (blog). https://www.spglobal.com/commodityinsights/en/market-insights/latest-news/energy-transition/031723-china-relaxes-compliance-carbon-market-rules-for-coal-fired-power-plants#:~:text=China%E2%80%99s%20environment%20ministry%20proposed%20the,a%20notice%20issued%20March%2015.

Yin, I. 2023b. "Commodities 2023: China's Carbon Market to Slow in 2023 as Energy Security, Economy Take Priority." *S&P Global Commodity Insights* (blog). https://www.spglobal.com/commodityinsights/en/market-insights/latest-news/energy-transition/011223-chinas-carbon-market-to-slow-in-2023-as-energy-security-economy-take-priority.

Zaman, R., O. van Vliet, and A. Posch. 2021. "Energy Access and Pandemic-Resilient Livelihoods: The Role of Solar Energy Safety Nets." *Energy Research and Social Science* 71: 101805. https://doi.org/10.1016/j.erss.2020.101805.

www.ingramcontent.com/pod-product-compliance
Lightning Source LLC
Chambersburg PA
CBHW041442210326
41599CB00004B/101